More Praise for

The Politically Incorrect Guide® to
Catholicism

"*The Politically Incorrect Guide® to Catholicism* envelops its deep learning in a breezy Chestertonian style that entertains as it informs. It offers a wry combination of the hilarious and the profound: truth delivered with razor wit. As a result, it is compulsively readable. Peppered throughout the text are recommendations of books 'You're Not Supposed to Read.' This nervy book now joins that honor roll. Read it."

> —Robert Reilly, former director, Voice of America, and author of *The Closing of the Muslim Mind* and *Making Gay Okay*

"John Zmirak is so brilliant, effervescent, and indefatigably entertaining that I'm much too embarrassed to mention it publicly."

> —Eric Metaxas, *New York Times* bestselling author of *Bonhoeffer* and *If You Can Keep It: The Forgotten Promise of American Liberty*

"John Zmirak has a deeply informed and accurate understanding of the real political and economic implications of the Catholic Faith, conveyed in gracious and highly readable language with more than a dash of healing humor. This book is the antidote to the leftist distortions of the Church that are all too ubiquitous today."

> —The Honorable Faith Whittlesey, former U.S. Ambassador to Switzerland

"John Zmirak has written an entertaining and enlightening book that will help you to think about Catholicism in ways you may not expect. His insights challenge conventional wisdom. Whether you come to agree or not with his at times provocative diagnoses of and remedies for the problems in the Church, reading this book will help you understand what is at stake."

—The Reverend Gerald E. Murray, J.C.D., pastor, Holy Family Church, New York, New York

"John Zmirak is the most articulate and learned defender of real Catholic social teaching of his generation. For decades, he has courageously spoken out for the life of the unborn, for the freedom of faith and families, and for the integrity of the Faith. *The Politically Incorrect Guide® to Catholicism* should serve as a vital textbook in classrooms of Catholic colleges—though of course, it probably won't!"

—Jason Scott Jones, producer, *Crescendo*, co-executive producer, *Bella*

"This book will help you learn a great deal about that greatly misunderstood subject: Catholicism. What's more, you'll laugh a great deal—something that is thoroughly Catholic!"

—Samuel Gregg, research director, Acton Institute

"John Zmirak is a joyful scandal, not scandal in the sense of leading anyone astray, but in the sense of telling the truth, which is always a scandal to modern ears. His new book is a wild and bumpy ride through Church teaching as it is—has been—will be, with immense dollops of orthodoxy's smoky incense and utterly bereft of heterodoxy's uncertain bells and whistles. Oh, and plenty of belly-laughs to boot."

—Austin Ruse, author of *The Littlest Suffering Souls* and president of The Catholic Family and Human Rights Institute at the United Nations

The Politically Incorrect Guide® to Catholicism

Be sure to check out

The Politically Incorrect Guides® to...

American History
Thomas Woods
9780895260475

The Bible
Robert J. Hutchinson
9781596985209

The British Empire
H. W. Crocker III
9781596986299

Capitalism
Robert P. Murphy
9781596985049

Catholicism
John Zmirak
9781621575863

The Civil War
H. W. Crocker III
9781596985490

The Constitution
Kevin R. C. Gutzman
9781596985056

**Darwinism and
Intelligent Design**
Jonathan Wells
9781596980136

**English and
American Literature**
Elizabeth Kantor
9781596980112

The Founding Fathers
Brion McClanahan
9781596980921

Global Warming
Christopher C. Horner
9781596985018

**The Great Depression
and the New Deal**
Robert Murphy
9781596980969

Hunting
Frank Miniter
9781596985216

Islam (And the Crusades)
Robert Spencer
9780895260130

The Middle East
Martin Sieff
9781596980518

The Presidents, Part 1
Larry Schweikart
9781621575245

The Presidents, Part 2
Steven F. Hayward
9781621575795

Real American Heroes
Brion McClanahan
9781596983205

Science
Tom Bethell
9780895260314

The Sixties
Jonathan Leaf
9781596985728

Socialism
Kevin D. Williamson
9781596986497

**The South
(And Why It Will Rise Again)**
Clint Johnson
9781596985001

The Vietnam War
Phillip Jennings
9781596985674

Western Civilization
Anthony Esolen
9781596980594

Women, Sex, and Feminism
Carrie L. Lukas
9781596980037

The Politically Incorrect Guide® to
Catholicism

John Zmirak

REGNERY
PUBLISHING
A Division of Salem Media Group

Cataloging-in-Publication data on file with the Library of Congress

ISBN 978-1-62157-586-3

Published in the United States by
Regnery Publishing
A Division of Salem Media Group
300 New Jersey Ave NW
Washington, DC 20001
www.Regnery.com

Manufactured in the United States of America

10 9 8 7 6 5 4 3 2 1

Books are available in quantity for promotional or premium use. For information on discounts and terms, please visit our website: www.Regnery.com.

Distributed to the trade by
Perseus Distribution
250 West 57th Street
New York, NY 10107

To my beloved sister, Patricia Marie Fain, who had to endure me as a teenager. Thanks for not strangling me, though I deserved it. See, "Damien" did eventually amount to something!

Contents

The Church: What It Says about Itself, the World, and What Will Happen to You When You Die

The Roman Catholic Church is like the weather: everybody talks about it, but nobody does anything about it. They can't, not in the most fundamental sense, any more than they can change earth's climate. The truths that the Church teaches about God and man, right and wrong, and the purpose of human history are simply *there*. You can embrace them enthusiastically as liberating and beautiful. (What the saints do) You can reluctantly admit that they are probable, and obey them to be on the safe side. (What most of us "bad Catholics" do) Or you can insist that some or all of them are false. (What non-Catholics do) What you can't do is alter those truths. (What liberal Catholics try to do) Not even a pope can manage that. Catholics believe that the Holy Spirit would intervene and prevent him, exercising the divine veto power that we call "infallibility."

Now I can't make you believe that tenet of Catholic faith. But the laws of logic bind us all. As you'll learn later on in this book, if a pope were to solemnly contradict the solemn teaching of a previous pope or council, he would thereby discredit his office, and with it the Roman Catholic Church. So he'd be a pretender pope of a ghost of a church, like a seedy exiled nobleman with documents that prove he is the Khan of the Golden Horde.

Did you know?

★ No pope can solemnly contradict the solemn teaching of a previous pope

★ The fact that you regularly meet Jews—but never Hittites—is evidence of God's existence

★ Medieval popes repeatedly condemned conspiracy theories about the Jews

Hence it's funny to read in the *New York Times* that liberal Catholic activists are pushing for a change in Church teaching on issues relating to—well, let's admit it, sex. Nobody is out there demanding the popes revisit the condemnation of Jansenism (don't ask), or settle the question of whether divine grace is or isn't resistible. No, journalists want to know what the Church thinks about whether one person should poke another and, if so, where, when, and how. What liberal Catholics and the journalists who love them are really asking is for the Church to admit that it was teaching a set of harsh, repressive errors for nineteen centuries and that now it is very, very sorry. Then it can toddle off like the Church of England to play dress up in empty Gothic buildings, and no one will ever have to pay attention to it again.

No doubt you have read breathless accounts in the press of the exciting new changes allegedly impending in Catholic teaching. Pope Francis has used his bully pulpit tirelessly to vent his private opinions on global warming, economics, immigration, and a long list of other issues on which he is less well-informed than the average American who watches Fox News. None of that matters. As you will learn, these subjects are outside the pope's scope of divinely appointed authority. He has no more claim to anyone's deference on these subjects than a traffic cop who stops you to offer gynecological advice. Peter and his successors were guaranteed infallibility not so that Catholics would know exactly what to do about greenhouse gas emissions and income inequality, but so that the signs identifying the narrow road that leads to heaven couldn't be switched out for the signs pointing to the broad way that leads to perdition. That, after all, is the purpose for which Jesus Christ established the papacy, and the Church itself, in the first place—to show us the way to eternal salvation, not to tell us how to vote.

But even on issues where the authority of the pope and the bishops really does apply, troubling things have been happening. In 2015, a significant percentage of bishops at the Vatican's Synod on the Family were playing with fire, floating proposals that the Church alter its teachings that declare divorce impossible, and sodomy a sin that "cries out to heaven for vengeance." Those proposals failed, but Pope Francis's sympathies on these and related issues are far from certain.

This book pierces through the pink fog of liberal wishful thinking and sketches what the teachings of the Church really are, why Catholics believe them, the main objections people raise to them, and how the Church answers those arguments. It's my task to throw a wet blanket on the hootenanny that began with the election of Pope Francis and help the reader discover:

★ ★ ★
What the Pope Can Do—and What He Can't

Pope Francis may continue to encourage liberals like the ones who want to change Church teaching on marriage, appoint more bishops who think like them, and say things that confuse and worry the faithful in silly press conferences and reckless interviews with atheist Italian reporters. Here's what he can't do: invoke his supreme authority and teach the opposite of what previous popes have taught. Until and unless that happens, the Church's core teachings are exactly what they have always been.

- Which aspects of Church practice and teaching can change, which ones can't, and why
- What authority popes have to speak about politics and economics—and the surprising things they have said on these subjects in the past
- The Church's long-time support for private property, free enterprise, self-defense and national defense, national sovereignty, states' rights, and border controls
- The positive vision the Church has of love, marriage, and sex—which treads a "golden mean" between the destructive extremes of seedy hedonism and world-hating Gnosticism

- The firm stands that the Church has taken over the centuries against evil ideologies, from Islam to feminism, Nazism, and communism

We won't gloss over the dark side. The Church has embraced billions of people over the centuries, millions of whom were jackasses. One of our first twelve bishops was a traitor who landed in hell. Many of the 266 popes were far from saints, and, as we'll see in the next chapter, only eight statements ever made by any of them are widely considered infallible. And while as a Catholic you do owe "religious assent" to non-infallible teachings of Church authorities,[1] as we'll also see, that doesn't mean you have to swallow every crazy thing that comes out of the pope's mouth at a press conference on his airplane, or get on board with your own bishop's asinine moral equation of the evil of abortion to the pain of unemployment.[2] That means we must think for ourselves—apologies to those of you who thought the whole point of joining the Church was that you'd never need to do that again!

★ ★ ★
A Pope? Yes. A Saint? No.

Alexander VI, a.k.a. Rodrigo Borgia, was one of three popes from the infamous family of Renaissance poisoners. He fathered numerous children with numerous mistresses, made his fifteen-year-old son a cardinal, and was rumored to have bribed his way into the papacy by paying off a rival candidate with so much silver that it had to be measured by the mule load. Then, when he died, there was a scandal about the difficulty of squeezing his body—bloated by his exorbitantly lavish lifestyle—into the coffin.

Freak of Nature or Piece of Supernature?

There's an old story about a group of blind men who encounter an unknown creature, so they each decide to explore it the only way they can—by touch. One calls out that it is like a tree, another a snake, another a wall, still another a sail. It turns out that what they have come across is an elephant. The first man is hugging its leg, the second petting its trunk, the third pressing his nose against its torso, and the fourth man stroking its ear. Only by piecing their separate reports together can they determine the truth. Or, if they were like modern liberals, they could dig in their heels and each insist on his point of view until the elephant got tired of being poked and prodded, and trampled them.

The Church, likewise, eludes any single viewpoint, discipline, or ideology. For one thing, it is enormous—not merely in space but in time. It embraces one-fifth of the whole human race, in every culture—far exceeding the reach of the Roman Empire. It has out-lasted every human institution on earth, including the second-place contender, the Chinese Empire. The Church has watched history unfolding, and changed its course, and in turn has been changed itself. The six-continent bureaucracy that spends billions of dollars, runs thousands of hospitals and schools, and serves as a moral authority to more than a billion people would have been unrecognizable to the eleven terrified nebbishes who hid in the Upper Room the night before Pentecost.

But the next day, the Holy Spirit touched them and set their souls alight, teaching them that their mission was to the world at large. *Those* apostles, speaking to the world with absolute authority of the One who had created and redeemed it…they would recognize the Church today. They would call their mission accomplished.

Because the Church has been around for what seems to us forever and has left its fingerprints everywhere in our history and culture, it is natural that myths and misconceptions hang about it. Most of them contain a kernel

★ ★ ★
Here Comes Everybody

As if to underline the point about the universality of the Church, on Pentecost the apostles were fitted out with the kind of "universal translator" that TV writers would later invent for *Star Trek*: they spoke of Jesus and His Resurrection from the dead in their native Aramaic, but the crowds heard the message in Latin, Greek, Syriac, Coptic, and even more obscure languages.

★ ★ ★

Good Things the Catholic Church Has Done for the World

- Built a new, better Western civilization after the fall of the Roman Empire
- Invented the university and the hospital
- Inspired—and in many cases financed—the world's greatest art
- Provided the strongest check in history on the power of the state
- Invented modern science (for the truth about the Galileo story, see chapter ten)

of truth. The Church makes a long list of claims about its mission and has built a vast pyramid of assertions about the ultimate ends of life and the truths of human nature. To reject these claims or dispute these assertions is not to be anti-Catholic. It is simply to be non-Catholic. To see the Church as a conspiracy, or to trade in half-truths and propaganda about it, on the other hand, is something else entirely. One of our purposes here will be to sift out the difference between sharp, legitimate questions and ignorant, hostile smears. Another goal of this book is to dismantle some widespread, long-standing distortions concerning the Church that are reinforced by the media, and accepted even by many Catholics.

There are people out there, including educated people, who believe that when you peel back the red velvet curtain, the Catholic Church is really:

1. The Roman Empire in disguise, a hierarchical institution whose secret purpose has always been to keep poor people distracted with promises of "pie in the sky when you die," so that they won't fight for their rights or demand back their "surplus value" from the bourgeoisie (the old-fashioned Marxist view)

2. The spiritual organization that Jesus created to form activist base communities of the marginalized to work despite structures of sin—such as capitalist economics and national

borders—for the final triumph of the poor over their oppressors around the world (the Liberation theologians' view)

3. A highly effective mechanism for disciplining and sublimating sexual energy into socially productive uses and explaining away the ordinary unhappiness that pervades all human life (the Freudian view)

4. The Whore of Babylon predicted in the Book of Revelation, which impersonates the true Church of Christ and leads souls to put their faith in their own empty works instead of the grace of Jesus Christ, so that they will fall into hell (the Protestant reformers' view)

5. A political pressure group that is more frequently useful than harmful, since its leaders push for ever more immigration and expansion of government programs; its irritating idiosyncratic objections to abortion and same-sex marriage can be safely ignored or suppressed through federal mandates that threaten its lucrative federal contracts (the view from the Democratic Party)

6. A traditional faith rendered untenable by research and reason, and presently undergoing inexorable dissolution into a smiley humanist social club that operates charities and engages in pretty rituals that people attend twice a year—in other words, the Episcopal church, without the good taste (the liberal Jesuits' view)

7. The greatest mainstay of the patriarchy, which is a male conspiracy that has been in place for all of recorded history to control female sexuality and maintain masculine power (the view of embittered feminist nuns in stretchy stirrup pants)

8. An organization that has many real Christians in it and that proved itself prophetic on the abortion issue, but whose leaders are inexplicably attached to expanding big government and weirdly reluctant to purge rank heretics from important positions (the ecumenically-minded Evangelical Protestants' view)

There are grains of truth to be found in most of these caricatures—except for maybe 4), which you don't hear that much anymore, except in little comic books that people leave lying around in Waffle House. But like that fabled elephant, the Church eludes the grasp of the visually differently-abled. It has had some of the this-worldly impacts laid out in the list above, though Catholics describe them differently. But all of these—from the Gothic cathedrals Freudians would chalk up to the sublimation of medieval man's sexual impulses to the political pressure the Church exercises, whether against legal abortion or the oppression of the poor—are side effects of a mission and an identity that reaches through all time and space, far beyond the confines of anyone's elephant cage.

★ ★ ★

Overripe Metaphor?

Think of the contributions of Catholicism to everything from economics to architecture as the Church's droppings. They have richly fertilized the culture, politics, art, and law of the West, but they aren't its reason for being.

It Started with Sin

If we want to get back to the living creature—the Church itself—we have to begin with the Garden of Eden. However literally or figuratively you choose to interpret the first chapters of Genesis—and since Pope Pius XII Catholics have been given a pretty wide scope—there are several central truths they tell that are essential to understanding the Catholic Church, and Christianity. Put briefly, they are:

- God made man on purpose, not as the unforeseen side-effect of a random biochemical process.

- All men are brothers, descended from a single set of original parents. (This was controversial back when Pope Pius XII insisted on it, since Nazis and other racists liked the biological fantasy that the various races of man were descended from different freak mutations all across the globe.)

- Man was not made to suffer and die but rather, in the original plan of creation, would have been somehow preserved from the death and decay we see all around us. Everything in the universe is ruled by entropy, the tendency of matter and energy toward chaos, absent a constant source of ordering energy from the outside. Bodies, like other things, fall apart. Well, according to Genesis, God's initial intent was to exempt man from this rule, to let us live in a paradisal state upon earth. St. Thomas Aquinas theorized that we would have been immune to physical harm, in perfect social harmony with each other, and able to communicate directly with God. (Even so, he thought that we would have still needed government, to coordinate our efforts at having fun and singing folksongs—was Aquinas a Democrat before his time?) Later theologians wondered how Adam and Eve's descendants, being fruitful and duly multiplying, would have fared as the earth filled up. The most plausible answer is provided by the example of the only ordinary human being after Adam and Eve to be spared Original Sin, the Virgin Mary. At the end of a certain span of years, her earthly life did end and she was taken body and soul to God in heaven. The same thing would have happened to a sinless Adam and Eve and their descendants, or so the theory goes.[3]

- But the first human beings, our primordial parents, rejected God's plan and sinned against Him, setting our species on a much darker, more arduous path. The Fall of Man, however you choose to picture it, had nothing to do with sex—no matter what you take away from the look on the face of Eve in late medieval paintings as she strokes the apple. Instead, it concerned the "knowledge of good and evil," a phrase that confuses people until they learn that "know" in this passage is used in the "biblical sense" (see "carnal knowledge"). By taking up Satan's offer to let them "be as God" by knowing good and evil alike in an intimate sense, Eve and then Adam were agreeing to *experience* them.

- And not just for themselves, but also on our behalf. Our first parents' decision affected something profound in what we might call our spiritual DNA, and the mutation has replicated itself in every generation. We knew evil all right, knew it good and hard, taking up the worst tendencies we see in our two closest primate relatives: the violence of chimpanzees and the promiscuity of bonobos. We got both drives in powerful doses—if you doubt me, take a look at the contents of R-rated movies. But the underlying sin that Adam and Eve committed, the one that bedevils each of us to this day, is the devil's favorite sin, which we call Pride. We shouldn't confuse this with self-esteem, or even the lesser (but still deadly) sin of Vainglory. Pride as the Church Fathers defined it is the systematic tendency to prefer our own will over God's, and our own selfish interests over those of our neighbors. Every evil decision in history can be traced back to this preference.

After the Fall, man's communication with God was fitful. The Lord tipped off Noah to the coming of the Flood, and after the ark landed He gave Noah a firm list of do's and don'ts for the human species, which Jews call the "Noachide Code." It's an abbreviated form of what we now call "the natural law," the code of ethics that God inscribed on the human heart—the inherent understanding that certain actions are wrong (and others right) that's hard-wired into the way our brains work. There is one problem: with Adam and Eve, it wasn't just human wills that were corrupted, prone to self-serving and cruelty. Our reason was also darkened. Our collective species IQ dropped by an unspecified number of points, and we no longer had direct access to God. So the human race's understanding of the natural moral law—and you may have noticed this—is not as clear and precise as it could be. It's as if a virus crept into our programming and promptly deleted both the manual and the "help" file, so we were left on our own.

Until Father Abraham. God chose the shepherd "Abram" to be the father of a very special people, whose very presence in history would be a sign of His love for mankind. The fraught and turbulent story of the Jews and the fact that they alone, of all the peoples of the ancient Near East, still exist at all, is a sign of God's existence; it has been called a divine fingerprint left on history. But we're getting ahead of ourselves. The key point is that the Jews became "the people of God," a title we'll hear again.

God promised the elderly Abraham that his old, infertile wife Sarah would bear him a son, whose descendants would form a great nation, through which "all the nations of the earth" would be blessed. The Jewish people would serve as the prism through which God would reveal His will for the whole human race. God fulfilled this promise in the person of Abraham's son Isaac. Then God put Abraham to the ultimate test of faith, asking him to offer Isaac as a human sacrifice. Of course, at the very last minute

★ ★ ★

"Where Are the Hittites?"

Pointing to the extraordinary survival of the Jewish people into modern times, Catholic novelist Walker Percy asked, "Why does no one find it remarkable that in most world cities today there are Jews but not one single Hittite even though the Hittites had a great flourishing civilization while the Jews nearby were a weak and obscure people?

"When one meets a Jew in New York or New Orleans or Paris or Melbourne, it is remarkable that no one considers the event remarkable."[4]

And in his last novel, *The Thanatos Syndrome*, Percy speculated that Nazi anti-Semitism was the fruit of the Nazis' pagan philosophy. They wanted to make themselves a race of "gods." To do that, they needed to wipe out any evidence of the real God.[5]

God intervened, sending down an angel to save Isaac's life and providing a ram as a substitute sacrifice. Christians believe this incident has a very particular meaning: it foreshadows the coming of Christ, a divine sacrifice of God's own Son on our behalf.

Remnant of Israel, People of God

This isn't a guide to the Old Testament, so we won't go through the ins and outs of the Jewish people's history, except to note that Moses was given the Ten Commandments, which reiterated and made more explicit God's requirements of mankind. In return for their obedience, the once-itinerant and later enslaved Hebrew people would be granted their liberty and a fertile homeland, the Holy Land, or Israel. It's a peculiarly strategic spot, the land of Israel—even in the ancient world standing squarely at the crossroad of several empires. The Hittites, Babylonians, and Egyptians would all need to pass through it as a chokepoint whenever they wished to invade each other's empires—which was often. So Israel was a risky place to live without the divine protection God promised.

As Israel's prophets themselves attested in fiery laments, the Jewish people were repeatedly unfaithful to God's law, especially in the core area of idolatry. The Jews were the only monotheists in the region, and the pagans around them were sunk in some particularly loathsome fertility cults involving temple prostitution and even child sacrifice. So the Lord had decreed that the Jews keep themselves apart from all their neighbors, practicing a strict dietary code. Sadly, many Jews, including some of their leaders, were beguiled by the military glories and religious rituals of their neighbors and, seduced by a kind of cultural peer pressure, began to emulate pagan ways. So Israel forfeited God's protection as a nation—and was conquered decisively by the Babylonian empire. The Jews were sent into exile there (eventually, via the Psalmist and an eighteenth-century English organist, inspiring a Don McLean hit: "By the waters of Babylon, we lay down and wept, and wept, for thee Zion..."), and at one point they were targeted for genocide (see the Book of Esther). But through some miracle, the Jewish people did not dissolve into the ethnic gumbo that was the ancient Middle East. In time, the Persian monarch Cyrus saw fit to return the Jews to their homeland, albeit as his subjects. Israel became just another province traded among empires, until the Jews finally ended up as subjects of the Romans.

Under the Roman Empire, the Jews divided into different factions with contrasting attitudes toward their Roman masters. The Sadducees, the sect that controlled the Temple and provided its priests, were religious minimalists and political collaborators. They rejected the later books of the Old Testament and disbelieved in life after death; they had no interest in politics, and helped provide legitimacy to the Roman occupation in return for being left alone. At the other end of the political spectrum, a loosely defined group of religious nationalists, the Zealots, tried to keep alive the dream of a revolt against the Romans, and looked for a military Messiah to come and lead their cause. But the bulk of religious Jews looked to the Pharisees, who saw the loss of Israel's independence as God's punishment for their ancestors' carelessness with the Law of Moses. They were determined to win back God's favor for their people by obeying its every jot and tittle. Still another group of Jews, the Essenes, lived in the desert and practiced asceticism; they are thought to have formed the core of John the Baptist's initial followers.

Each of these groups may have treasured the claim that it was the loyal "remnant" of Jews who had stayed faithful to God, treasuring His promise that a Messiah would come and restore their forfeited privileges. In fact, He would do even more, and make them a light to the Gentiles—taking the Law from their tiny kingdom and spreading it across the earth.

It was to fulfill that promise that Jesus came, but He did so in a most unexpected way, clearly answering some of the prophetic predictions about the Messiah—that he would be a "suffering servant," for example—while leaving others apparently hanging, such as the promise that God's people would be freed from bondage and come to exercise authority across the earth. Jesus' death on the cross, Christians believe, did indeed free God's people from the bondage of sin—but it didn't free the Jews of the curse of Roman occupation. The Church that Jesus founded would become a world-wide moral authority, teaching the Ten Commandments to tribes in North America and New Guinea. Jesus died and rose from the dead, as attested by many witnesses. But the political nation of Israel did not see a resurrection.

Jesus' claims surprised many Jews, who hadn't understood the prophetic references to the "Son of Man" as predicting that God Himself would become incarnate; that He Himself would replace the "scapegoat" that Jews drove into the desert as the bearer of their sins; or that He would replace their Passover dinner with a miraculous sacrifice of His own flesh and blood, which they would consume as spiritual food. They hadn't seen that coming. It was at best a divine surprise—or at worst a bizarre set of assertions by a false prophet guilty of blasphemy, which was the charge on which the high priests and Pharisees arraigned Jesus and had Him condemned to death. So while the whole of the Christian church would remain entirely Jewish for at least a decade after the Resurrection, many Jews rejected Jesus—and banned His followers from worshiping in the Temple at Jerusalem. They even put at least one of His apostles, James, to death. A zealous Pharisee named Saul served as a kind of Jewish inquisitor, hunting down the Christians whom he regarded as renegades and idolaters.

In the face of rejection and even persecution on the part of Jewish authorities, the Jews who *had* accepted Jesus made the claim that *they* were the faithful "remnant" of the Jews—that the bulk of the Jewish people had fallen away from perfect obedience to God by refusing His last and greatest prophet, John the Baptist, and rejecting His Messiah. This observation, tragically, led to nearly two millennia of persecution of Jews by Gentile Christians, on the theory that the Jews were spiritual renegades and rebels, in essentially the same state as the Samaritans of New Testament days, in fact, worse than that, guilty of "deicide"—God-murder. St. Augustine even wrote that God had kept the Jewish people in existence, in exile and oppressed, as an object lesson in what happens to those who disobey Him. But what medieval anti-Semites who took the passage in St. Matthew's Gospel where the crowd tells Pilate, "His blood be on us and on our children" as inspiration to start pogroms were missing was the fact that Jesus' death has to be blamed on the *human* race, all of which—Jews and Gentiles alike—is in need of salvation.

They were also ignoring the advice of the popes. Contrary to popular anti-Catholic opinion, the horrific violence against the Jews in the Middle Ages was more frequently led by secular rulers—such as Emperor Charles IV, who gave city leaders in Nuremberg (a place name that would come up again in the annals of anti-Semitism) advance approval for a pogrom in 1349—than by religious ones. The papacy actually has a long history of defending the Jews against violence and the conspiracy theories that fueled it—including the infamous "blood libel" accusing Jews of human sacrifice and cannibalism. Pope Innocent IV (1243–54), for example, issued a papal bull declaring it wrong "to accuse any Jew of using human blood in their rites, since it is clear in the Old Testament that it is forbidden to them to consume any blood, let alone the blood of human [beings]." Gregory X (1271–76) made adhering to the blood libel an excommunicable offense. Paul III (1534–49) issued yet another bull against that conspiracy theory, astutely observing that, "those accusing the Jews of drinking the blood of children are blinded by avarice, and only want to rob their money."[6]

Still, the idea that the Catholic Church was the faithful remnant of the Jewish people has certainly contributed to Christian anti-Semitism over the centuries, so Vatican II attempted to clarify Church teaching on that point. The Vatican II document *Nostra Aetate*, promulgated at a time when the Nazi Holocaust was still a recent memory—and before a smear campaign (likely set rolling by the Soviet propaganda machine)[7] had succeeded in tarring Pius XII, a man whom Golda Meir (among many others) praised for saving the lives of Jews threatened by the Nazis, as "Hitler's Pope" in the popular imagination—declares, "Although the Church is the new people of God, the Jews should not be presented as rejected or accursed by God...." A couple of decades later, Pope St. John Paul II asserted that the Old Covenant "has never been revoked by God."[8]

Today, controversy still swirls around the question of whether the Church ought to (a) leave Jews alone, assuming that they can get to Heaven on their own track, without our help; (b) aggressively target Jews for conversion, as Christians did throughout the Middle Ages, sometimes employing force, without much success; or (c) accept gratefully from Jews the many gifts they gave us—monotheism, the Ten Commandments, and Jesus come to mind—and hope that our prayers and friendly witness will somehow contribute to their eventual acceptance of the

A Righteous Gentile

"It cannot be true that the Jews, by such a heinous crime, are the cause or occasion of the plague, because through many parts of the world the same plague, by the hidden judgment of God, has afflicted and afflicts the Jews themselves and many other races who have never lived alongside them."

—**Pope Clement VI in 1348, defending the Jews against another conspiracy theory, which accused them of spreading the Black Plague by poisoning wells[9]**

Messiah who came first of all for them. Option (a) appeals to theological liberals, who believe that any person of good will who follows his conscience is in effect an "anonymous Christian." Option (b) is beloved of traditionalists, who regard any criticism of past Church practices as a surrender to secular humanism. Option (c) is the one endorsed by St. John Paul II, Pope Benedict XVI, and the Vatican under Pope Francis. In light of the role that Christian anti-Judaism played in preparing the ground for the Holocaust, and of the paranoid anti-Semitism that appears to be bleeding over into Europe and America from the Muslim world, option C seems both the humbler and the more effective approach to this complex, vexing question.

A Book You're Not Supposed to Read

The Myth of Hitler's Pope: Pope Pius XII and His Secret War against Nazi Germany by David G. Dalin (Washington, DC: Regnery History, 2005).

The Mystical Body of Christ

But the Church still claims the title "people of God." And an organization of Jewish Catholics currently uses "Remnant of Israel" as its name. Another, quite different appellation that popes and councils have adopted to describe the Church emphasizes Jesus as the central focus of Christian faith: the Mystical Body of Christ.

This is a title that the Church has used for itself for many centuries. It taps into a way of thinking about the human race that we modern individualists find deeply unfamiliar, even off-putting—as a family, a collective entity that reaches across all national lines and through every century, back to the Garden of Eden. But if we refuse to think of humanity this way, it's impossible to make any sense of Christianity. If each of us were ultimately an isolated monad—Ayn Rand's idea of what a human being is—then what could it possibly mean to say that we all fell with Adam and Eve? That we were redeemed by Christ? Not just by Christ, but in Christ. From the earliest days of the Church, theologians (beginning with St. Paul) referred to Jesus as the "new Adam," who by His perfect obedience reversed the worst effects of Adam's rebellion against the Creator. In fact, the old sinful Adam died on the cross, and what was raised up on Easter morning was not just the physical body of Jesus of Nazareth, ex-carpenter and itinerant preacher. It was the whole human race, renewed and remade, reconnected with God and eligible for heaven.

On this understanding the Church is the public face of the new humanity, the transhistorical organization—existing both on earth and in heaven—that was formed on Pentecost when the Holy Spirit descended upon the apostles to equip them to wake up the whole human race to its new, radically improved situation. It's through the Church that every human being is offered a new life on earth, and eternal life in heaven in a resurrected body exactly like the one Jesus walked around in for forty days after Easter. The Church must obey Jesus' command to teach this truth to the nations and incorporate any willing person, regardless of race, sex, or nation, into visible communion. The means of doing that are the seven sacraments:

- Baptism, which enacts the death of the "old" fallen man and his resurrection with Jesus from the depths
- Holy Communion, which perfects the Passover dinner that marked the deliverance of the Hebrews from bondage and feeds us spiritually, making it possible to carry on a friendship with Jesus
- Confession, by which the Church's ministers, standing "in the person of Christ," dispense to the penitent the forgiveness of sins Jesus promised

- Confirmation, which seals believers with the Holy Spirit and is meant to give them the strength to face even martyrdom if need be. (For this reason, it was traditionally administered with a light slap on the face.)
- Marriage, which elevates something that was already naturally sacred—the fruitful love between man and woman that propagates the human race—and makes it an image of the union between Christ and the Church, and Jesus and every human soul
- Holy Orders, which empowers certain selected men to offer sacraments and lead the Christian community
- Anointing of the Sick, by which priests carry on the healing ministry that the apostles took on even during the earthly ministry of Christ

Catholics believe that the power to offer these sacraments, and to pass that same power along to other men so that they can benefit mankind, was given to the apostles at a particular place and time: on Holy Thursday, when Jesus gathered his closest disciples for a Passover that turned out to be something quite different—a farewell meal, and the first Eucharist.

Sacramental Christians (Catholics, Orthodox, Anglicans) believe that at this dinner, the twelve apostles—including Judas—were ordained not just as priests, but also as bishops. We trace the powers and authority of our bishops by direct ordination, through one man's laying his hands on another's shoulders, all the way back through the centuries to Holy Thursday night. One weak link in that chain would render null and void all the orders of every priest or bishop in a given "line" of apostolic succession, ever after.

Thinking of the Church as a "mystical body" helps us understand why it needs a hierarchical structure. The Church is not some amorphous spiritual

★ ★ ★

Only as Strong as the Weakest Link

"Apostolic succession" became an important issue for Anglo-Catholics—Anglicans who were rediscovering the treasures of their ancestors' Catholic patrimony—in nineteenth-century England. During the Reformation three centuries earlier, anti-sacramental radicals had gained control over the English church under King Edward VI and Queen Elizabeth I. Determined to banish the "superstitions" of the Roman Church, they purposely altered the ceremonies used in ordaining priests and bishops to eradicate the Catholic theology of the sacraments, especially the Eucharist—which the new Anglican authorities, like the most radical Protestants on the Continent, saw as purely symbolic. When Anglicans of the Oxford Movement in the 1800s, such as John Henry Newman, wanted to revive the medieval and apostolic devotions of their religious ancestors, they began to worry about whether the orders that they had received were valid—or if the chain of ordination had been purposely broken. In 1896, Pope Leo XIII studied the issue at the request of Catholic-leaning Anglicans—and concluded, sadly, that because of the Reformers' tinkering with the rituals, Anglican orders had been rendered "absolutely null and utterly void." So Anglican Eucharists, however lovely, really *were* purely symbolic, just as the founders of Anglicanism had intended, and their clergy were pious laymen in handsome chasubles. (When the world-famous Newman eventually followed his own logic into the Roman Church, he was treated as a simple seminarian applying to be ordained.) Only marriage and baptism, which don't strictly require a priest in order to be valid, remained as valid sacraments in the Church of England. To answer Leo's objections, "high church" (Catholic-leaning-over-backwards) Anglicans went so far as to get themselves ordained or re-ordained by Eastern Orthodox bishops, who carry on the apostolic succession just as Roman Catholic bishops do. Today, of course, in many Anglican and Episcopal churches, a new breed of theological radical has taken over, and flouts Christ's example of only ordaining men. The women chosen as priests and bishops in such churches are in Catholics' eyes merely laymen (heh, heh), and the Apostolic succession hits another dead end.

amoeba that engulfs all human beings whether they like it or not, as liberal theologians like to imagine, taking everyone willy-nilly to heaven. Nor is it a secret Gnostic virus, carried by a tiny elect of ultra-spiritual ascetics that rescues only a tiny elite from hell, as rigorist and pessimistic Christians have sometimes suggested. In fact, the Church is fallen mankind redeemed and transfigured, which makes it a primate—the highest primate. So its complex body needs faculties, structures, and parts. It needs to be hierarchical, with a brain, a heart, and hands. It needs a rational faculty that will help it make decisions and a firm will that renders some of its judgments definitive and final.

This is where the bishops and the pope come in.

★ ★ ★

A Conversation You're Not Supposed to Have

Why Should We Believe Any of This Stuff?

Q: Why are you a Christian?

A: Because, out of all the worldviews I've ever encountered, Christianity seems most attuned to human flourishing on earth. It makes the most sense of life, fosters more just societies, promotes the dignity of the person, restrains and undermines tyrannical systems of government, and encourages virtuous conduct, generosity, and kindness. While the record of Christian societies is far from perfect, they embody all these values much more clearly than any other arrangement. That tells me that those people are on to something.

Q: What are they "on to"?

A: A truthful explanation of who man is, what he's here for, what's wrong with him, and how to fix it. Or rather, Who had to come here to fix it, and what we should do in response.

Q: OK... even assuming all that, does that prove that Christianity is true?

A: It's hard to see how you could prove that a religion is true. I'm not sure that anyone who didn't meet the resurrected Christ has ever had the kind of "proof" you're talking about—and even they could have questioned themselves. If Christ appeared to a roomful of atheist psychiatrists today, I doubt that they'd all convert. More likely, they'd put themselves on medication to suppress hallucinations.

Q: But haven't you had personal religious experiences that serve for you as evidence?

A: As it happens, I have. But so have Muslims and Buddhists. Such things are not proofs but clues. They could all be delusions, wishful thinking, or the neurological side-effects of having an Irish-American mother. As ex-Marxist philosopher (then anti-communist dissident, then convert back to Catholicism) Leszek Kolakowski points out, there is literally no sign that God could give us that would be so big and miraculous that it could prove the vast array of unlikely, even paradoxical assertions entailed in

★ ★ ★

Christian faith.[1] A skeptical scientist who saw the sun dance at Fatima could find a dozen less implausible explanations than "It's a miracle! The Virgin Mary appeared here in Portugal."

Q: So why choose the Catholic Church?

A: Because it has the original claim to be the Church Christ founded, continuity with Him, a powerfully convincing intellectual account of what the Gospels mean and what they don't, and a record of faithfully passing along apostolic beliefs—however unattractive to the culture that surrounds it. Also it has produced by far the best body of art, literature, architecture, and music. I'm not sure beauty will save the world, but it makes the place much more livable.

Q: What could convince you that the Catholic Church isn't true?

A: Should a pope get up one day and teach ex cathedra (that is formally, solemnly, from the chair of Peter) that...let's say...Mary was NOT assumed into heaven. In short, if any pope solemnly denied any dogma that had previously been solemnly affirmed by the Church.

Q: What would that prove to you?

A: Here's what it would not prove: that Jesus isn't God, that the sacraments are invalid, or that life is a meaningless series of incidents that winks out at the grave. It would prove just one thing: that the pope is not infallible, hence Vatican I wasn't valid, and hence that the Eastern Orthodox have been right for the past thousand years. That might ruin my day, but it wouldn't wreck my life. Perhaps I would walk down the street to that nice Greek church I've been passing for forty years, pray in front of its icons and eat baklava after the liturgy instead of donuts.

Q: Is there anything that could convince you that Christianity isn't true?

A: Yes. If I came to believe that in fact what Christians teach did not foster human flourishing, that it made earthly life unbearable, and hence was in fact not in tune with the human nature it claims that God created "good."

Q: Give me an example.

A: Okay, let's say the Church took literally Jesus' words about cutting off your hand if it causes you to sin. Every teenage boy on earth would look like Captain

Hook—and the more enterprising ones would castrate themselves, becoming "eunuchs for the kingdom of heaven." One of the Church's most central functions, I think, is letting us know when Jesus was using hyperbole, and when He wasn't.

Q: But your example is just absurd.

A: Is it? One of the most brilliant men in Christian history, Origen, made this exact mistake—and castrated himself. More broadly, for hundreds of years, our monks and theologians had a very hard time seeing how marriage could really be holy. Witness the relentless pressure monastic confessors often put on pious couples to "live as brother and sister." Pascal would famously call marriage unworthy of Christians, and convince his sister to drop the man she loved. While it's often the theological Left that calls attention to this anti-sexual heritage (which never rose to the level of doctrine), Pope St. John Paul II alluded to it as the reason he needed to articulate the "theology of the body."

Q: But no one takes such ideas seriously now.

A: Don't be so sure. I talked for two hours to one of the most famous popular theologians in America, and this subject came up. I mentioned the passage where Jesus appears (at first glance) to be saying that it would be better if everyone were celibate, and pointed out that Christ obviously couldn't have possibly meant that literally, since it would destroy the human race in seventy years. You know what the theologian said? "Well, I could envision Christ issuing a prophetic call on the human race to live one final generation of holy witness, to be crowned by the Second Coming."

To that I responded, "No, if Jesus had called on the human race to die out, that would prove to us that he wasn't the Messiah, but some false prophet who was the enemy of our kind."

There are other strands in the Gospel that could be wrenched out of context to distill that kind of poison, and if the Church were to start prescribing the stuff, we would know that its message was false.

Q: Such as?

A: Pacifism. Throughout her history, the Church has not taken Christ's command

★ ★ ★

to "turn the other cheek" as a call for Gandhian non-violence—for fathers to stand by passively as their wives are assaulted, their daughters raped, their neighbors robbed and pillaged, or their countries overrun by neighboring tyrants. That kind of non-violence is profoundly evil, because it is incompatible with decent human life. It denies the most fundamental human drives, implanted by God: to preserve your life and that of your loved ones, to be free, and to keep the fruit of your labors. Any faith that taught us to mortify such drives would be fundamentally Gnostic; it would teach that our human nature, and hence that creation, is evil down to its roots.

Q: What if some future pope embraced Franciscan poverty and called on every Christian to practice it?

A: He'd be calling for mass starvation, of the sort that Stalin imposed in the Ukraine. Some of St. Francis's followers did exactly that, demanding that every Christian live like a friar. These "spiritual Franciscans" were anathematized by the pope—a fact that deeply affirms my faith in the papacy.[2] Likewise, if (to give you another a crazy hypothetical)

a pope asserted that every Christian was bound by monastic obedience and that he had to treat his local pastor's commands as the voice of God, that would create a totalitarian theocracy that we would be right to reject.

Q: What if the pope issued an ex cathedra declaration calling on the wealthier nations to open their borders wide to everyone who wishes to move there?

A: With the outcome that these newcomers could vote to impose their religion on the Christians, or to use the modern redistributist state to confiscate their property and tax them into serfdom? That's what happens when one civilization conquers another, either by war or other means. Any Church that taught that would prove itself Gnostic by denying people's right to preserve their heritage, keep their freedom, and pass on the fruits of their labors to their children. It would die out like the Shakers, and deserve to.

Q: So you're saying that the content of the Church's moral message, including its application to society and politics, is not some secondary question.

★ ★ ★

A: For me and millions of other thinking Catholics, these applications are vital reasons to believe. And so we need to talk about them, to swat down misconceptions and counter new teachings that pretend to be more "radical" embraces of the Gospel, but that are really ancient heresies of a toxic and Gnostic sort.

Q: **Is that why you sound so angry sometimes when these issues arise?**

A: It is. When someone claims that Christian faith demands something life-denying —that it calls for mass celibacy, total pacifism, the end of private property, or anything else that would cripple or kill off the species—they are attacking not my politics, but my faith. The Church is the servant of the Father who created us, and hence the friend of the human race. Those who claim that it is a civilizational suicide cult are saying (though they don't mean to) that Jesus was an imposter who deserved to die in obscurity.

The Pope, the Other Bishops, and When and Why Catholics Have to Believe What They Say—and When and Why We Don't

When most people think of the Roman Catholic Church, they summon to mind the face of the current pope, and perhaps of the nearest bishop. This is not an accident. The only reason we know more about the story of Jesus than the brief allusions that appear in secular literature is that his followers, starting with Peter, the first pope, and the other apostles, the first bishops, spread the Word—energetically, with the confidence that knowing who Jesus is and what He did was essential to transforming people's lives and giving them the access to the sacraments that he laid out as the ordinary, reliable means of God's grace to human souls. The Church calls Jesus' command to preach His gospel "the Great Commission." Christians believe that the Holy Spirit came down on the apostles at Pentecost, giving them the power, courage, and conviction to spread the message of Jesus to the whole of mankind.

But what was that message, exactly? There was no Bible yet: its first books wouldn't be written for at least a decade, and eventually dozens of "Gospels" would appear, each claiming authenticity, many of them teaching some strange and repugnant doctrines. (For instance, some taught

Did you know?

★ Dozens of "Gospels" were written by early Christians, but only four of them were declared canonical by the Catholic Church

★ The word "Trinity" is not found in the Bible; the three-Persons-in-one-God dogma that nearly all Christians believe was clarified only by Church councils

★ The New Testament itself says that it doesn't contain everything that Jesus taught His disciples

★ ★ ★
Lost in Transmission

If you have ever played the game of "telephone" as a child, you know how easily even a simple statement can get garbled in transmission. How much more a complex and mysterious re-interpretation of ancient Jewish tradition, extending its offer of a relationship with God to the whole human race? If you start out with something like "There are seven sacraments that serve as the ordinary means of grace for mankind," it would be easy enough, after it passed from person to person a few dozen times, to end up with "The hair of eleven statues' syrup is fortunately green or gray—the banned kind." I think you'll agree that this formula is much less theologically exact.

that the body itself is evil, and that Jesus had to come to earth to liberate us from the corruption of fleshly existence. This theory, always popular in hot climates where people eat garlic and bathe infrequently, is called Gnosticism—from the Greek word for "know it all.") It wouldn't be until 397, at the Council of Carthage, that the Church would finish weeding through those books and clarify which ones had divine inspiration, while the others were merely "inspirational" or frankly demonic. In one "infancy Gospel," a boy who accuses Jesus of breaking the Sabbath and another who runs into Him and knocks Him down are both struck dead.[1]

However wacky some of the "apocryphal Gospels" are, there are religions running around today calling themselves Christian that are equally distant from the authentic Gospel in their teachings about key moral issues—because their leaders have severed themselves from any controlling authority. So even when they claim to follow the Bible, in fact what they are obeying is a vague and sentimental reading of the Scriptures that would have been unrecognizable to any Christian in the fourth century, tenth century, or even the seventeenth century. Sadly, many who call themselves "progressive" Catholics are just as guilty as any liberal "mainline" Protestant of garbling the Gospel—while some of the most anti-hierarchical Protestant denominations cling to it fairly closely.

Why Popes? Because the Buck Has to Stop Somewhere

For practical as well as theological reasons, the Church needed a hierarchical structure from the beginning, to reconstruct what exactly Jesus had said, from the memories of those who'd heard Him say it, and to ponder what it meant. The next step was to translate it into terms that would make some sense to people who'd never met Jesus in the flesh—some of whom weren't even Jewish. So the apostles (bishops) began to have meetings (councils) that made decisions about their message (doctrines).

And every group needs a leader, someone who can break a deadlock, stick up for embattled minorities when they're right, browbeat pig-headed majorities when they're wrong, and generally serve as the place where the perennial buck goes to stop. Happily for the Church, Jesus had already picked a leader for it, and thereby suggested a mechanism for creating a succession of leaders for the future. Peter wasn't the smartest apostle, or the most devoted. His three-fold denial of Jesus on Holy Thursday suggests that he wasn't the bravest. He wasn't Jesus' half-brother (or cousin) the apostle James. And perhaps that was Christ's point: in choosing the apostle who would serve as the final authority for the others, the "rock" upon which He would build His Church (Matthew 16:18), Christ was taking an utterly ordinary man and making his position as leader of the Church entirely dependent on supernatural help—what Christians call "grace," a free gift of God that requires only our humble willingness to accept it. Students of history agree that the men who ended up as popes—sometimes after a flurry of bribery, scheming, and influence peddling, or the murder of their predecessors—were not the best men available on earth to serve as religious leaders. They weren't always towering intellects or—as we have already seen—even virtuous men. Their everyday pronouncements on politics, science, and even religious matters were often riddled with mistakes.

A Book You're Not Supposed to Read

The Bad Popes by Russell Chamberlin (Stroud: Sutton History Classics, 2003).

There is just one thing that Catholics believe about every pope who legitimately held that title: not one has ever taught ex cathedra ("from the chair" of Peter)—that is, when he was making a solemn pronouncement of a dogma for the whole Church—anything on faith or morals that contradicts "the Deposit of Faith." (That crucial term refers to the body of teachings that Jesus gave to the apostles in oral form, that they passed on to the bishops whom they ordained, and that the inspired authors partially recorded in the form of the New Testament.) That's quite a claim—astonishing in its boldness, but surgically narrow in its scope. Only two statements by popes in history are universally accepted as infallible—Pope Pius IX's declaration in 1860 that the Virgin Mary was conceived without original sin, and Pope Pius XII's statement in 1950 that she was assumed into Heaven at the end of her life. There are six others whose wording and scope probably meet the criterion, and they are on equally technical questions of theology. None of them has to do with sex, economics, or politics—which might explain why they attract little interest from the media.

Does that mean that apart from two (or eight) narrow definitions, Catholics are free to believe whatever we please? You might get that impression if your religious education consisted of lackluster CCD classes and the average of two (often ecumenical or progressive) "religious studies" classes required at most Catholic colleges.[2] Loudly "Catholic" politicians such as Joseph Biden and Nancy Pelosi who dissent from crucial Catholic doctrines would be pleased if you thought that. But of course it's absurd. Before we get into the history, let's consider the question logically: Catholics believe in papal infallibility...exactly why? Because a council of the bishops of the Church taught it...infallibly. That was the First Vatican Council, in 1870. It's just one example of how, from the very beginning of the Church, it has been in meetings of the apostles, and then of their successors the bishops, that Christians have discerned which teachings were true to what Jesus had told them, and which ones were weird innovations or crackpot theories—in theological jargon, "heresies."

Virtually everything that Christians share in common as points of faith was not found unambiguously stated in the Bible or determined by popes, but arrived at as the decision of often contentious councils of bishops. For instance:

- Christ's equal divinity with the Father (Nicaea I, 325)
- The equal divinity of the Holy Spirit (Constantinople I, 381)
- That Mary is the Mother of God (Ephesus, 431)
- That Jesus has both a fully human nature and a fully divine nature (Chalcedon, 451)

Church Councils or the Bible, Which Came First?

The first Church council, which is actually described in the fifteenth chapter of Acts, took place in Jerusalem. The bishops present included the original apostles and Paul, who had offered the curious theory that non-Jews could join the Church without first becoming Jews via circumcision and obeying the complex kosher laws. Initially, Peter opposed Paul's acceptance of Gentile converts as dangerous, perhaps because the innovation might discredit the Gospel with Jews. But Paul's arguments convinced him, and Peter stood down, opening the Church to every nation on earth. It would be councils like this one, composed of the men chosen by these apostles, and then the men those men had chosen, that would preserve and promulgate the verbal traditions and scriptures that make up the Christian faith.

Even the word "Trinity" is not found in the Bible, and the doctrine of three divine Persons in one God was not the subject of any of the eight probably infallible declarations from the popes. That understanding of the Divinity only became clear as it was hammered out in the early Church councils.

These councils would continue over the centuries, generally being summoned by a pope or another leading bishop to resolve a theological controversy or address some festering scandal. Until 1054, the bishops of the East and the West met in common, and generally acknowledged the Bishop of Rome as having a leadership role in the Church; councils that he condemned were dismissed as having no authority.

Councils that the pope approved were treated as having infallible authority on matters of faith and morals. It is the teachings of those councils that form the core of Christian faith, shaping the way that later Christians would read the Bible—even Christians like Martin Luther and John Calvin, who rejected the principle that such councils were infallible.

It was not until 1870 that the Church—in a council, albeit one boycotted by the bishops of the Orthodox East—declared that a pope could teach with the same authority as a council, on his own and without the consent of bishops. In the years since Vatican I, a pope has done so only once.

★ ★ ★
Thieves in Bishops' Clothing

Ephesus II (449), the council that denied that Jesus has two natures (human and divine), is known as the Latricinium or "Robber Council." The pope was not in attendance, but the papal legate (the pope's representative) Hilarius voted against the decision of the council—before fleeing for his life from angry bishops attempting to impose the Monophysite heresy by force. Ephesus II and its declarations were condemned at the Council of Chalcedon (451).

It's important to know all this because it is easy for Catholics to fall into the trap of overemphasizing papal authority, even seeming to deify the pope, treating his every statement, encyclical, or policy decision as being straight from the mouth of God. In fact, by historical standards, some 99.9999999999 percent of papal statements come with no guarantee of infallibility. That doesn't mean they are wrong. But insofar as they are authoritative, it is because they repeat and explain what Christians have always believed—at least implicitly—since Jesus taught it to His apostles face to face. The Church has no authority to add to or subtract from the Deposit of Faith—the totality of the Gospel revelation was complete at the time of the death of St. John, apostle and evangelist—but must simply pass it along unchanged, occasionally clarifying it or restating it in more comprehensible terms.

The Magisterium: A Backstop against Creeping Unitarianism

This is where that mysterious (and to some, menacing) institution "the Magisterium" comes in. Magisterium just means "teaching authority," and the "Extraordinary Magisterium" is the infallible teaching authority vested in popes and councils when they define dogmas. Infallible teachings of the Extraordinary Magisterium—that is, of the pope defining dogmas either in union with the bishops at a Church council or speaking on his own ex cathedra—are dogmas of the faith that can never change. We owe them "the assent of faith." In other words, being Catholic means you have to believe them, from the divinity and humanity of Jesus Christ (established at the Council of Nicaea in 325) to the Assumption of the Blessed Virgin Mary (solemnly defined by Pope Pius XII in 1950). The "Ordinary Magisterium," on the other hand, refers to the pope's and bishops' authority to pass along the teachings of Christianity that came down to us from the apostles—teachings that, for one reason or another, no pope or council ever got around to defining infallibly via the "Extraordinary Magisterium." Those "Ordinary" teachings demand not "the assent of faith" from all Catholics, but only the lesser category of "religious assent." We are to accept what the pope and the bishops teach on faith and morals, if we want to be faithful Catholics, not "dissenters."

Why do we need the Magisterium at all—Extraordinary or Ordinary? So we can know for sure what the Gospel really is. Christians were spreading the faith for decades before the text of the New Testament was complete and centuries before it was officially canonized, and even after that they had no access to printing presses. The followers of Christ reported to the world what they had seen and what Jesus had told them, and the Gospels were

★ ★ ★

Ordinary and Yet Infallible

Confusingly, a teaching of the "Ordinary Magisterium" can actually be infallible, too. But only if an important condition is met: all the bishops in the world have to teach it in union with the pope. Interestingly, the argument that the teaching of *Humanae Vitae*—that contraception is wrong—is infallible rests not on Paul VI's reiteration of that moral principle in *Humanae Vitae* itself, but on the case that he was reiterating a doctrine in consonance with centuries of previous Church teaching—as even John Noonan admits in his impressive (if dissenting) Contraception. *Humanae Vitae* does not solemnly declare dogma, the papal spokesman who presented it denied that the pope was speaking ex cathedra, and the pope did not contradict him. Nor have subsequent popes taught solemnly on the subject of contraception, even when they have reiterated that authoritative teaching. So the case that we can know for sure that contraception is always wrong rests on the argument that, from the beginning of the Church, the bishops and popes all condemned it.

composed from these oral traditions as well as from—in the case of the apostles Matthew and John—eyewitness reporting by the Gospel authors themselves.

But the New Testament doesn't contain everything that Jesus taught the apostles. As we read in John 21:25, "But there are also many other things which Jesus did; were every one of them to be written, I suppose that the world itself could not contain the books that would be written." Catholics and Eastern Orthodox Christians believe that this is a reference to the oral teachings that Jesus passed on to the apostles, which they put into practice and passed along without including them in the Gospels. It was against the rich body of Christian oral teaching that the bishops judged the very books of the New Testament when they drew up the canon of Scripture, weeding out dozens of inauthentic, even heretical "Gospels." Thus the Deposit of the Faith comes to us by way of two sources: Sacred Scripture and Sacred Tradition. That's why the Vatican II document *Dei Verbum* refers to "the word of God, whether written or handed on."[3]

And the Magisterium of the Church interprets the body of what all orthodox Christians throughout the world have believed since the very beginning, because it was taught to them accurately by evangelists who were passing along what their bishops had learned from the apostles—except for those truths that people misunderstood so seriously that councils or popes were forced to define them infallibly, which really is Extraordinary. As *Dei Verbum* explains, "This teaching office [that is, the Magisterium of the Church] is not above the word of God, but serves it, teaching only what has been handed on, listening to it devoutly, guarding it scrupulously and explaining it faithfully in accord with a divine commission and with the help of the Holy Spirit, it draws from this one deposit of faith everything which it presents for belief as divinely revealed."[4]

★ ★ ★

Anti-Magisterial Children's Lit

In *His Dark Materials*, a series of explicitly anti-Christian children's novels, author Philip Pullman calls the evil, oppressive conspiracy that his heroes struggle against "The Magisterium." Of course, Pullman's insult to our Faith was greeted by world-wide condemnation for his bias against Catholics…no, I'm just kidding. Almost no one complained.

The Law Written on the Human Heart

Of course, Christians don't just have faith. When we're doing it right, we also have morals. Those morals have two sources: divine revelation via the Deposit of the Faith, and the natural law that's written on the human heart by our Creator. Often these two sources overlap: nine of the Ten Commandments can be demonstrated by honest reasoning from accurate premises. C. S. Lewis wrote in *The Abolition of Man* about what he called "the Tao," the core principles of moral decency that virtually all cultures share to one to degree or another—don't steal or murder; respect your parents; take care of your children. Divine revelation sharpens, clarifies, and makes these moral insights more persuasive by showing how they are essential to our relationship with God in this life—and, more ominously, in the next.

From the very beginning, the apostles (including St. Paul) and then the bishops whom they appointed as their successors imitated Jesus by drawing

★ ★ ★
"What We Can't Not Know"

We don't have to have the pope, the Church, or even the Bible to know that abortion is wrong. As the great pro-life physician and research scientist Jerome Lejeune said without hesitation when a journalist asked him what he would do if the Church were to approve abortion: "I would leave the Catholic church." The immorality of killing an unborn baby is just one of those things that's clear from the natural law, which Catholic philosopher J. Budziszewski describes as "what we can't not know."[5]

moral conclusions from His message. They taught those morals with the authority of their office, which came from Christ, and Christians listened. That is why Christians know better than to imitate King Solomon and marry hundreds of women, or try to get to heaven quicker by committing suicide. (Neither point is explicitly addressed in the New Testament.) From the very beginning, Christian bishops followed the Ten Commandments and the clear dictates of reason in rejecting abortion at any point in pregnancy, almost two thousand years before scientists fully understood the biological details of sperm and egg. Because the condemnation of abortion was shared by all faithful Christians since the beginning, it is considered part of the Ordinary Magisterium.

The Catholic Faith makes claims on our belief because, on top of everything else, it encapsulates and reaffirms the most profound moral insights that we have as human beings, which our God-given reason provides us. In fact, the sources of divine revelation—Scripture and Church Tradition—which have been interpreted and clarified by the Magisterium of the Church in the pronouncements of the popes and councils of bishops, call us to standards that are even higher than the natural law we know from our reason alone; unlike the Koran, they never dip below it.

Here's an easy test of whether a question is subject to the authority of the Church. Just answer these questions:

1. Can it be deduced from the contents of divine revelation?
2. Can it be deduced from the moral law written on our hearts?

If you answer "no" to both, the issue is beyond the authoritative teaching of the Church and the bishops. That principle applies whether we're talking about the Extraordinary or the Ordinary Magisterium. In the former case, Vatican I made it clear that the guarantee of papal infallibility applies only to teachings on faith and morals by limiting it to those instances "when, in the exercise of his office as shepherd and teacher of all Christians, in virtue of his supreme apostolic authority, he defines a doctrine concerning faith or morals to be held by the whole Church."[6] And the same thing is true about the teachings of the Ordinary Magisterium, as the *Catechism of the Catholic Church* explains, citing the Vatican II document *Lumen Gentium*: we owe "religious assent" when the bishops "teaching in union with the successor of Peter…propose in the exercise of the ordinary Magisterium a teaching that leads to better understanding of Revelation in matters of faith and morals."[7]

A Book You're Not Supposed to Read

Triumph: The Power and the Glory of the Catholic Church: A 2,000 Year History by H. W. Crocker III (New York: Three Rivers Press, 2003).

Everything else the pope and the bishops do and say is fair game for criticism. The Christian faith does not teach us the *details* of medicine, chemistry, astronomy, metallurgy, economics, or political science, although it offers moral standards on the proper use of each. Catholic doctors must not kill—even fetuses with Downs Syndrome or terminal patients—but there's no specifically Catholic way to treat cancer of the pancreas. It is intrinsically impossible for the pope, as pope, to speak with authority on the details of climate science. Nor is he better suited than you or I to evaluate the so-called "consensus" of actual scientists. He might as well be picking stocks or rewriting the scores of Broadway musicals, for which he has equal divine authority: none.

He can do his best to apply the truths of revelation and the moral law to subjects and situations outside the ambit of his authority. But in that case, his judgments are said to be "prudential," and his conclusions are not binding on Catholics who judge the facts on the ground to be different from the pope's understanding of them.

There Is No "Catholic" Ideology That We Have to Believe In

The concept of the Magisterium is easily abused. It's often applied where it doesn't belong—to specific, detailed questions of economics and politics. On such issues, the Ordinary Magisterium of the Church offers broad, general guidelines and unshakeable core principles drawn from natural law and divine revelation. Those teachings hold together and have been consistent since the beginning. When popes attempt to apply these principles to concrete situations, however, that's a horse of a different feather, as we shall see.

Some Catholics sympathetic to big government, open borders, massive social spending, and radical environmentalism have suggested that there is a coherent and morally binding body of papal teaching on politics and economics from which we can derive specific policy initiatives and firmly condemn alternatives as "un-Catholic" or even dissenting.

Hence defenders of market economics or opponents of mass immigration who disagree with what a recent pope has said on one of these issues can be tarred with the same brush as those who favor women's ordination or homosexuality. And we are led to believe that we can actually build up a Catholic political economy that is a "third way" between capitalism and socialism, that bravely "cuts across" the lines dividing Left and Right and between America's political parties.

We can start with papal statements about "hot" issues of the day, ranging from encyclicals on economics and the environment to casual comments to reporters on the papal airplane. We can move forward bravely by reading the fruits of bishops' conferences and statements by the Vatican's various social justice officers. As we proceed, compiling divinely approved answers to each burning current question, we can fill in the empty spaces of politics and economics, then present the Catholic program for the perfect earthly society to a rudderless world like a completed crossword puzzle.

Obiter Dicta

One of my favorite reference books is *The Pope Speaks*, which collects the allocutions and conferences of Pope Pius XII on subjects ranging from ophthalmology to beekeeping. It's amazing how well informed and thoughtful that good man was.

There are smart, sincere people out there who seem to believe that the papacy is a Delphic oracle, that the "spirit-led authority of the Magisterium"[8] inspires the statements of popes about economics and politics, and guards them from error. Even if such statements are not infallible, these Catholics claim that we are obliged to grant the pronouncements a docile religious submission, as we are to non–ex cathedra assertions of Catholic teaching on faith and morals.

I have read earnest attempts to collect everything that popes have said on these subjects since Leo XIII and treat them as a kind of divine wish list that Catholics are obliged to accept as the first principles of politics—and defend against every criticism.[9] Such attempts show love for the papacy and ought not to be sneered at. Nor should we simply disregard the papal statements in question, which are largely wise and often profound, and in fact serve as worthy digests of some of the best that has been written or thought.

But is there really a "spirit-led" Magisterium that works by accretion over the centuries, gradually building up a coherent, defensible program of economics and politics, which can be implemented by simply reading what popes have said and fitting those statements together like Lego blocks to construct a Catholic city? Is that what Jesus intended to give us when He founded the papacy?

That's not what the Catholic Church teaches. Even on subjects that are part of our faith (and morals), we don't believe that the pope and the bishops are inspired with new teachings. They are only authorized to teach (which includes interpreting and settling disputes about the meaning of) what's in the Deposit of Faith, which, as we have seen, has not been added to since the death of St. John the Evangelist. And even when they are teaching from the original Deposit of Faith, we do not believe that God guarantees that they'll teach those truths in the most felicitous way—only that their statements will be protected from error (and even that only under the specific circumstances we have discussed).

A pope has the power to invoke his infallible teaching authority to settle any question of natural law, but there is no consensus that any pope has ever done so. We have seen, for example, that in *Humanae Vitae*, Pope Paul VI was exercising the Ordinary Magisterium as applied to contraception, an issue of natural law, and that the argument that Church teaching on that subject is infallible rests not on the authority of *Humanae Vitae* itself, but on the fact that the Church—the pope and the bishops teaching in union— has consistently condemned it throughout its entire history.

If the believers in the "spirit-led" Magisterium are right, then we should be able to survey papal statements over the centuries on economics and politics and find in them the same exquisite consistency we see in papal teachings about contraception, abortion, the two natures of Jesus Christ, and the sacraments—the slow, organic unfolding of the implications of the divine revelation that came to a close with the death of St. John the Apostle.

But if we find—by, say, comparing and contrasting the various papal statements over the centuries on lending money at interest—that the papal teaching on economics and social issues does not exhibit the same crystalline consistency, we might be tempted to leave the Church, or else to resolve the cognitive dissonance by blocking out or distorting the inconvenient facts of history in bad faith—literally. We'd be clinging to a "faith" that had morphed into a modern-style ideology. I am not sure which of those two temptations would be more deadly, to abandon faith or to corrupt it.

But those are not the only choices. A third way is to accept that Catholic social teaching is not really analogous to Eucharistic doctrine and Marian dogmas, which are 100 percent "Deposit of the Faith" issues, with the councils and popes simply handing on what was originally revealed and, when necessary, stepping in to settle doubts and clarify what it has always meant. When popes have weighed in on the economy and the right way to organize civil society, revelation and natural law are involved, but so are prudential judgments—which makes Catholic social teaching a mixed bag.

Where popes teaching on politics and the economy are espousing moral principles, they're exercising their ordinary magisterial authority (which covers both faith and morals) to hand on and interpret the Deposit of Faith, so we have seen Catholics must render "religious submission" to their judgments. Thus, there are clearly defined moral teachings that set limits on what Catholics can believe about politics and economics. A Catholic economist can't embrace Ayn Rand's "virtue of selfishness" or adopt the communist notion that "all property is theft." Both of those positions clearly fall afoul of commandments that Catholics must believe and obey: "Love your neighbor as yourself," which makes it pretty clear that selfishness is not in fact one of the virtues, and "Thou shalt not steal," which demands respect for other people's property rights. Those doctrines can be found in divine revelation (see Mark 12 and Exodus 20) and also in the natural law written on our hearts. And they have been underlined by popes using their ordinary teaching authority, such as when Leo XIII defended both private property and our obligation to use it for others' benefit in his encyclical *Rerum Novarum.* But the broad moral principles that have been clearly and consistently taught by the Church for the past two thousand years do not add up to a detailed "third way" politico-socio-economic program. Any such program could never be binding on the faithful, as it would necessarily include many prudential judgments about facts. Because, remember, the Church's teaching authority simply doesn't extend beyond faith and morals.

Where the popes have opined on the details of economics and social policy, making their own prudential judgments in applying the moral principles from divine revelation and the natural law to concrete factual situations—assessing the social and economic conditions on the ground, as it were—what they have left us is not magisterial teaching, but something much more akin to the Catholic literary tradition—a treasure trove of often brilliant insights and deep investigations into the best ways for men to live that claims our respectful attention.

So instead of attempting to apply Catholic social teaching as the blueprint for the perfect Christian society, we could quote a papal encyclical where it is apropos as we might cite a piercing insight from Dante or Walker Percy, aware that when popes spoke on the details of economics and politics, they were addressing key implications of natural law as best as their intellects and advisors advised them.

Christ never intended the papacy to serve an oracular function on current events, party politics, and the details of economics. The popes try to act as shepherds, consulting their knowledge of Church tradition and natural law, to come up with the wisest, most prudent ways to apply the timeless principles drawn from both at a given moment in time...and sometimes they make mistakes. Jesus never meant to leave behind an oracle. When we invent one for our convenience, we are forging a golden calf.

Does God Pick the Popes and Put Words in Their Mouths?

There's a popular belief current among some pious Catholics that God chooses each man who's elected pope, and that for this reason we must suspend our critical faculties in the face of strange papal statements, puzzling papal decisions, and counterproductive papal policies. After all, God knew what He was doing when He inspired the cardinals to choose this particular man and

★ ★ ★

Contrary-to-Fact Condition

Take the magnificent condemnation of Nazism in Pius XI's encyclical *Mit Brennender Sorge* (*With Burning Sorrow*)—ghost written by the future Pius XII, who has been wrongly pilloried as "Hitler's Pope"—as an example of the popes' social teaching, an application of the morality we learn from revelation and the natural law to a concrete political situation. In fact, the encyclical is an accurate and damning exposure of Nazi evils. But suppose that we imagine—to propose an obviously counter-factual scenario—that a Catholic reader of that encyclical had known for a fact that Hitler was really a nice guy who was just getting bad press, that he wasn't really an anti-Semite working for the dominance of the Aryan race, and that the Nazis only had the best interests of the Jews at heart. That reader would have been justified in disagreeing with the pope's conclusions about Nazism. But he still would have been obliged, as a Catholic, to render religious assent to the underlying principles that the pope was teaching: that that no group of human beings has a right to dominate other groups on the basis of "race and blood" (morals) because we're all one human race descended from Adam and Eve (faith).

foresaw everything he would say and do in office. Hence, the pope's words are God's words, and his actions are the result of the providential will of God. Some pious Catholics took St. John Paul II's election as a sign that they should learn Polish, or adopt his idiosyncratic philosophical views. More recently, others have taken the election of Pope Francis as a hint from God that they should adopt his economic and political views.

There are just a few problems with this theory. For one, the Church has never taught it—anywhere, ever. Never even hinted at it. As we have seen, Vatican I said that the pope is infallible in his ex cathedra pronouncements on faith and morals—not in every idle comment he makes to the press corps on an airplane. And even in his exercise of the Extraordinary Magisterium to define dogma, the pope's statements are not necessarily inspired, only protected from error.

For another, it amounts to idolatry, elevating the merely human actions and opinions of a mere man, chosen by men, to the same level as Jesus' own deeds and sayings. The kindest word that an orthodox theologian would use to describe this inflation of the papacy is "pious superstition," but in fact by conflating man with God it breaks the First Commandment, making the pope a graven image whom we effectively worship. Protestants who are exposed to this ultramontane attitude have good reason to mutter "Antichrist" under their breath. Read the account in the Book of Revelation, and you will see that they have a point.

As for the idea that the Holy Spirit takes over the wills of the cardinals and chooses His own candidate for pope each time…let's get real. The cardinals who elect the pope are not infallible in their choice; they're not even protected from obvious errors, let alone inevitably inspired by the Holy Spirit. Yes, we have had an excellent run of pious and learned men for the past couple of centuries—but the papacy didn't always attract such holy souls.

People don't believe superstitious nonsense about the papacy because the Church has taught it; instead it is a psychological phenomenon. Understandably, we want to look to the pope as a spiritual father figure, and each of us has at some point in our childhoods imagined our fathers as perfect. Because the pope is the public face of the Church that leads us to God, it is easy—if we are lazy—to confuse the sign with the thing it points to. That confusion is touching, but deeply dangerous, because it suggests that we can give up the arduous task of thinking for ourselves and clinging to the Deposit of Faith passed on from previous popes. Hence if this pope contradicts the views of a pope who lived in the past, some even act as if God had changed His mind—that the pope is an ongoing oracle revealing bold new truths that Christ has whispered to His Vicar. Now this is not a Catholic or even a Christian theory. It is what the Mormon church holds about its earthly leadership: that God has granted a committee of elected elders an

★ ★ ★

Uninspired Choices

We've already met the clichéd choice for an obvious bad pope: Alexander VI. In addition to his other faults, that Borgia pope used papal funds to promote the military exploits of the robber barons in his family. But he was even better known for dishonesty and violence. As Machiavelli remarks (admiringly, of course) in *The Prince*, "Alexander never did anything, nor ever thought of anything, but how to deceive men...."[10] Then Leo X, a Medici pope, is supposed to have said, "God has given us the papacy. Let us enjoy it." But these popes were far from the worst ones the Holy Spirit has allowed the Church to elect over two millennia. That honor really must go to Pope Stephen VI, who dug up the corpse of one of his predecessors, Pope Formosus, to try the dead pope for heresy. As I recounted in *The Bad Catholic's Guide to the Seven Deadly Sins*:

"In the course of the festively named 'Cadaver Synod,' the rotting form of Pope Formosus was disinterred (minus the three fingers used for papal blessings, lopped off at Stephen's orders), vested in papal robes, propped up in a chair, and charged before a court of bishops with a long list of crimes. These ranged from perjury and impersonating a priest to an attempt at seizing the papacy by force—but all were merely pretexts for the new pope to vent his rage upon his predecessor, who'd taken the opposite side in the struggle for power in Rome. The reigning pope (surprise!) won a guilty verdict against the dead one, and the court declared that even the priestly ordinations Formosus performed had been invalid. Formosus's body was thrown in a potters' field, then dug up again and tossed into the Tiber.

"Legend tells that Formusus's body bobbed back up in the Tiber and began performing miracles. This comeback so impressed the Roman mob that they rose up and deposed Stephen, who was promptly strangled in prison. This sordid Dark Age prequel to *Godfather III* was mitigated only by the absence of actress Sofia Coppola."[11]

Was Pope Stephen the Grave Robber the best candidate available, in the eyes of the Holy Spirit? Or maybe, just maybe, his election was the result of human actions, such as bribe-taking and coercion...

ongoing revelation, which can flatly reverse the contents of previous revelations. Hence when the state of Utah sought admission to the Union but was held back by the "divinely revealed" Mormon practice of polygamy, a

★ ★ ★
The Development of Doctrine

If the Church just keeps teaching the same truths of the Gospel and the moral law, all of which were already revealed in the apostolic age, then why do popes, bishops, and councils need to make declarations at all—and especially, how can they newly "define" dogmas that haven't been defined before? With apologies to blessed John Henry Newman, who explained "the development of doctrine": the teaching of the Church is like your foot. From time to time a heresy comes along, like a pebble that gets into your shoe. As a result, your foot doesn't really take a new shape, so much as its original shape takes on a clearer definition and a new hardness in response to the pebble. Thus it wasn't until Arius came along claiming that Jesus was created that the Council of Nicaea had to solemnly define the dogma that the Son was eternally begotten of the Father—though that had been a truth of the Gospel all along.

new revelation could come from God via His elders, and polygamy went from being obligatory for Mormons to outright prohibited. If the Catholic faith really worked this way, why should we bother with it?

The results of such papal idolatry (or "papalotry") has been plain to see in the Catholic press, especially after the election of Pope Francis: a childlike credulity in the wisdom, insight, and supposed prophetic qualities of the pope, and a willingness to defend his every assertion—even those that are clearly just personal reflections, casually offered on airplanes by an exhausted man in his seventies, speaking on subjects of which he has little personal knowledge. Some Catholics are willing to twist the plain meaning of Francis's words, or twist logic into pretzels, or toss out centuries-old understandings of such issues as immigration, capital punishment, or private property, to match their imperfect understanding of perfectly fallible words that might have been carelessly translated. More ominously, some Vatican officials are willing to play off this popular superstition and use it to enforce a kind of top-down groupthink on issues that fall entirely outside of the pope's proper authority. The most infamous instance occurred when Bishop Marcelo Sánchez Sorondo, a close advisor to Pope Francis, addressed a contentious public colloquium on global warming, on December 3, 2015, in Rome. As LifeSite News reported:

[I]n his address Bishop Sorondo spoke of "global warming" saying that in *Laudato Si* "for the first time in the Magisterium" Pope Francis "denounces the scientifically identifiable causes of this evil, declaring that: 'a number of scientific studies indicate that most global warming in recent decades is due to the great concentration of greenhouse gases released mainly as a result of human activity.'" He repeated the point later, saying, "faith and reason, philosophical knowledge and scientific knowledge, are brought together for the first time in the pontifical Magisterium in *Laudato Si.*"

This led to a heated exchange with panel presenters at the conference, especially journalist Riccardo Cascioli, who objected to the suggestion that Catholics must submit to pronouncements on "scientific theories" rather than "faith and morals."

Sorondo retorted by saying, "When the Pope has assumed this, it is Magisterium of the Church whether you like it or not— it is the Magisterium of the Church just as abortion is a grievous sin—equal (it is the same)…it is Magisterium of the Church … whether you like it or not."[12]

So Catholics who deny that human beings are causing catastrophic global warming that must be ameliorated through drastic restrictions on our use of energy are morally equivalent to pro-choice politicians like Nancy Pelosi—who by Church law should not even be receiving Holy Communion. Or so says the learned Bishop Sorondo, the chancellor of both the Pontifical Academy of Sciences and the Pontifical Academy of Social Sciences.

Sorondo was willing to admit—under pressure from questions by fellow participants, including Father Robert Sirico of the Acton Institute and Father Joseph Fessio, S.J.—that Pope Francis's climate forecasts are not taught infallibly. That is, in his opinion they are not part of the Extraordinary Magisterium

★ ★ ★
Magisterial Equivalence

Sorondo's assertion is staggering, and it has staggering political implications. Count on dozens of social justice Catholic bloggers to use Sorondo's statement relentlessly to try to convince Catholic voters that, according to the Vatican, global warming is an equivalent issue to abortion. Given that premise, pro-life candidates such as Ted Cruz and Marco Rubio, who reject the Paris Climate agreement, are no better than Hillary Clinton and Bernie Sanders, who want to fund Planned Parenthood's baby-parts business. So you're free to vote for Bernie Sanders.

but merely of the Ordinary Magisterium, which is not generally infallible but demands religious assent from Catholics, who may not publicly dissent from it without committing a serious sin.[13]

Now the pope does have the authority to promote and reaffirm the truths that clearly follow from natural law. So if Pope Francis were to say simply, "It is sinful to render the earth uninhabitable," he would be correct, and within his authority. But on questions of whether that is in fact happening, why it's occurring (if it is), or what's the best way to remedy it (assuming it's a real problem in need of a solution), he has no special authority.

Don't tell that to high-level Vatican diplomats, like the one who argued—in a talk at a U.S. think tank conference I attended—that Catholics must learn to suppress their rational doubts about what Pope Francis says on economics and politics and heed his "prophetic voice." Apparently the pope is a veritable fountain of new revelation, or radical new readings of existing revelation that are binding on every Catholic.

Such a statement is quite at odds with the Church's real teaching on papal authority, but it sums up an attitude very common among editors of Catholic newspapers and magazines—as those of us who have tried to defend older doctrinal formulas, more traditional understandings, and more conservative economic and political views have learned by bitter experience. In effect, inside the hermetically sealed world of professional Catholics, the Mormon theory is what is actually practiced.

Cafeteria Catholics...and Feeding Tube Catholics

"Cafeteria Catholic" is a term for people who pick and choose from the Church's non-negotiable teachings on faith and morals, based on what seems right to their private consciences formed by the secular culture around them, their own urgent desires, and the writings of disaffected Jesuits and radical nuns who have traded in Thomas Aquinas for Karl Marx, Carl Rogers, or Carl Jung. Do you find the Church's historical teaching on divorce too much of a "hard saying"? There are theologians, up to the level of Cardinal Kasper (the friend of the zeitgeist), ready to nuance it into oblivion. Do you feel that the Church's condemnation of abortion or homosexual "marriage" is too "patriarchal"? Here's a coven of nuns ready to teach you all about the love of the goddess.

But when faithful Catholics question the current pope's exotic economic views, which he himself has said are not binding on Catholics,[14] suddenly those who dissent from core Church teachings are ready to break out the thumbscrews. What we might call Feeding Tube Catholics crave the certainty that the Holy Spirit has guarded every single step taken by the Church through its two thousand years of history, picking each pope and guiding his daily actions, public statements, and decisions. So whatever the pope is saying at the moment, you should simply shut down your critical faculties and believe it—regardless of what previous popes and councils might have taught. Those go into the Memory Hole, and *pfft!* they never existed.

Before he became Pope Benedict XVI, Cardinal Ratzinger addressed the threat of what we're calling Feeding Tube Catholicism, which would reduce Catholics to the kind of mindless zombies imagined in the worst stereotypes of anti-Catholics like Jack Chick. Ratzinger had already pointed out one case where a pope (Pius IX) had issued a comprehensive manifesto of political statements (the Syllabus of Errors), only to be later contradicted by a Church council (Vatican II in *Gaudium et Spes*).[15] Ratzinger also spoke of the case of Pope St. John Paul II, whose teaching on the death penalty differed from that of previous popes. Ratzinger sharply distinguished between dissent on issues where the church has spoken clearly and consistently, such as abortion and euthanasia, and disagreement with a pope who is saying something new. He reminded us that the teaching of the Church is not some Moscow-style "party line" meant to wipe the minds of believers clean like the shake of an Etch-a-Sketch.[16]

Let me propose, instead of either Cafeteria Catholicism or Feeding Tube Catholicism, a kind of Thomistic golden mean. Let's call it Knife-and-Fork Catholicism. No, we won't pick and choose from the Church's teachings as if we were scanning for our favorite flavor of muffin at a Shoney's breakfast bar. Nor will we lie back, brain-dead, as the latest pope's latest statements are downloaded into our brains like one of Apple or Microsoft's non-optional updates.

Instead we will sit up like men and women with knives and forks at a restaurant. We will accept the balanced, healthful meals sent out by a chef whom we trust. But if there seems to be some kind of mistake, if we find on our plates gorge-raising dollops of stale Cuban, Venezuelan, and North Korean prison rations, we drop our forks. We assume there has been a mistake, since none of this was on the menu. We send the chef a message that we will pass, in the happy faith that the restaurant's Owner will agree and understand.

★ ★ ★ ★ ★ ★

A Conversation You're Not Supposed to Have

The Pope Is Not an Oracle

Q: Is the pope infallible?

A: The safe answer is no.

Q: What do you mean by "safe answer"?

A: That if you say no, you will be right some 99.9999999999 of the time. If I asked you, "Are American women in labor right now?" your answer would be the same. But in both cases there would be rare exceptions. A tiny percentage of American women are giving birth as you read this, and an even tinier percentage of statements made by popes throughout history were infallible.

Q: Which ones?

A: We aren't entirely sure.

Q: You're kidding, right?

A: No. There are only two statements that popes have made that the Church explicitly labels as infallible. There is a list of six other papal statements that are *probably* infallible, and a raft of popes' teachings that some people claim are infallible, while others disagree.

Q: That seems...less than helpful. Which two statements are Catholics sure about?

A: In 1850, Pope Pius IX taught that all Catholics must accept an ancient Christian belief about Mary, the mother of Jesus: that God granted her a kind of baptism at her conception. Since God stands outside of time, He could give her the graces of Christ's redemption in advance. So when she was born, she was just like Adam and Eve at their creation: free of original sin. She started with a blank slate, instead of the toxic inheritance of warped will, blinkered reason, and constant temptation to sin that afflicts the rest of us. She was still nothing more than human, and was completely free to sin. But unlike Adam and Eve, she never did. Without this special gift from God, she absolutely would have sinned, just as the rest of us do. So there's nothing special about Mary in herself; she is simply the most transparent example of God's saving grace in action.

Q: I don't buy it, but go ahead. What's the other one?

A: It's tied to the first teaching. Because Mary was spared, through the grace of Christ, the stain of original sin, she was also spared one of its consequences: her body dying and rotting in the ground. Instead, at the moment of her death, she was assumed into heaven—in much the same way that the Old Testament teaches Elijah was. This is another ancient Christian belief, which Pope Pius XII declared in 1950 was not just opinion but fact.

Q: **What about the other six, the probably infallible statements?**

A: They address complex questions of faith:

- The natures of Christ (He has two— divine and human)
- The two wills of Christ (ditto)
- What happens to your soul after you die (you are judged right away)
- The role of free will in salvation (it's decisive)
- And the authority of the pope over local bishops, despite the interference of secular monarchs (bishops get their authority from God via Rome, not through politicking)[1]

Q: **So is the rest of Christian doctrine and morality up for grabs—er, I meant to say, "left to the individual conscience"?**

A: Absolutely not. Almost all of the central teachings that Catholics believe, which most faithful Orthodox and Protestants share, came from teachings at councils of bishops in the early Church. The bishop of Rome presided over some of these, played a role in others, and approved still others from a distance. These councils (such as Nicaea and Chalcedon) were the key means the Church used to figure out which books to accept as authentic books of the Bible and how to interpret what they mean. We believe that the teachings of the councils in union with the pope were protected by the Holy Spirit from error, and hence that their statements on faith and morals are infallible.

Q: **Okay, so you people believe that these Church councils were universal and could declare infallible teachings?**

A: Yes. Our Orthodox brothers argue that there were no such infallible councils after the Eastern and Western churches split, whereas Catholics hold that the councils of the Western churches continued to be infallible. And according to the next-to-last such council, Vatican I

★ ★ ★

(which ended in 1870), we believe that on rare occasions the pope can act alone with the same authority as a council. This doctrine of papal infallibility was very controversial in its time, and many Catholics opposed the idea. They argued that such a doctrine was unnecessary, divisive, and an obstacle to reunion with the Orthodox.

Pope Pius IX, on the other hand, thought that a declaration of papal infallibility was essential to shore up the authority of the pope in an age when nationalism was sweeping through the West, including the Church, pitting French cardinals against German ones, as Catholics were becoming more loyal to their nation states than to the church. In fact, as the world would see in 1914, Catholic bishops on both sides of World War I would bless the armies marching to the trenches and speak of the war as a holy crusade. So Pius IX had a point: it would be very hard to run the Church via councils of bishops in those circumstances.

Had Pius had his way, Vatican I might well have made virtually every papal statement on any important subject binding on every Catholic—enshrining the pope as a kind of oracle. But the Holy Spirit does protect ecumenical councils from error, and what Vatican I approved was much more modest. It taught that in a narrow set of very special circumstances, when the pope explicitly announces that his statement is infallible, then Christ will grant him protection from error.

Q: So on those occasions what he says is considered divinely inspired, almost prophetic?

A: No. And we don't think that of councils either. Catholics believe that God wouldn't let a council or a pope solemnly teach heresy. He'd prevent it, as He prevented the Church from accepting forged documents as Gospels. Think of it as a divine veto power, which might take the form of a still, small voice in a pontiff's heart. Or maybe a sudden heart attack.

Q: What about when the pope writes or speaks on politics and economics?

A: Most of the time, those topics involve specific disputes about how to apply moral principles, questions of facts on the ground, or arguments over what's prudent. Infallibility can't apply to any of those "prudential" judgments. When he's writing on those subjects, the pope is just an ordinary man—although in most cases a wise and learned one, whose ideas we should take seriously. For instance, when Pope Paul VI wrote in *Populorum Progressio* that the right way for rich countries to help poor ones was to tax their citizens and send money to Third World governments, that was a suggestion worth considering. But faithful Catholics can and did disagree. Many have noted that such foreign aid now—almost forty years after he made that suggestion—has an extensive track record of all too often ending up in Swiss bank accounts or being spent to prop up corrupt regimes. Pope Paul VI made a prudential judgment, and faithful Catholics are perfectly free to reject it. The same applies if a pope speaks out on immigration policies, welfare programs, or Middle Eastern politics.

Q: A lot of Catholics seem to disagree with what you just said. They suggest that the Holy Spirit picks who's elected pope, then protects his everyday statements and policies from error.

A: The Church has never said any such thing—out of deference to the First Commandment, and perhaps to avoid becoming the laughingstock of even Catholic historians.

If the Holy Spirit directly picked the popes without human agency, we'd have to ask why He picked so many close relatives of previous popes and so many cardinals who bribed their way to the throne. We've done much better with choosing popes since the Council of Trent, but the process never became magical. Sometimes the cardinals pick a weakling, a coward, or a bully. Popes do have original sin. The Holy Spirit oversees the selection process, of course, but allows a lot of scope for human freedom—and folly.

The pope can't infallibly predict the weather, draw up the U.S. budget, or tell us which wars are just or unjust. Think of the five "crusades" against "heresy" that Pope Martin V launched on cities full of Christians. Popes misused their authority so often and so egregiously that it helped cause the Reformation.

The Church has never pretended that Jesus made each pope a magical fountain of new divine revelations or brilliant policy ideas. We do the Church no favors by inflating the papacy's claims like a balloon. Our history is full of needles that could pop it.

CHAPTER 3

One, Holy, Catholic, and Thoroughly Splintered Church

Before the Second Vatican Council (1961–65), the Catholic Church was a byword for unity and rigorous, centralized leadership. As recently as the sixteenth century—and given a Church that thinks in centuries, that's considered recent—the Church had been split along national lines, with German and French and Spanish cardinals voting as blocs at the Council of Trent and putting the interests of their countries ahead of the Church's. But the trauma of the Reformation and the persecution of the Church at the hands of the French Revolution had shown the importance of a powerful papal hand at the wheel. The Jesuits, founded by St. Ignatius of Loyola with a special vow of personal obedience to the pope, had fanned out around the world, running elite academies and colleges, disseminating the message that the Church was ruled from Rome.

In the nineteenth century, Pope Pius IX (1846–78) had pushed back hard against explosive European nationalism, whose adherents sometimes made idols of their "fatherland," even composing "catechisms" that laid out their eternal faith in things as temporal and passing as Italy or Germany.[1] We've already seen how he proposed papal infallibility—defined at Vatican I, the council he convened for that purpose—as a corrective to bishops'

Did you know?

★ Pius XII, who has been called "Hitler's pope," actually collaborated in an assassination plot against the Nazi dictator

★ Until just after Vatican II, the Roman Catholic Mass had not changed significantly in fifteen hundred years

★ Paul VI wept when he encountered the effects of his liturgical reform

competing loyalties to their nation states. Pius IX raised the profile of the papacy, defended the Church's interests against aggressive monarchs, and broke the backs of national bishops' groups.

Pius's successor, Leo XIII (1878–1903) reached out to the working classes of Europe, issuing the first papal document addressing modern economic problems, *Rerum Novarum*. (We'll explore that fascinating encyclical later, in chapter seven.)

Pope Pius X (1905–14) reacted to the rise of "Biblical criticism" that put the often shaky opinions of scholars above Church tradition and even the literal sense of Scripture, harshly suppressing those "Modernists" who urged the Church to revise its doctrines to suit "modern times." He removed professors from Catholic universities, cracked down on seminaries, and demanded that every priest and bishop swear a sacred vow rejecting the Modernist idea that the truths of religion could be relativized or abandoned to suit the changes in secular thought.

Pius XII (1938–59) vigorously denounced both communism and Nazism—the pope even collaborated in a conspiracy to assassinate Adolf Hitler[2]—and squelched efforts to replace the philosophy of St. Thomas Aquinas with more recent thinkers' systems.

But the Church could only delay its confrontation with secular modernity, and rally its forces. It couldn't outright avoid it—any more than the Anglican or Orthodox churches have been able to avoid reckoning with the greatly changed circumstances of life in the modern West.

Bishops in Western Europe, who were living comfortable lives—often with their incomes guaranteed by their countries' governments, thanks to "concordat" treaties with the Church—were especially prone to pressure from theologically liberal professors in their own Catholic universities. As Europe had become more secular and prosperous, some Catholics had become impatient with the disciplines and dogmas of a Church whose institutions had evolved in a much tougher world, in centuries when life was usually short, often lived in fear of hunger or under the whip of autocratic governments. In the unprecedented prosperity of postwar Western Europe, the Catholics in the wealthiest (and hence most influential) countries, such Germany, the Netherlands, Belgium, and France, began to demand that the Church adopt a more "human" face. Whether this would entail turning the Church's face away from God would be the subject of much debate—such as took place during the Second Vatican Council, which the moderately liberal but orthodox Pope John XXIII summoned in 1960, shocking the world.

Vatican II: Pope John XXIII's Fragmentation Bomb

Entire books have been written that detail in depth the theological and ideological battles that were waged at Vatican II. Don't worry, we won't get into all of that here. Suffice it to say that the summoning of the council raised enormous expectations among many Catholics who had chafed for years under one constraint or another that they were living under—nuns

Books You're Not Supposed to Read

If you want to know what the stakes really were at Vatican II, how far from the traditional Catholic Faith radical theologians really wanted to go, and how hard orthodox bishops had to fight to stop them, *The Rhine Flows Into the Tiber* by Ralph Wiltgen (TAN, 1991) exposes how the most bleeding-edge leftist theologians (such as Hans Küng, Karl Rahner, and Edward Schillebeeckx) were leading by the nose bishops from the wealthiest churches on earth, in Germany, the Netherlands, and Belgium.

These progressive bishops worked with avante garde theologians, and secular journalists on the outside, to keep up pressure for radical changes in Catholic doctrine. One theologian who served at Vatican II and took part in the orthodox resistance was Romano Amerio, whose book *Iota Unum* (Angelus Press, 1996) reveals how poisonous some of these new ideas really were, and tells the story of the close-run but successful struggle of faithful bishops at Vatican II to keep the Faith.

who disliked their habits, Jesuits who wanted to get involved in revolutionary politics, intellectuals who wanted to replace Thomas Aquinas with Kant or Jung or Sartre. Intense debates at the council resulted in mostly modest changes—but Vatican II was followed by some much more radical changes in practice, especially in the liturgy.

Only a single document of the council could be said to amount to a development of doctrine, revising a major teaching on religious liberty (or, rather, against it) that had often been repeated throughout Church history. Since shortly after the Roman Empire had ceased to persecute the Church under Constantine, many leading Catholic thinkers had argued that the empire should go further and promote the true religion as it promoted just laws, sound public order, and public health. It was St. Augustine's position, for example, that the government should further the common good, and that that included the salvation of souls—through membership in the Catholic Church. Pope after pope and council after council had said the same, right up through Pope Leo XIII in the late nineteenth century.

Put into practice, this theory meant that the state would disadvantage other religious groups, from Jews to dissenting Christians ("heretics" in traditional Catholic parlance). Harsh restrictions were placed on Jews living in newly Christian countries; pagan temples were not just defunded but destroyed or seized and turned into churches. Over many centuries, preachers whose doctrinal positions diverged from the Church's official teachings could be arrested, imprisoned, and in the worst cases burned alive—a practice that Christians learned from Muslims in Spain. The cruelties of the Inquisition—both the Roman version that was directly controlled by the pope, and the much harsher Spanish one that often defied his wishes, for instance in its persecution of Jews—made a deep black mark on the record of a Church that preached free will, mercy, and a loving God.

★ ★ ★

Everybody Expects the Spanish Inquisition

The crimes of the Inquisition were real, and no Catholic should try to whitewash them. But they have also been grossly exaggerated by secular historians, and used as a shabby argument against Catholicism—and against Christianity itself, since most Protestant countries also employed persecution against their own dissenters. The notorious Spanish Inquisition executed only about 2,250 people.[3] And adding up all the people directly killed by the various versions of the Inquisition, but setting aside the victims who died as a result of mistreatment and neglect in prison, the total figure is around six thousand. In fact, the Inquisition was invented in the first place partly to bring the prosecutions of heretics under stricter controls, so as to prevent secular rulers from waging crusades against heretic communities, burning innocent parties at the stake, and using heresy prosecutions to settle political scores.[4]

These figures cover hundreds of years. By comparison, according to R. J. Rummel, communist regimes murdered some 110 million civilians in the seventy years after 1917.[5]

The hunting of heretics seemed to backfire in the long run; for instance, in Spain and France, which had once been fiercely intolerant of dissenters from the Church, anticlerical movements rose to power and used the long-ago cruelties of the Inquisition to justify much harsher attacks on clergy and believers. Catholics subjugated under communist regimes from Poland to China made arguments for their own religious freedom—and were answered by their jailors that their own Church did not believe in freedom as a principle. Franco's Church-friendly regime still outlawed Protestant churches, and at one point non-Catholic evangelists were outlaws in much of Latin America. And today, even in the United States, where Catholics have never been in a position to impose our religion on anyone, and religious liberty has been the law of the land since the American Revolution (partly as a result of the work of Founding Father Charles Carroll, the only Catholic who signed the Declaration of Independence) those on the other side from Catholics on any political issue regularly invoke the Church's past endorsement of coercion. "Keep your rosaries off my ovaries" would have a lot less resonance if the defenders of legal abortion weren't subtly invoking the ancestral fear that Catholics are secretly angling to bring back the Inquisition.

Most influential of all the factors affecting the bishops' decision to endorse religious liberty was the success of the Catholic Church in America, which had never enjoyed any favor from the government, but had flourished in the face of deep popular suspicion and the occasional anti-Catholic law. A curious coalition of three quite different groups of bishops put *Dignitatis Humanae* over the top at Vatican II: patriotic Americans such as New York's Francis Spellman who saw the American experiment with religious liberty as a roaring success; liberal Western Europeans, such as Belgium's Leo Suenens, who were embarrassed by the Church's authoritarian past; and Eastern European conservatives such as the young Karol Wojtyla (the future Pope St. John Paul II) who urged the Church to embrace the principle of liberty that they needed to make their case against communist repression. This unlikely alliance prevailed over conservative bishops such as Marcel Lefebvre, who warned that reversing course on an issue on which so many popes had spoken in authoritative terms would open the door to demands by liberal Catholics for many other radical changes. On that point, even those of us who welcome the Church's revised teaching on religious freedom have to admit that Lefebvre proved prophetic.

But the Church's new position on religious freedom was a relatively obscure point compared to the much more visible and practically important subject of the liturgy. Going into Vatican II, Catholics of the Latin Rite (more than 90 percent of the Catholic Church) had a highly formalized liturgy that had not changed significantly in almost fifteen hundred years. It was conducted by a priest who faced a marble altar with his back to the congregation and softly recited prayers in a dead language (Latin), with responses quietly offered by altar boys, while the congregation either flipped through bilingual missals or prayed the rosary. Back when that liturgy had originally been codified in fourth-century Rome, Latin was the language of ordinary people, who typically gave the responses themselves and joined in the Church's liturgical chants. In some other Catholic rites, such as the Ukrainian and

Melkite, liturgies had been revised and translated into new vernaculars, but the Roman Rite was frozen, beautifully, in amber—which kept it safe from doctrinal diversions and fashionable meddling, retained its universality across a Church with hundreds of languages, and made it the subject of some of the greatest music ever written, exquisite compositions from Palestrina's polyphonic masterpieces to Mozart's *Requiem*, even to music by the Lutheran Johann Sebastian Bach. That changelessness also made the liturgy less than satisfying as the main worship vehicle of ordinary Catholics.

In 1960, no one was especially happy with the state of the Roman liturgy, which various popes had tried to revitalize by teaching more people Latin or urging the rebirth of Gregorian chant, whose beauty they hoped would engage ordinary Catholics. (Sadly, none of these initiatives had had much effect.) But conservatives feared that tinkering with the liturgy would make the Church's central rite subject to improvisation by freelancing priests, dumbing-down in the name of reaching everyday Catholics, and countless abuses that would reduce the reverence that laymen had for the Body and Blood of Christ. The modest revision of the liturgy that Vatican II approved in its document *Sacrosantum Concilium* sought to guard against such dangers by mandating that Latin would remain the language of the liturgy (with the readings and certain prayers permitted in the vernacular), that Gregorian chant would retain pride of place as the music of the Mass, and that the priest would continue to lead the people in prayer with his face toward the altar against the wall of the church—as priests did in every other Catholic rite, as well as in the Eastern Orthodox churches.

That compromise might well have worked, but it was never really tried. Pope Paul VI, the pope who followed John XXIII, overrode the decision of the council and handed the revision of the Catholic liturgy to a small committee of experts, one of whose leaders was Rembert Weakland, (who worked with a number of other proponents of ecumenical dialogue), and even some Protestant advisors, to craft a new liturgy that would minimize

★ ★ ★

Not the Dream Team

Paul VI's Consilium for the Implementation of the Liturgy included not only Rembert Weakland, who would later resign as archbishop of Milwaukee after a gay payola scandal, but also the infamous Annibale Bugnini, who had opined, "We must strip from our Catholic prayers and from the Catholic liturgy everything which can be the shadow of a stumbling block for our separated brethren that is for the Protestants." In 1975 Bugnini was suddenly removed from his position in liturgical reform and sent to Iran as the Apostolic Pro Nuncio—apparently because Paul VI had been convinced that he was a Freemason, something incompatible with the position or the presumed faith of a Catholic archbishop.[6]

the elements of the Mass that underlined doctrinal differences dividing Catholics, Anglicans, and Lutherans—in the hope of crafting a liturgy that would promote the healing of denominational splits. What resulted instead, of course, is all too familiar to church-going Catholics today: a liturgy that is radically different from parish to parish, depending on the orthodoxy and personal tastes of the pastor, but reliably uninspiring virtually everywhere. Further changes either approved by Paul VI—or adopted without permission and then presented to that weak pope as faits accompli—such as Communion in the hand, turning the priest to face the congregation, standing for Communion, and lay Eucharistic Ministers, all combined to radically change the weekly experience of Catholics.

Instead of a starkly formal, impressive, if somewhat distant ritual that was clearly an extended sacrificial offering focused entirely on God, the Novus Ordo (New Order) liturgy that now dominates most parishes around the world is comparatively folksy—even without the atrocious "folk music" that guitar-banging nuns foisted on Catholics throughout the 1970s. The priest faces the people and treats them as an audience, with microphones making sure that his every word—including his improvisations and chit-chat—is carried to every believer. An ethos of entertainment has largely displaced the solemn gravity that once marked the Mass. Instead of kneeling at a marble rail to extend their tongues over a gold plate and receive the Body of Christ from the blessed hands of a priest, Catholics now troop up to reach out their hands and take it from a layman. Perhaps it is not surprising that Mass attendance has plummeted in every country—even America and Ireland, whose churchgoers were once the most dutiful—while popular surveys show that only a small percentage of Catholics still believe that the host is the miraculously transformed Body and Blood of Christ. How could they, after forty years of watching it be treated like a movie ticket?

The "Spirit of Vatican II" vs. the Texts of the Council

The change in Catholic liturgy, and in other "externals" such as nuns' habits and mandatory abstinence from meat on Fridays, had a huge cultural impact on Catholics. If the central ritual of their faith, the only event that Catholics were bound on pain of sin to attend, could undergo this kind of transformation, Catholics asked themselves—or the secular media asked for them—what else could change? In every revolution, the first thing that radicals change is the flag. Once that has been replaced, in the public mind all bets are off—which is one reason why the commies and the Nazis, when they took power, filled every available space with their banners. Imagine, for a moment, that a newly elected president replaced the Stars and Stripes with the Confederate battle flag. Or that he replaced our fifty stars with the flag of Mexico. Let's say he got away with doing this, and wasn't carried off to an undisclosed location by

★ ★ ★
Hoist on His Own Petard

Even Pope Paul VI was disoriented by the liturgical changes he had promulgated. When he arrived in his chapel to vest for Mass on Pentecost Monday, 1970, he asked the papal master of ceremonies why the vestments laid out for him were green, instead of red for the Octave of Pentecost. The MC told him, "It is green, now. The Octave of Pentecost was abolished."

"Green? That cannot be!" said the pope. "Who did that?"

"Holiness, you did."

And Paul VI wept.[7]

the Secret Service. What would that signify for his administration? If people accepted the change, what else would they be likely to accept? Would anything be off the table?

For progressive Catholics, the answer was clearly, "No." While the approved texts of Vatican II had not opened the door for the alteration of any core Catholic teaching, or even de-emphasized the authority of the pope, still, bishops, clergy, nuns, and Catholic "activists" pretended that they had—that the "spirit of Vatican II" must prevail over its "letter," and that a permanent revolution in Catholic teaching, morals, and mores must be conducted, with no end in sight. The event of Vatican II began to be treated, as penitent liberal Joseph Ratzinger (later Pope Benedict XVI) reflected, as a "super-dogma" that trumped all the authority of past councils and popes.[8] For disgruntled feminists, practicing homosexuals, would-be Catholic Marxists, and other dissenters from settled Catholic doctrine, Vatican II had wiped the slate clean and issued them an invitation to rewrite the Catholic faith from scratch.

Of course, there are many counts on which the traditional Christian faith, especially in its Catholic form, is frustrating and demanding. We wouldn't need the sacrament of Confession if living a Christian life came naturally to us, like breathing, eating, or asserting our will at other people's expense. The explosion of secularism in the past three hundred years has encouraged Westerners to believe that our own claims to self-expression and the outcome of our own (often poorly informed) reasoning ought to trump the dry, stuffy statements of a faith that comes down to us from the apostles—which insists that the will of God, the claims of others, and the structure of creation as ordered by its Creator are somehow more important than our transitory whims. (Even Martin Luther finally had to admit that the Bible doesn't interpret itself, and that human authorities are necessary to rule out selfish, perverse, or ideological misreadings of Sacred Scripture.)[9]

Indeed, one of the main advantages of having a hierarchical Church with the power to make authoritative judgments is that it can resist popular opinion, reject passing fads, defy secular elites, and cling to the core of the timeless teachings of Jesus. It's for this reason, as G. K. Chesterton once observed, that orthodoxy is never "fashionable": it is designed precisely to slough off current fashions, and prevent them from adulterating the authentic Deposit of the Faith. But how can the Church do that crucial job when leading members of its hierarchy, clergy, and academic institutions keep insisting that, in the wake of the Second Vatican Council, the Church's own creeds and anathemas from the past no longer apply—that we must continually reinvent the contents of Christianity by following our secularized "conscience"?

The answer is that it can't, any more than the "mainline" Protestant denominations that have been hemorrhaging members since the early 1960s. For all the excitement and apparent renewed energy that convulsed the Catholic Church in the wake of Vatican II, the profound doctrinal and political divisions that the council exposed and deepened have virtually crippled the Church in the developed world, even in America—which once was seen by as unsympathetic a British Catholic as Evelyn Waugh as

★ ★ ★

Standing Up to the Zeitgeist for Two Thousand Years

The early Church swam against the tide of pagan culture in the Roman Empire, rejecting infanticide and caring for plague victims.[10] In the Dark Ages, Catholicism ended the revenge culture among the evangelized barbarian tribes.[11] A millennium later, when socialism was turning intellectuals' heads and sweeping through the working classes at the end of the nineteenth century, Pope Leo XIII did not embrace it but condemned it. Then, when nationalism and racism were getting Germans drunk on "blood and soil," Popes Pius XI and Pius XII duly condemned such heresies, too. The whole point of having a Church is to keep a line to the "permanent things" and avoid falling down before the idols of the moment—which today are worshiped under the titles of "diversity," "tolerance," and "inclusiveness."

the future of the Catholic Church, because of the high rates of Mass attendance, burgeoning Catholic schools, and thriving seminaries that produced thousands of new priests every year.[12] All that is over now, and according to Pew Research, 40 percent of American adults raised Catholic have left the

Church and not returned.[13] If it were not for mass immigration from Latin America, the Catholic share of the U.S. population would be shrinking, instead of just holding steady. And alarming percentages of those immigrants or their children leave the Catholic Church, either ceasing to practice the faith altogether, or leaving Catholicism for enthusiastic, Bible-basic Pentecostalist storefront churches. Latinos in America, and increasingly in Honduras, Brazil, and other South American nations, are finding doctrinal certitude and spiritual uplift in churches that cling to traditional understandings of morality more firmly than the tepid compromised parishes that their local Catholic churches often provide them.[14]

The Second Vatican Council and the liturgical revolution that followed it certainly played their roles in the fragmentation of what had seemed a unified Catholic Church until the middle of the twentieth century. But the issue that fundamentally split the Catholic Church after Vatican II was not the change in liturgy, and certainly not the embrace of religious freedom. No, it was a much more practical matter that touched every Catholic family, and involved the clash of a long-settled Catholic moral teaching with profoundly new realities of life in the twentieth century. I speak, of course, of birth control.

The split that occurred over *Humanae Vitae*, Paul VI's encyclical confirming the perennial Catholic teaching against contraception, persists. Indeed it has only widened and deepened, forming fissures in the Church that remain to this day.

CHAPTER 4

How Birth Control Tore the Church Apart

Whole books have been written about how birth control divided the Catholic Church. Let's start with the awkward facts of the matter.

FACT: Up until 1900 or so, the whole Christian world was pretty much united in its condemnation of contraception—that is, of anything that interfered in the sex act to prevent the conception of a child. Catholics, Protestants, Orthodox, even Quakers were all largely on the same page. The Christian condemnation of artificial birth control can be traced back for many centuries, and Catholics are fond of unearthing the scorching words of Martin Luther and John Calvin on the subject. We can go back much further, of course, and find condemnations in the writing of St. Augustine and the Didache, an early Christian document rediscovered in the nineteenth century. For nearly two millennia, Christians saw contraception as the tool of hedonists who wished to cream off the pleasure from the sexual act, while denying its natural consequence and only biological rationale: reproduction. Theologians on both sides of the Tiber denounced sexual acts between married people using contraception as the moral equivalent of sodomy or masturbation: mortal sins that turned the marital act from an

Did you know?

★ Margaret Sanger popularized birth control by playing on the WASP elites' fears of poorer, darker people

★ Eugenics was invented by Charles Darwin's nephew

★ A mistranslation in the first English edition of *Humanae Vitae* gave the false impression that it's moral to limit family size only in life-threatening situations

But Tell Us What You Really Think

The Protestant reformers on contraception:

"This is a most disgraceful sin. It is far more atrocious than incest and adultery."

—**Martin Luther**[1]

"When a woman in some way drives away the seed out of the womb, through aids, then this is rightly seen as an unforgivable crime."

—**John Calvin**[2]

occasion of grace into a sin that "cries out to heaven for vengeance."

FACT: By around 1900, thanks to the good offices of modern medicine and hygiene (see capitalism, in chapter seven), the infant mortality rate in the developed world had plummeted. A couple who wished to replace themselves now no longer needed to have five or six children in the hope that two or three would live to adulthood; outside of certain backward regions, most children born alive would make it to adulthood. (One of those backward regions was the Hell's Kitchen neighborhood of New York City where my own Irish-American grandmother bore eleven children, only five of whom lived past the age of four. That was once the global norm.)

FACT: Throughout most of human history, the overwhelming majority of people lived in rural environments. In such a setting, children needed only a rudimentary education to become productive adults; they also could begin taking part in productive work at an early age, either around the house or on the farm. Given the low cost of having children and the need for large families just to replace the population, limiting births was indeed usually the act of a reckless hedonist, as the Church Fathers had written. But with the Industrial Revolution, as people saw that higher incomes and longer lifespans were available in cities, millions and then hundreds of millions moved there—and, out of habit, put their children to work, now in factories. Since factory work is far less healthy for children than gleaning grain or milking cows, child labor soon became a social scandal, and prohibiting it an important social cause. So new laws spared children work in unsafe conditions and freed them up for school. They also made every child a pure economic cost to his parents for the first fourteen years of his life (when an eighth grade education was the standard)—or twenty-two (now that completing college is expected) or indefinitely (with millennials nearly impossible to dislodge from their parents' basements). In the U.S., the proportion of people working on farms has plummeted from 64 percent in 1850 to 2 percent in 2015.[3]

Partly as a result of the combined pressure of these realities, many Christians began to reconsider whether sinful hedonism was always to blame for contraception—particularly when married couples used it to limit their family size. In 1930 the Anglican church's leaders, gathered at the Council of Lambeth, decided that under grave circumstances, Christians could use the existing technology (condoms, diaphragms) to frustrate conception. As the Church of England bishops said:

> Where there is a clearly felt moral obligation to limit or avoid parenthood, the method must be decided on Christian principles. The primary and obvious method is complete abstinence from intercourse (as far as may be necessary) in a life of discipleship and self-control lived in the power of the Holy Spirit. Nevertheless, in those cases where there is such a clearly felt moral obligation to limit or avoid parenthood,

★ ★ ★

Mixed Motives?

The urbanization, wealth, and health brought in by capitalism and the industrial revolution clearly made large families more problematic. But those easier circumstances may also have created a different reason for modern people to question the formerly widespread belief that contraception was wrong. After all, it's easier for a camel to get through the eye of a needle than for the rich to enter the kingdom of God; or, as less authoritative sources have noted, rich people tend to be spoiled rotten. So it's quite possible that selfish hedonism was actually on the rise—and partly fueling the impulse to revisit the ancient Christian condemnation of artificial birth control—at the same time that people had some new (and actually reasonable) reasons for thinking that selfish hedonism wasn't the only motivation for limiting family size.

and where there is a morally sound reason for avoiding complete abstinence, the Conference agrees that other methods may be used, provided that this is done in the light of the same Christian principles. The Conference records its strong condemnation of the use of any methods of conception-control for motives of selfishness, luxury, or mere convenience.

But in that same year, in the encyclical *Casti Connubii* (*Of Chaste Marriage*), Pope Pius XI reiterated the Catholic Church's condemnation of artificial means for limiting births: "In order that [the Catholic Church] may preserve the chastity of the nuptial union from being defiled by this foul stain, she raises her voice in token of her divine ambassadorship and through our mouth proclaims anew: any use whatsoever of matrimony exercised in such a way that the act is deliberately frustrated in its natural power to generate life is an offense against the law of God and of nature, and those who indulge in such are branded with the guilt of a grave sin."

This statement was clear and definitive: contraception was intrinsically immoral, not just wrong if it was being used for selfish reasons. The encyclical also reaffirmed that bearing and educating children were the primary purposes of marriage, to which lifelong faithfulness and love were added benefits, and included powerful condemnations of other social phenomena that were challenging marriage—particularly the growing legal and social acceptability of divorce. Pius also forthrightly condemned the popular eugenics movement, a pseudo-science that applied the model of cattle-breeding to human beings, in social engineering schemes intended to improve the "stock" of the human population and supposedly eliminate criminal and other anti-social behavior. This then-respectable discipline—invented by Charles Darwin's nephew, Francis Galton[4]—was especially relevant to the birth control debate in the United States, where the activist leading the charge to legalize birth control and make it socially acceptable was Planned Parenthood founder Margaret Sanger. Sanger began as a sexual radical and libertine, a close associate of early sexologist Havelock Ellis. She was an apostle of "free love" who practiced what she preached, abandoning her husband and young children to travel Europe and conduct a series of casual affairs.[5]

Sanger had grown up in a large family, and seen her mother die shortly after giving birth. She chafed at the grim biological fact that the ecstasy of sex was chained to pregnancy, to medical risk and physical pain, to squalling brats and stinking diapers. Why should the best, most exciting moments in life be yoked by a pulsing pink umbilical cord to years of sacrifice and self-denial? Just as Marx looked at how men interact economically and saw a dark conspiracy, Sanger stared at the facts of mammalian reproduction, and saw them as a crime against women. An unplanned pregnancy was a biological injustice, and this "Woman Rebel" (the title of Sanger's first magazine) would lead a revolution to correct it. As she suggested in 1922, in *Woman and the New Race*, "...the most merciful thing that the large family does to one of its infant members is to kill it."

Sanger campaigned for sexual license for years with no success—even landing in jail several times—before she discovered a useful political "wedge issue": the deep anxiety of Anglo-Americans over mass immigration from Southern and Eastern Europe. As Robert Marshall and Charles Donovan show in exhausting detail, Sanger used the Protestant elites' tribal fear of displacement by browner people to make discussion of birth control

Two Books You're Not Supposed to Read

Blessed Are the Barren: The Social Policy of Planned Parenthood by Robert G. Marshall and Charles A. Donovan (San Francisco: Ignatius, 1991).

War against the Weak: Eugenics and America's Campaign to Create a Master Race by Edwin Black (New York: Four Walls Eight Windows, 2003).

acceptable—if at first only as something for the law to impose on other, "lesser" people. She would campaign successfully in thirteen American states for laws that mandated the forced sterilization or even castration of those who failed that era's primitive, culturally biased IQ tests. Sanger's laws would be used as a model by Nazi Germany, which imported one of Sanger's closest associates, Harry Laughlin, to advise them on implementing their plan to reduce the number of "inferior" children born to German mothers.[6] The last of those American eugenics laws would only be repealed in 1974.

Even as she claimed to advocate sexual freedom, Sanger favored massive, federal involvement in the reproductive life of every American. As she wrote in "America Needs a Code for Babies":

> Article 1. The purpose of the American Baby Code shall be to provide for a better distribution of babies, to assist couples who wish to prevent overproduction of offspring and thus to reduce the burdens of charity and taxation for public relief, and to protect society against the propagation and increase of the unfit....
>
> Article 3. A marriage license shall in itself give husband and wife only the right to a common household and not the right to parenthood.
>
> Article 4. No woman shall have the legal right to bear a child, and no man shall have the right to become a father, without a permit for parenthood....
>
> Article 6. No permit for parenthood shall be valid for more than one birth....
>
> Article 8. Feeble-minded persons, habitual congenital criminals, those afflicted with inheritable disease, and others found biologically unfit by authorities' qualified judge should be sterilized or, in cases of doubt, should be so isolated as to prevent the perpetuation of their afflictions by breeding.[7]

Sanger also took a particular interest in limiting reproduction by African-Americans. As she wrote to a colleague in the birth control movement, "We should hire three or four colored ministers, preferably with social-service backgrounds, and with engaging personalities. The most successful educational approach to the Negro is through a religious appeal. We don't want the word to go out that we want to exterminate the Negro population, and the minister is the man who can straighten out that idea if it ever occurs to any of their more rebellious members."[8] She agitated for the government "to apply a stern and rigid policy of sterilization and segregation to that grade of population whose progeny is already tainted, or whose inheritance is such that objectionable traits may be transmitted to offspring."[9] Everything connected with the woman most responsible for making contraception socially acceptable is repugnant.

But it wasn't only racism, WASP insecurities, or dreams of a master "race of thoroughbreds"[10] that drove Sanger's successful campaign to legitimize contraception. Birth control was also seeming more acceptable on account of the practical demographic questions that we have seen were facing modern couples because of the suddenly blessedly low rate of infant mortality and the growing cost of childrearing and education. For those reasons, many Catholics were seeking to rear smaller families, and in 1951 Piux XI's successor addressed birth control in an allocution to Italian midwives. In that statement, Pius XII allowed that the goal of reducing the number of births or spacing them further apart was legitimate and urged doctors to perfect the only morally acceptable method for achieving it: periodic abstinence during the times when a woman is fertile.

This in itself was a theological development, since that very practice had been condemned by St. Augustine, whose statements on marriage were the primary source in Pius XI's teachings on the subject. And Pius XII even said that "grave motives" might exempt some couples "for a long time, perhaps even the whole duration of marriage" from the

★ ★ ★
What's in a Name?

In the 1950s and '60s many Catholic couples used the "Rhythm Method," which depended on assuming that the fertile time in a woman's monthly cycle could be predicted from her previous cycles. Unfortunately, as we've all heard, past performance is no guarantee of future results. Today, the tiny percentage of Catholics who still take the Church's teaching on birth control seriously use "Natural Family Planning," a term that covers a variety of more accurate methods for identifying a woman's fertile days and avoiding conception by means of abstinence during that time.

responsibility to become parents. The pope was clearly accepting that something better than hedonism was at work among married people who sought to regulate their fertility; what remained controversial between the Church and the opinion of the rest of the world was what means could be used to achieve that end morally.

Meanwhile, two developments in the broader culture were influencing the thinking about birth control. Eugenics had been disgraced by its associations with Nazi genocide. But another factor was distorting and grossly exaggerating demographic concerns: the alleged looming threat of "overpopulation." Just as with the eugenics movement, Planned Parenthood also played a role as a key propagandist for the overpopulation panic. Social scientists, ecologists, and social engineers (there's a lot of overlap among those groups) looked at the unprecedented rise in human population that had taken place in the nineteenth and twentieth centuries as the result of better nutrition, modern medicine, and sanitation—themselves the results of capitalism, as we have seen. The death rate, especially among infants and young children, had plummeted. Now, on the face of it, this would seem like very good news: by the second half of the twentieth century women in Ireland, Africa, India, Brazil, and the Philippines—like women in Europe and North America in the previous century—were suddenly much less likely to die in childbirth, and to have to mourn lost babies and toddlers. But as a result the global population, which had been doubling every hundred and fifty to two hundred years, now seemed likely to double in mere decades. And this possibility panicked the world's movers and shakers, such as the sponsors of the Malthusian Population Research Bureau, which noted with alarm, "World population growth accelerated after World War II, when the population of less developed countries began to increase dramatically. After millions of years of extremely slow growth, the human population indeed grew explosively, doubling again and again; a billion people were added between 1960 and 1975;

Take Your Choice

"The Church's stand on birth control is the most absolutely spiritual of all her stands and with all of us being materialists at heart, there is little wonder that it causes unease.... Either practice restraint or be prepared for crowding."

—**Flannery O'Connor in 1959**[11]

another billion were added between 1975 and 1987. Throughout the 20th century each additional billion has been achieved in a shorter period of time. Human population entered the 20th century with 1.6 billion people and left the century with 6.1 billion."[12]

Even as the fruits of amazing modern technologies were transforming human life in much of the world, the elites in the most prosperous and influential countries had abandoned the Christian humanism that—by teaching Europeans that the world was an orderly mechanism that followed discoverable laws, with man as its prudent steward—had unleashed the scientific revolution in the first place (see chapter ten). A grab-bag of ghastly ideologies competed for the intellectual loyalty of the educated Western elites—and subtly influenced even those who never became true believers in any of them. The "dialectical materialist" Marx convinced many leading thinkers that economics was simply how men cooperate to pool their resources and talents but a dark struggle for dominance between social classes locked in irreconcilable enmity. Others became drunk on Darwin, who pictured all life as a relentless and brutal fight for "survival of the fittest" in a world of scarce resources. A century of increasingly radical

The Difference between Nationalism and Patriotism

"'My country, right or wrong,' is a thing that no patriot would think of saying. It is like saying, 'My mother, drunk or sober.'"
—G. K. Chesterton[13]

nationalism (1848–1945) taught millions of Western Christians to dehumanize members of other "racial" groups.

The combined effect of these grim anti-Christian philosophies, drummed into the public through government schools, state propaganda, and popular entertainment, was to make the explosion of human lifespans across the planet seem more like a plague than a blessing. And in the wake of the Second World War, but especially in the 1960s, governments around the world began to take the advice of their pessimistic experts and plan for ways to stem the tide of human reproduction within their borders. Having long ago lost faith in God, the educated classes lost faith in man, and accepted the warnings of dour environmentalists that Earth's resources would soon be exhausted. Professional pessimists like Lester Thurow and Paul Ehrlich wrote bestsellers and appeared on popular TV shows to warn of a "population bomb" that would inevitably cause mass famines, resource wars, and the brutal deaths of hundreds of millions of people. Governments promptly took action, imposing forced birth control (often sterilization) on poor women in their countries, sometimes as the price of food or medicine.

In the democratic West, there were few overt attempts to impose birth control by force—though some Western governments, including that of the U.S., conditioned foreign aid to poor countries on coercive schemes of birth control and sterilization.[14] And elites convinced by the new pessimism about population poured millions into private organizations like Planned Parenthood, which promised to offer solutions in the form of more advanced birth control. Indeed, that organization helped to fund the research that produced the birth control pill, which was introduced in

★ ★ ★

Planned Parenthood and Communist China Led a Gendercide against Baby Girls

The worst population control program was in China, imposed by the communist regime that had ruled that country since 1949. In 1980, that government adopted a "one-child" policy as a means of stemming population growth and maintaining its absolute control over Chinese society. (That same government, just nine years later, would roll over student protesters with tanks in Tiananmen Square.) A Chinese communist official boasted in 2015 that this policy had cut Chinese population growth by 400 million people as of 2011.[15] In a secretive dictatorship such as China, it is impossible to know how many of these casualties were the result of forced abortions. The Chinese branch of Planned Parenthood helped to enforce the policy on the ground, shaking down peasants for crippling fines to punish "illegal" births.[16]

A climate of fear and coercion has dominated Chinese family life ever since, as informers and spies hunt down women with "illegal" pregnancies, and families desperate for at least one son to support them in their old age have resorted to sex selective abortion on a massive scale. According to Lifenews, in China, "more than 120 boys are born for every 100 girls. This has created a bachelor society of men who will be unable to marry and has given rise to more crime, sex trafficking, prostitution, and other problems."[17] China has the highest female suicide rate on earth. In 2015, the Chinese government announced a "generous" concession to its people, expanding its one-child policy to two. Any Chinese who have more than two children are still subject to persecution.

the U.S. for contraceptive use in 1960—coincidentally, the first year of the Second Vatican Council.

The Church and the Pill

Theologians eager to stay in tune with the times urged the Church to approve use of the Pill in order to stem the tide of "overpopulation." Pastors heard the stories of women who felt overwhelmed by childbearing, or who faced economic problems, and hoped for a change in Church teaching, which didn't seem impossible in a climate where so much else—the liturgy, nun' habits, Church rules about the sacraments—was seemingly up for grabs. What is more, the fact that the Pill (unlike the condom) did not directly interfere in the mechanics of sexual intercourse made it seem like a more acceptable method.

For all these reasons, Pope John XXIII, and then Pope Paul VI, agreed to revisit the issue. For the first time in history the pope created a theological commission—staffed by theologians from around the world, and eventually including some married laymen and women—to advise him on a controversial question. The commission deliberated from 1963 to 1966, and its final report (delivered in secret but leaked to the media) approved the use of artificial contraception. But dissenters from the committee's report worked privately with Pope Paul VI, urging him to maintain the teaching of Pope Pius XI and Pope Pius XII—and twenty centuries of Christian condemnation of artificial birth control. And in 1968 the pope issued *Humanae Vitae*, which again condemned contraception, but offered broad permission for the use of Natural Family Planning for "just" and "serious" reasons, in accord with the virtue of prudence. (Unfortunately, the hasty and imprecise translation in the first English edition of *Humanae Vitae* led many Catholics to view even NFP as acceptable only in life-threatening emergencies—and others to reject the teaching altogether.)[18]

The bottom line of *Humanae Vitae* was that the goal of limiting families could be justified under a wide array of circumstances. However, using artificial means of contraception was intrinsically evil—meaning that (like other intrinsically evil acts, such as sodomy and adultery) it can never be justified, even to save one's life. Neither alteration of the sex act nor sterilization, whether permanent or temporary (as in the case of the Pill), could ever be a moral act. In extreme cases where a pregnancy could be fatal, marital celibacy was the only option.

Pope Paul's logic was compelling, and it arose from the solid core of Catholic teaching on natural law. It advanced on what Pope Pius XII had taught, that parents have the right and even the duty to limit their fertility to match their resources. Ever since Augustine, the Church had recognized that educating children, both in the Christian faith and in the skills needed to go on and become independent adults, was every bit as important as bearing them in the first place.[19] As St. John Paul II—who would remind married couples that they must be "open to new life" and accept it "generously"—would also explain, responsible parenthood sometimes "demands renunciation of procreation" when "any further increase in the size of the family would be incompatible with parental duty" including the couple's "mutual sense of responsibility for the birth, maintenance, and upbringing of their children."[20]

But the Church had also always rejected interventions that violate the very nature of the sexual act by separating its "unitive" from its "procreative" purpose. And that teaching, too, was reiterated in *Humanae Vitae*. To re-use an analogy I employed in *The Bad Catholic's Guide to Good Living*: Pope Paul approved of weight loss, but he insisted we do it through dieting, not bulimia. Natural Family Planning, which Catholic doctors helped to pioneer, entails carefully

★ ★ ★

The Roots of the Birth Control Battle

Contraception (Harvard University, 1986) is a scholarly historical study by John Noonan, who favored changing the teaching on the issue, but scrupulously documented its deep roots in the thinking of Church Fathers. Nevertheless, he argued that the issue had never been decided infallibly and made the case that traditional Church views on marriage had been developed entirely by celibates and were marred by an anti-sex bias, with insufficient attention to the experience or sanctity of married couples. A new emphasis on love and mutual self-giving, Noonan argued, should broaden the traditional view that marriage is mainly justified by biological reproduction.

Catholic Sexual Ethics (Our Sunday Visitor, 2011) by William E. May, Ronald Lawler, and Joseph Boyle Jr. restates the underpinnings of Pope Paul's teaching on contraception—and of the rest of Church doctrine on sexual sins, including homosexual acts—in Scripture, Church history, and natural law thinking.

observing the natural process of fertility and trying to work around it—instead of blocking its action. It shows respect for God's design, and it requires patience, sacrifice, and close coopera-tion of a couple. It has no medical side-effects—unlike the Pill, which imposes significant health risks on women.

The immediate response to *Humanae Vitae* was a firestorm of public and private dissent on the parts of bishops, theologians, professors, and "activist" Catholics. For several noisy years Catholics had been told by their pastors that there was good reason to believe that Church teaching would change, and millions of them around the world had adopted contraception in good faith. Many felt betrayed by *Humanae Vitae*—and were unwilling to go back to old habits, or a "rhythm method" whose effectiveness was still uncertain. (Later studies have shown that Natural Family Planning is at least as effective as condoms, perhaps less effective than the Pill.)[21] The majority of the pope's own commission had argued for the opposite conclusion, and some of its members went public, condemning what they considered the back room politicking that had undermined their work.

As we have seen, a papal spokesman denied that *Humanae Vitae* was an infallible declaration—and Pope Paul VI did not contradict him. The case that the teaching against contraception is infallible is that the Church has always taught contraception is wrong. But absent a papal declaration to that effect, there will be some doubt about the teaching. Nevertheless, Catholics are sup-posed to give their religious assent to this (and every other) teaching of the

Ordinary Magisterium on faith and morals, to obey the teaching and not to publicly dissent from it. Not many comply.

Prominent theologians, bishops' conferences, and high-profile academics at Catholic universities announced their public dissent in 1968, and did so with virtually no consequences from the Vatican. A kind of truce set in, whereby successive popes restated Pope Paul's teaching while doing very little to drive it home to most married Catholics—for instance, by requiring that it be taught in high schools, colleges, or the Pre-Cana programs required before a Church wedding. To many ordinary Catholics, whose pastors never mentioned the teaching from the pulpit or in the confessional, it seemed as if this papal position was one that was likely someday to change—as the Mass had changed from Latin to the vernacular.

The acceptance of *Humanae Vitae* has not grown over time—despite the fervent efforts of

★ ★ ★
Two Views on *Humanae Vitae*

In *Turning Point* (Crossroad Publishing, 1997), which tells the story of one married woman who was part of the papal commission, Robert McClory argues that Pope Paul VI issued *Humanae Vitae* not so much out of conviction on the issue but out of concern that by contradicting two of his predecessors he would undermine the moral authority of the papacy itself.

Anne Roche Muggeridge, in *The Desolate City* (Harper & Row, 1990), argues that the whole collapse of doctrinal discipline and the chaos that has prevailed ever since in Catholic seminaries and universities, can be traced to the rejection of Pope Paul VI's authority at the time of *Humanae Vitae*.

Pope St. John Paul II to reaffirm and deepen the teaching in his writings and talks on "the theology of the body." A 2012 Gallup poll showed that 82 percent of American Catholics believe that contraception is morally acceptable, which is only 8 percentage points lower than the figure for non-Catholics.[22]

Humanae Vitae did play a powerful role in the Church, though, by becoming the touchstone of orthodoxy for many Catholics on the right, as it remains to this day. For the Left, the highly unpopular and widely unenforced teaching on birth control became a powerful wedge issue that convinced millions of Catholics to disregard Church teaching on a wide range of moral issues. Soon priests such as Father Charles Curran, who had in 1960 been arguing that contraception was compatible with traditional Catholic sexual morality, were embracing dissent on many other issues, even making arguments that homosexual behavior could be reconciled with Catholicism.

CHAPTER 5

Progressive Catholics and Their Permanent Revolution

The revolt sparked by *Humanae Vitae* found its most enthusiastic supporters among those Catholics who felt that the proceedings at Vatican II had not gone nearly far enough in "opening" the Church to the currents of secular modernity, such as feminism, sexual freedom, modern Biblical criticism, and "social justice" (socialism). In fact, such progressives would complain, the actual documents of Vatican II were a disappointing compromise, hobbled by the need to capture the votes of conservative and moderate bishops who clung to traditional doctrinal positions. The "real" meaning of the documents themselves, and the phenomenon of Vatican II as a whole, the much-invoked "spirit of Vatican II," must be understood by consulting expert theologians—men such as Karl Rahner, Hans Küng, and Eduard Schillebeeckx, who had sat at the elbows of the hugely influential Dutch, Belgian, and German bishops who in turn had promoted the most radical changes at Vatican II. These theological experts would explain what the documents *really* meant—and secular media hungry for headlines and often unsympathetic to Catholic claims would broadcast

Did you know?

★ Purportedly neutral academic Biblical criticism actually has a built-in bias against Christianity

★ In the dissent and chaos after Vatican II, weekly Mass attendance dropped from three out of four Catholics to one out of four

★ The archdiocese of Chicago paid for Barack Obama to learn community organizing from an organization founded by Saul Alinsky

their interpretation to millions of Catholics, often with no correction from the bishops, who were typically timid, or progressive themselves. Liberal Catholic publications such as the *National Catholic Reporter, Commonweal,* and the Jesuit-run *America* magazine provided sophisticated defenses of increasingly radical departures from traditional Catholic teaching, talking points for pastors and religion teachers whose task it was to re-educate ordinary believers in the new avante-garde Catholicism—which increasingly began to resemble nothing other than liberal mainline Protestantism.

The explosion and radicalization of progressive dissent in the Church shocked many Catholics, including Pope Paul VI, who had long been seen as a liberal reformer and was so wounded by the open contempt he received from former allies after *Humanae Vitae* that he never issued another encyclical.

Everybody's a (Biblical) Critic!

The revolution had many causes.

The crackdown on "Modernism" under Pius X in the early twentieth century meant that the Church had postponed for half a century its reckoning with the radical implications of academic Biblical criticism—whose methodology takes for granted as a fundamental premise that *miracles are impossible.* That methodology had come to dominate Protestant academia, especially the most prestigious divinity schools around the world. Catholics engaging in ecumenism, or keen to fit in the top-level academic circles outside of Catholic organizations, were bound to encounter such criticism. Far too many, it seems, let themselves be convinced by the "hermeneutic of suspicion" that Biblical criticism adopts toward any claims of divine inspiration, supernatural events, or assertions of theological orthodoxy.

A Book You're Not Supposed to Read

Politicizing the Bible by Scott Hahn and Benjamin Wiker (Crossroad, 2014) shows in scholarly and historical detail how the allegedly neutral and rigorous methods of much Biblical criticism are explicitly based on politicized, secularizing premises. The authors show how, again and again, critics claiming to find the "real" meaning of Biblical passages—as opposed to the meaning that the Church had historically seen in them—were simply gutting the religious content from the Bible. Often, such critics found new meanings for Scripture passages in order to deliberately weaken the institution of the Church and strengthen the hands of secular rulers—whose payroll those critics were sometimes on. Hahn and Wiker trace back the intellectual parentage of some of the key principles of such Biblical criticism directly to writings of Machiavelli, Thomas Hobbes, and others who favored state control over the Church and the secularization of society. In other words, when your pastor gets up on Sunday to explain to you that when Jesus multiplied the loaves and fishes, what "really" happened was a miracle of generosity in which people coughed up the loaves and fish they'd brought with them but selfishly hidden, here's what that pastor is really doing: *relying on an utterly cynical method of Bible reading that was thought up by power-hungry philosophers working for politicians who wanted to steal gold from the monasteries and make the Church into an arm of their unelected governments.* Carried to its logical conclusion, that method of reading the Bible debunks the Resurrection and the Eucharist, and makes priests completely unnecessary, so they should go out and get real jobs at Hobby Lobby instead of accepting salaries for confusing people. Keep that in mind when the collection comes around. Maybe instead of a check, you can drop in a photocopy of this page, and see if your pastor gets the hint.

Camel Finding It Really Difficult to Get through the Eye of That Needle

Sociological and cultural factors also played a role. As we saw in the last chapter, postwar prosperity made Catholics impatient with Church structures and teachings. The West in 1965 was a very different place from what it had been in 1930 or 1940. Catholics in those earlier periods had often faced economic privation and political or social exclusion. Many were preoccupied with the threat of totalitarian movements in their countries, or the shadow of war. But the postwar explosion of wealth and the long peace enforced by the presence of nuclear arsenals changed the face of life in the West for hundreds of millions, including Catholics. Assertions that would have seemed absurd in any previous era, such as predictions that mankind was progressing to a world of peace, plenty, and universal harmony, were suddenly much more plausible to people who had watched their standard of living rapidly increase, whose countries had banished perennial hunger and disease. The bishops who presided over the Church from Vatican II up through the 1980s came of age before and during the Second World War. Many of them associated strict adherence to theological orthodoxy—such as they had seen in their childhoods—with other attributes of that older, bleaker world: political repression, scarcity, and casual bigotry.

If the economy could open up wealth to millions of previously impoverished and undereducated people, and society could open up to minorities, who were churchmen to say that the Church itself could not open up as well? And who was to say where that opening might stop? Not the papacy, which, many bishops thought, had spectacularly failed to understand the needs of modern families by rejecting contraception.[1] So the bishops left the birth control question open-ended, presumably trusting in the good will of ordinary Catholics, as guided by the theological experts.

The Priest (and Nun, and Lay Catholic) Shortage

One of the phenomena that makes nostalgic Catholics wring their hands about Vatican II and its aftermath is the collapse in priestly and religious vocations in the wake of the council. In 1970, there were 419,728 priests in the world, serving 653.6 million Catholics in 191,398 parishes. As of 2014, there were only 414,313 priests, ministering to some 1.229 billion Catholics in 221,740 parishes. The number of religious sisters dropped from 1,004,304 in 1970 to 705,529 in 2014, and religious brothers dropped from 79,408 to 55,314 over the same period. The number of parishes without a resident priest rose by 20 percent in that time, from 39,431 to 49,153.[2]

Indeed, today many parishes are short of the priests they really need to offer the sacraments. And Catholic schools can no longer offer free tuition, relying on the free labor of tens of thousands of religious sisters and brothers to compensate for the costs of anti-Catholic laws passed in the nineteenth century forbidding many states to direct parents' school tax money to the schools their children actually attended. On the positive side, Catholic school children no longer endure the ample corporal punishment that such unpaid celibate laborers (mysteriously!) dished out to the kids of their married, salaried neighbors. Instead, what Catholic schools remain—thousands have closed—employ mostly lay teachers, who accept lower salaries than they would be paid in public schools in return for the chance to advance Catholic education and, let's be candid, for safe working conditions.

Observers have often been puzzled at the fact that many priests, brothers, and religious sisters who had willingly joined quite strict religious orders, or been trained in rigorous traditional seminaries, emerged as theological and political radicals in the tumult after *Humanae Vitae*. How could a nun such as Mary Daly move from earnestly trying to reconcile the feminist writer Simone de Beauvoir with St. Thomas Aquinas in one book, *The Church and the Second Sex*, to embracing man-hating feminism, even lesbian separatism, as she did in a later book *Gyn/Ecology: The Metaethics of Radical Feminism*? One infamous passage in the latter book has Daly explaining away transubstantiation as a pitiful male attempt to mimic the "miracle" of menstruation. When Boston College tried to fire Daly for what she proudly admitted was heresy, the result was a student strike that cowed the administration into backing down, surrendering any attempt to keep its theology department recognizably Catholic. Daly slipped ever further into a feminist fever dream, at one point refusing to accept male students in her classes—then agreeing under pressure from the college to admit some, provided they "filtered" all questions through female students. She died in 2010, a gnarled relic of the high hopes that had accompanied the launch of Vatican II.

Daly's case is extreme, but her career is mirrored to one degree or another in the lives of the thousands of nuns who rejected the very habits that they had voluntarily chosen to wear, the spiritualities of the saints who had founded their orders, and the routine of prayer that had presumably attracted them to religious life in the first place. Many sisters renounced their vows and left the convent, and thousands of priests suddenly discovered that they had not been called to celibacy, after all, and requested "laicization" by the Vatican. Thousands more quietly engaged in homosexual relationships, while the boldest, such as "hippie priest" Paul Shanley of Boston, openly promoted sexual behavior the Church had always condemned as sinful. Shanley served as the chaplain of Dignity, a pressure group, social club, and often hook-up site for gay Catholics, including clergy. He would later be laicized (and sent to prison) for the sexual abuse of teenage boys to whom he had claimed to "minister." It turned out he was also involved in the founding of NAMBLA (the North American Man/Boy Love Association) and that his extracurricular activities were well known to Boston's then-cardinal Umberto Medeiros—whom Shanley was blackmailing: the gay activist priest had threatened to go public about the rampant homosexuality in the Archdiocese's seminary.[3] (Cardinal Medeiros had even made the gay activist his "representative for sexual minorities," and he was also appointed to the Young Adult Ministry Board of the USCCB.) Madeiros's successor Cardinal Bernard Law also allowed Shanley to continue in his distinctive ministry.[4]

To one degree or another, Catholic institutions were occupied by the revolutionary forces, which kept pushing the edge of their revolution into

A Book You're Not Supposed to Read

Ungodly Rage: The Hidden Face of Catholic Feminism by Donna Steichen (Ignatius Press, 1991) is the fruit of years of investigative reporting by a Catholic wife and mother who was troubled by the radical feminist rhetoric she kept hearing from officially Catholic organizations, such as the Leadership Council of Women Religious—the Vatican-recognized umbrella group for most religious women in America. Steichen decided to cut off her hair and dress frumpy so she could fit in with all the angry nuns and started attending their conferences and retreats with tape recorder in hand. What she found shocked her profoundly: long, angry rants by mother superiors about the evil "patriarchy" that rules the Church; rejections of celibacy; spiritual justifications for lesbian relationships; defenses of legal abortion; arguments for paganism as more "inclusive" than Christianity; and clear evidence that some convents were practicing Wiccan rituals instead of Christian prayer. The next time you hear about "the nuns on the bus" touring America to denounce Republican politicians, you might want to consult Steichen's book on what else those religious sisters have gotten up to.

more extreme territory. In 1968 the issue of contention had been whether it was moral for responsible married couples to use artificial means if they needed to limit the size of their families for good and prudent reasons. By 1977 the Catholic Theological Society of America was promoting a book that defended bestiality.[5]

Perhaps the most emblematic instance of the post–Vatican II meltdown was the fate of one large and successful female order: the Sisters of the Immaculate Heart of Mary. Keen to follow Vatican II's call for renewal, that religious order interpreted this dictate differently than the well-meaning bishops had probably intended. In 1966, the IHMs contracted with secular psychologist Carl Rogers to work with him and his teams of facilitators, who engaged the sisters in touchy-feely "humanistic" therapy sessions—the key to which was "values clarification," whereby sisters were encouraged to look for answers to ethical questions, not in the doctrinal tenets that they had learned but rather within their own emotions.

William Coulson, one of the psychologists who worked with Rogers, came to deeply regret this experiment, which inspired hundreds of nuns to leave the order. Coulson notes that quite a number of the sisters who had gone through his therapy sessions soon "discovered" that they were lesbians, and either left the order to pursue relationships or simply carried them on within the convent.[6]

Dozens of other religious orders, male and female, unraveled less dramatically, over years instead of months, as the therapeutic mentality displaced traditional spirituality and tools for self-discipline (such as physical mortification) were thrown aside in favor of counseling. Nuns streamed out of convents, and brothers out of monasteries. (The Christian Brothers' quarters at my Catholic high school in Queens had emptied completely by the time I enrolled.)

With historical perspective, it is possible to speculate that what looked like a radical vocations crisis was really the end of a century-long vocations glut, the end of an era when young adults who were never really called to the priesthood or religious life in the first place entered for misguided reasons, and were admitted by superiors eager to boost their recruitment numbers—a profound disservice both to those young adults and to the Church. How many young women reached age twenty-three, panicked at being "old maids," and entered the convent? How many young

The Religious Life Shipwrecks on the Authority of the Inner Self

"The IHMs had some 60 schools when we started; at the end, they had one. There were some 615 nuns when we began. Within a year after our first interventions, 300 of them were petitioning Rome to get out of their vows. They did not want to be under anyone's authority, except the authority of their imperial inner selves." —**William Coulson to** *Latin Mass* **magazine**[7]

men with zero attraction to women decided to put the celibacy that God demanded of them to good use and joined the priesthood? We will never know for sure, but that would explain why so many apparently pious nuns turned into man-hating, pope-hating radical feminists and why the rate of homosexuality among priests is so much higher than that of the general population.[8]

A Book You're Not Supposed to Read

Goodbye! Good Men: How Catholic Seminaries Turned Away Two Generations of Vocations from the Priesthood by Michael S. Rose (Milford: Hope of St. Monica Inc, 2002).

And from the moment that the sexual libertines achieved positions of power within the Church (or that the men already in those positions discovered their inner libertine), they perpetuated themselves in the clergy and hierarchy. Or, if they couldn't exactly perpetuate themselves—their movement having turned out to be as sterile as the sex acts they preferred—they blackballed potential priests and sisters who still believed in the Church's doctrines. Countless young men were forced out of seminaries as "psychologically immature" for taking celibacy seriously or as "rigid" for harboring a literal belief in the dogmas and moral teachings of the Catholic faith.

And it wasn't just the ranks of the priesthood and religious orders that were melting away. Mass attendance by lay Catholics plummeted amidst the dissent and confusion in the wake of Vatican II. Polling found that three of four Catholics regularly attended Mass in 1958; by 2002, only one of four did.[9] And the people still showing up for Mass weren't as Catholic as they used to be. By 2002, more than half of Catholics said that you could get a divorce or an abortion and stay Catholic, and only 10 percent of lay teachers in Catholic schools still believed that contraception was wrong. Even more disturbing, a 1994 poll found that nearly two-thirds of Catholics from ages eighteen to forty-four believed the Eucharist was only symbolic.[10]

Progressive Politics as a Substitute Religion

When a large group of highly educated people who have dedicated themselves to an organization with firm doctrines, strict rules, and stern demands—such as the Catholic Church—reject those doctrines, rules, and demands, what do they do with themselves instead? Shrug and join the United Methodist Church? Leave their homes and careers and go find apartments and jobs as high school guidance counselors? When families (like the Kennedys or the Bidens—and millions of less famous Irish and Italian-American clans) have strong ethnic and historical connections to the Church, what do they do when they reject its teaching authority? The history of the Catholic Left after Vatican II gives us the answer: such people focus on the parts of the original mission *that still appeal to them*—and jettison the rest.

The Church has an almost two thousand–year tradition of offering the needy education, health care, and a voice in the face of genuine oppression. Many Catholics had joined the Civil Rights Movement and marched for integration. And in the late 1960s, there were new and exciting causes that modeled themselves on the Civil Rights movement's tactics and rhetoric, but whose agendas were not so compatible with traditional Christian teaching as the noble fight against institutionalized racism had been. Feminists, homosexuals, and anti-war activists began to throng the streets and demand radical changes in American law and policy, and many Catholics with left-wing sympathies and deep roots in the Democratic Party began to exert their energies on behalf of these new movements—assuring themselves that they were acting as Jesus had when he denounced the scribes and Pharisees.

So Catholics who had once taken part in Freedom Rides for black Americans denied basic civil rights got swept up in a "Women's Liberation" movement that sought to fast-track divorce, legalize abortion, and finally dissolve the traditional family itself. That movement's greatest success was *Roe v. Wade*, which gave the U.S. the laxest abortion laws on earth—outside of communist countries—and has resulted in the deaths of more than a million American unborn children every year since 1973.[11]

Catholics joined Marxist-organized antiwar marches and demanded an end to the U.S. intervention in Vietnam, which had been launched in part to protect millions of South Vietnamese Christians from communist oppression. Some Catholics even joined the "gay liberation" movement, which began with attempts to stop police harassment, but evolved to demand that the law make no distinction between heterosexual marriage and homosexual relationships. In 2015 we saw that movement culminate with the Supreme Court decision *Obergefell v. Hodges*, which has endangered the religious freedom of millions of American Christians. As time went on, the Catholic Left became increasingly hard to distinguish from just the Left, except in its use of Biblical metaphors and the very selective employment of cherry-picked quotations from Church documents to further its agenda. The

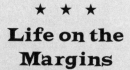

Life on the Margins

Many grandchildren of Catholic immigrants to our overwhelmingly Protestant country still clung to the pretense that they were outsiders—excluded and marginalized enemies of the existing American establishment. So they felt bound to make common cause with every other group of "outsiders," regardless of the justice of their claims. This outsider illusion made it easy for them to be right about Civil Rights...and then poisonously wrong about feminism, gay liberation, and socialist economics. In the 1950s, this same cultivated sense of alienation had led Catholics to join secular Jewish groups in petitioning to throw out prayer from the public schools; they wanted it removed because it was Christian, while we opposed it because it was Protestant.

fact that the U.S. bishops had enjoyed a long-standing friendly relationship with the Democratic Party—since back when that party was socially conservative and solidly anti-communist—made it easy for leftist activists to gain access to bishops and their staffs. Soon the position papers issued by the U.S. Catholic Conference were largely indistinguishable from Democratic Party talking points except on the issue of abortion. And even on abortion, progressive Cardinal Joseph Bernardin (1928–96) succeeded in blunting the impact of the Catholic witness with his "seamless garment" argument, as we shall see.

Bernardin was the most influential Catholic prelate in America. He reigned from 1982 to 1996 as archbishop of Chicago, and in that time was credited as the guiding force behind some of the most politically activist statements from the U.S. Catholic Conference. Under his tutelage, the American bishops embraced positions on economics, welfare policy, and defense that were a virtual mirror image of the Democratic Party platform.

Bernardin was the Catholic Left's key rhetorician and strategist. In 1983 he invented the term "seamless garment" to describe a supposedly consistent pro-life philosophy which must bind every Catholic. To be truly pro-life, Bernardin claimed, one must go far beyond opposing abortion and euthanasia—which entail the direct killing of innocent human beings. It was equally important, he suggested, to take correct Catholic stands on a long list of topics including military spending, Medicaid funding, pollution control, the minimum wage, food stamps, and pretty much every subject dear to the Democratic National Committee.[12] By presenting such disparate issues as a "seamless" whole, and pretending that their own progressive views on these subjects bore the stamp of Church authority, leftist Christians could claim that while Republicans might be sound on just one of those topics—abortion—Democrats were better on all the others. So pro-lifers not only could but probably should vote for liberal pro-choice candidates, since on balance their record was better. And hey presto! Proponents of abortion had an argument that being a pro-choice Democrat was compatible with being Catholic: "Sure, I may differ with the Church on one or two issues, but so does my Republican opponent. Unlike him, I stand with the bishops' conference on Medicaid, immigration, and U.S. policy toward Neeka-RAO-gu-WAH."

Today, the "seamless garment" banner has been picked up by the current archbishop of Chicago, the progressive Blase Cupich. When the gruesome videos exposing Planned Parenthood's profiteering in unborn children's organs were released, Cupich wrote an op-ed for the *Chicago Tribune* in which he said, "While commerce in the remains of defenseless children is particularly repulsive, *we should be no less appalled* by the indifference toward the thousands of people who die daily for lack of decent medical care; who are denied rights by a broken immigration system and by racism; who suffer in hunger, joblessness and want; who pay the price of violence in gun-saturated neighborhoods; or who are executed by the state in the name of justice [emphasis added]."[13]

Pro-life activist Jason Scott Jones, my colleague and sometimes coauthor, who lost a daughter to a forced abortion, responded to Cupich with a poignant open letter, in which he asked the archbishop, "Do you really not see what is uniquely evil about murdering children and selling their parts for profit? As Jesus told us, the poor we will have always with us, and we must advance their interests. But how can you compare the malice of organ-profiteering abortionists with the 'indifference' that you (uncharitably?) attribute to fellow citizens who disagree with you about the optimal public policies helping the poor, reducing unemployment and violence and reforming immigration?"

Jones went on to point out:

> Historically…the seamless garment served, not to elevate issues in addition to abortion but as a bulletproof vest for pro-abortion zealots like Geraldine Ferraro and Mario Cuomo, whose places at the communion line have been filled in our time by Nancy Pelosi and Joseph Biden. Cardinal Bernardin's clever piece of rhetoric still helps such politicians to believe that they are free to reject fundamental moral principles such as sparing the lives of the innocent, so long as they work with the bishops on expanding health care or funding food stamps.

★ ★ ★

The Catholic Campaign for Obama's Development

Cardinal Bernardin's most important legacy may be the political career of an obscure but promising young activist named Barack Obama. As George Neumayr and Phyllis Schlafly show in their book *No Higher Power: Obama's War on Religious Freedom* (Regnery Publishing, 2012):

"In the 1980s, the Catholic archdiocese of Chicago contributed to the training of Obama in the very Alinskyite radicalism that would culminate in such anti-religious measures as the HHS mandate [requiring the Little Sisters of the Poor to pay for contraceptive and abortifacient drugs]. In fact, in the course of writing this book, we met a source who once had access to copies of documents from the archives of the Chicago archdiocese. This source supplied us with never-before-published copies of invoices, checks, and letters that confirm the Church's support for the man who would one day seek to destroy its religious freedom.... In a series of appendices, we have reproduced the check and invoice showing that the archdiocese of Chicago paid for Obama's plane trip to a conference in Los Angeles run by the Industrial Areas Foundation, the community organizing group founded by Alinsky.

"Alinsky had always targeted churches for radical infiltration, and to a certain degree he succeeded. The Catholic Campaign for Human Development (CCHD) was the Alinskyite branch of the United States Conference of Catholic Bishops which had offices in dioceses across the country. It was founded in 1969 by priests and bishops close to Saul Alinsky, such as Monsignor John Egan, who sat on Alinsky's Industrial Areas Foundation board. The group was originally called the Campaign for Human Development, with 'Catholic' added later as its socialist work began to draw criticism.

"Alinsky had initially won favor with some in the Archdiocese of Chicago by appearing to be an advocate of justice for the poor. In the 1950s, in fact, Alinsky received tens of thousands of dollars from the Church to 'study' poverty and racism."[14]

Saul Alinsky was a socialist organizer who eschewed revolutionary violence in favor of a strategy of "community organizing," which gathered members of disaffected communities and taught them how to apply political pressure to achieve their demands. Alana Goodman, of the *Washington Free Beacon*, documented Alinsky's mentorship of the young Hillary Clinton, and summed up Alinky's approach: "A self-proclaimed radical, Alinsky advocated guerilla tactics and civil disobedience to correct what he saw as an institutionalized power gap in poor communities. His philosophy divided the world into 'haves'—middle class and wealthy people—and 'have nots'—the poor. He took an ends-justify-the-means approach to power and wealth redistribution, and developed the theoretical basis of 'community organizing.' *The Prince* was written by Machiavelli for the Haves on how to hold power,' wrote Alinsky in his 1971 book. *'Rules for Radicals* is written for the Have-Nots on how to take it away.'"[15]

These same politicians can smear as "dissenters" the vast majority of pro-life politicians, who are conservatives and therefore differ with some bishops on how to best help America's poor. Pro-choicers manage this smear by hijacking Catholic "social teaching." But that kind of teaching, which specifies budget levels for poverty programs or particular immigration quotas, does not exist! As Popes Leo XIII and St. John Paul II taught, the Church does not impose a particular political agenda on believers. That goes beyond the Church's mission. We can argue about the impact of a higher minimum wage or border patrol. But any Christian church must demand that the innocent be protected. There is no gray area on abortion, as there wasn't on slavery: Human beings have rights. Will we protect them, or not?

Some church leaders have spoken clearly about the radical difference between laws that protect the innocent, and particular public policies which might be best for the common good. In his time, Cardinal John O'Connor of New York taught, as your colleague Archbishop Charles Chaput recently has written, that protecting innocent life is a fundamental and non-negotiable

★ ★ ★

"But let your 'Yes' be 'Yes,' and your 'No,' 'No.' For whatever is more than these is from the evil one."

On July 10, 2016, Chicago Archbishop Blase Cupich—whom Pope Francis has assigned to be one of three men essentially picking future bishops for the United States—was asked by the local ABC News TV affiliate the following question:

"If someone is in a gay relationship, should they be able to have any leadership positions within a local parish?"

Archbishop Cupich answered:

"I think that if a person is in a, uh, in a, in any kind of relationship that does not, um, uh, that, that is not, uh, a relationship that, uh, is uh, is open to, uh,

the three promises of marriage, any kind of relationship outside of marriage, that is a cause of concern that the, the individual, uh, should take serious what the teachings of the Church are with regard to living that kind of life. Uh, we do have people who, uh, are, uh, in so-called irregular situation, in a situations that are working with their pastors in trying to, um, ah, look at their situations individually, in an individual cases. But, uh, to make a blanket statement would be, uh, I think ignoring the fact that you have to, uh, make sure that you see where people are, and then you go from there."[16]

condition for social justice. It is not in any way comparable to public policy questions where Christians have clear moral goals we must pursue, but must use our prudence to determine by open debate what mix of policies are the most just, and the most welcoming to Christ's poor.[17]

Sloppy "seamless garment" thinking smooshes together the intentional murder of unborn children for convenience with the sad but stubborn fact that in a fallen world, man is mortal. There is a radical, absolute difference between directly killing someone, on the one hand, and, on the other, not diverting all your resources to postponing his death. Otherwise, every time you switch the channel away from some hunger appeal on TV, you might as well have hired a hitman to knock off a neighbor—since either way, people die. To use "pro-life" this way is to make it mean everything and nothing, which is handy if your other political priorities make you lean toward the rabidly pro-choice Democratic party.

There is a long, complex, and detailed heritage of Catholic moral reasoning on issues of family life, war and peace, and economics (as you'll see in subsequent chapters). But liberal Catholics threw this long tradition aside as "pre-conciliar," as somehow cancelled out by Vatican II (despite the fact that nothing in the council's texts remotely supported this interpretation). Having flouted the reigning pope over birth control, why should they feel bound by the statements of long-dead popes on other issues? In fact, as progressive theologians assured them, they were following the promptings of the Holy Spirit in helping to disentangle the Church from "sinful structures" such as the bourgeois family, the nation state, and market economics, which had "compromised" the Christian mission for many centuries. Some went so far as to take up the old Protestant theory that the Church had lost its way in the time of Constantine, when it accepted protection and help from the Roman government. Now it was time for Catholics to follow the "Spirit of Vatican II" and return to the (imagined) purity of the Church of the Apostles.[18] They could at once throw off burdensome sexual mores, join the Spirit of the Age, embrace the causes then fashionable among educated elites, and prove that they were truer and better Catholics than the pope. What was not to like?

And that, dear reader, explains how politicians like Nancy Pelosi and Joseph Biden can support partial-birth abortion, same-sex marriage, and legal mandates that nuns such as the Little Sisters of the Poor distribute the "morning after" abortion pill—and still go to Holy Communion. They haven't abandoned the Church. They are in fact its progressive vanguard, helping to restore it to its original mission—as the partisan of the marginalized and the enemy of repression.

Nice work if you can get it.

★ ★ ★

Two Views of the Catholic Crackup

The Trojan Horse in the City of God by philosopher and heroic anti-Nazi activist Dietrich von Hildebrand (Sophia Institute, 1967) is a scathing analysis of the alien thought systems, imported from the secular world, that bishops, Catholic professors, and pastors allowed to replace traditional Christian modes of understanding faith, morality, and politics in the wake of Vatican II—often in defiance of its actual texts. Von Hildebrand shows how the same modes of thinking (utilitarianism, relativism, progressivism) that had already undermined clear moral reasoning in the world at large, but had been kept at bay for decades within Catholic institutions, finally burst the dams and flooded Catholic life and practice. Discontented with a pastoral renewal that kept the Deposit of Faith intact (which is what Pope John XXIII had wanted), dissenting progressive Catholics promoted the nebulous "Spirit of Vatican II"—an amalgam of wishful thinking and radical chic—as a "super-dogma" (in the words of then–Cardinal Ratzinger)[19] that canceled out twenty centuries of authoritative Catholic teaching and prudent practice.

Bare Ruined Choirs (Paulist, 2014) by progressive Catholic gadfly and journalist Garry Wills, offers an irreplaceable historical snapshot of what it was like to grow up in the solid, insular, but smoothly functioning and apparently orderly Catholic subculture of the 1940s and 50s—and then to be swept up by the hope for a newer, "freer" faith, to the point where no change seemed too radical. Wills powerfully and honestly portrays what made the pre-conciliar Church so attractive and reassuring in a world of reckless ideologies and fading faith. So the reader is surprised in the latter part of the book by the glee he takes in that subculture's almost total destruction. Wills's subsequent books on Catholicism, especially *Papal Sin* and *Why I Am a Catholic*, are intellectually dishonest attempts to pulverize the last few remaining piles of rubble.

They Kept the Faith: The "Orthodox" and Traditionalist Response to Post–Vatican II Chaos and Dissent

G iven that many of the brightest, most committed, and highly placed Catholic academics, clergy, religious, and even bishops allowed the split on *Humanae Vitae* to detach them from the Church's traditional teachings on a long list of issues and embraced a radical political agenda as a new object of faith, what was the impact of this on all those Catholics who looked to them for leadership—the people sending their impressionable children to Catholic schools, with every confidence that the Church-vetted sisters, brothers, priests, and teachers would pass along to young people the same faith that those schools had been built to defend?

Remember that the entire Catholic school system had been built with the hoarded pennies of impoverished immigrants, in the face of anti-Catholic laws passed specifically to prevent Catholic parents from directing their school taxes to the schools that their children actually used. Right up through the 1950s, public schools in many parts of the country were effectively Protestant, offering Protestant prayers and inculcating a broad-church Christian ethos that was surely good for America—but markedly incompatible with Catholic doctrine on many issues. It was to prevent the faith of Catholic immigrants from melting in that pot that the Church erected, from

Did you know?

★ A meeting of Catholics appointed by their bishops endorsed women's ordination and the primacy of conscience over the Church's teaching on birth control

★ Archbishop LeFebvre, founder of the Society of Saint Pius X, pioneered the ordination of native black Africans to the priesthood

★ Marketing research shows that "orthodox" book buyers are less than 5 percent of the Catholic population

purely private funds, a vast national network of primary schools, high schools, and colleges.

Now that so many of the priests, religious, and teachers were adopting a brave new religion based on the "Spirit of Vatican II," how would that change the shape of Catholic education in the parishes and their schools? Let me share how it altered my own quite typical immigrant-founded New York City parish in Queens, and remade the faith of my own generation of Catholics, who came of age in the 1970s and 80s. The story is quite typical. I have read dozens of similar accounts from all across America.

First there was the liturgy, which during my childhood went from being a solemn affair dominated by silence and rousing doctrinal hymns (such as "Faith of Our Fathers" and "O Lord I Am Not Worthy") to an event celebrated in our grammar school cafeteria with crude felt banners with slogans like "God Don't Make Junk" and (as I seem to recall) "Rejoice, Damn It!" Sacred music was replaced with "folk songs" such as "Where Have All the Flowers Gone?" and a hymn called "Blowin' In The Wind" by some obscure church composer named "B. Dylan." I grimly read the impenetrable lyrics—and figured that they must be from the Old Testament. And I wondered what had happened to the mysteries that just a few years ago had seemed so awesome and…serious. The perception that the Church was in a constant state of doctrinal flux was confirmed by the reality that her most central, sacred mystery was being monkeyed with.

In the Catholic high school my father had helped to raise the money to build by walking door to door with a can collecting money—in his off hours from carrying the U.S. Mail on his back—I sat in religion class and listened. The teacher, an ex-seminarian trained at Catholic University, explained to us how the Catholic Church had once been sunk in darkness and superstition, subject to a harsh authoritarian system that suppressed all dissent and enforced obedience to its arbitrary decrees with the help of the Inquisition. Among the absurdities it used to teach before Vatican II was the notion that Jesus' mother, Mary, had given birth to Him by some sort of miracle—but this, of course, relied on an ancient mistranslation of the Hebrew word for "virgin." The same Church had also once taught that Jesus had somehow stopped being dead and walked around like a real living person—but this, too, rested on unreliable accounts written decades, even centuries after the fact; their real meaning was surely that Jesus' message was still alive in his followers' hearts. The Church had once taught that the pope was some sort of wonder-working oracle, whom we must all obey on every issue—a clear affront to us as Americans, since the man wasn't even elected by popular vote! The students, who had never been taught much of anything on these subjects before, nodded solemnly and took notes.

Lest the Irish, Italian, and Hispanic teenagers hearing all this think that our teacher had nothing positive to offer, he offset his debunking of these medieval strictures with some reassuring news: the old, pre-conciliar teachings on human sexuality were now recognized as mistaken. They had been devised by angry, white-knuckling celibate monks who hated women and sexuality itself. Not only was the "pre-conciliar" teaching on birth control invalid—as all the pope's own experts, he said, had agreed—but so were the former solemn condemnations of masturbation, premarital sex, and homosexual relationships. All these old taboos had been the tool of a patriarchal system designed to keep medieval peasants breeding obediently.

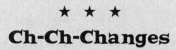

Ch-Ch-Changes

This is how it felt to be young and Catholic in the 1970s: every sacred thing had to be changed, every old thing replaced with a new one, everything delicate and beautiful plastered over with the cheap and the easy. The message was subliminal, but all the more powerful for that reason. I remember being in grammar school when they told us, "The pope wants us to receive Communion in the hand now." (He didn't; it was an abuse that was forced on the Vatican through relentless disobedience until it became a local norm, but never mind.) Then, a few years later, "The pope wants us to stand for Communion." A few more grades, and we heard, "The pope wants us to go to Confession face to face." What had seemed a solid bulwark of formality and seriousness was suddenly shifting with every year's hemlines—which is precisely what progressives conspiring to change the Church's teaching had in mind. That is why they pushed for these futile, pastorally destructive changes of "inessentials"—as a way of beating down resistance to changing essentials.

In a subsequent class, a stocky nun who wore a pants suit, dangling earrings, and blood-red lipstick explained the patriarchy to us. She showed us how women were unjustly excluded from the priesthood, in order to reinforce the "systemic sexism" in which the Church had colluded for centuries as the price of political power. Then she taught us about another set of peasants—in Nicaragua and El Salvador, whom the U.S. government was cooperating with right-wing death squads to repress. She showed us films depicting the courageous struggle of the Sandinista government to dismantle "structures of sin" and retold the stories of heroic priests and nuns who had pioneered Liberation Theology.

While I was little dubious about the attacks on Ronald Reagan and praise for Marxist governments, I was just as pleased as all the other students that we were being taught stark, modern truths that our parents had never suspected. The new, lax sexual ethic that Vatican II had apparently adopted was music to the ears of any teenaged boy.

Then one of the teachers crossed a line. The chairman of our religion department exposed another medieval fetish that the Church had taught our benighted parents: the claim that the Eucharist was a piece of hocus pocus (two words that he wrote on the chalkboard), that some celibate priest had the magical power to change a piece of bread into the literal Body of Christ—a disgusting idea, if you thought about it. He teased the students, "Do you think you're eating a leg, or maybe just a finger?" They shuddered, and got his point: the whole thing was just a symbol, intended to "build community," to unite the congregation—who in fact were the *real* Body of Christ.

It was at that point that I heard a little voice inside my head: "What if these teachers are just... *evil?*" Then, like a good little nerd, I trooped off to the public library and started working my way through the dusty, cracked volumes of the 1907 *Catholic Encyclopedia*—to get a less biased glimpse of the dreaded "pre-conciliar Church." I took out books on Vatican II by conservative authors and started hitching a ride with one of our few old-fashioned teachers—who was kept far away from our classes on religion—to sit in on graduate seminars with a lonely orthodox Jesuit, Father John Hardon, S.J., at St. John's University. It was from him and the people I met there that I learned of a large, poorly organized, and disenfranchised movement of Catholics like me—who had discovered that the authorities in charge of us, whom we'd duly obeyed and listened to, were peddling something quite different from the Church's official teachings. Like me, they were completely power-less to do anything about it—since the very Church authorities who should have taken their complaints seriously were in on the conspiracy, too.

The Catholic Folk Resistance: The "Orthodox Catholic" Subculture

There are countless colorful stories of other conservative Catholics who "woke up" to the dominance of dissenters in positions of Church authority. And so there grew up across America, and in other countries, too, a net-work of institutions that were run by Catholics who called themselves "orthodox"—because they still believed in the same Catholic Faith that the Church had always taught—outside the direct control of bishops and Church institutions, to push back against the radical, even dishonest read-ing of Vatican II that progressives were peddling from pulpits, episcopal thrones, and tenured chairs at venerable Catholic universities. Historians of the Church will someday recognize the lonely efforts of writers at outlets that, because they operated outside of any bishop's control, were able to monitor and criticize the officially sponsored and often lavishly funded programs that promoted non-Catholic agendas in local churches. And then there were the letters, hundreds and thousands of letters like the one I sent to my own local bishop and the papal ambassador to the U.S., letters sent to Vatican congregations reporting astonishing abuses of authority by teachers, pastors, and bishops. These letters were part of what let the newly

★ ★ ★

That'll Look Good on Your College Application

Here's how I explained the phenomenon of Catholic dissent to the baffled Jewish Yale alum who interviewed me when I applied there and who asked me what high school extracurriculars I'd engaged in:

I truthfully answered: "Not much. Mostly, I just prosecuted my religion teachers for heresy."

He chuckled. "No, seriously." Then he saw the look on my face—and whipped out his note pad.

I recounted how I'd compiled a dossier on two of our religion teachers, who'd repaid my parents' tuition by denying...pretty much everything which any martyr has ever died to affirm—from the virginity of Mary to the authority of the pope, from the bodily Resurrection to the Eucharist. I explained how I'd moved from confronting them in class, to notifying the principal, then the bishop, then at last the papal nuncio—the pope's ambassador to the U.S.

"What did your school do?"

"They threatened to expel me. But I had my attorney draft a letter warning them we'd sue. They backed down after that."

"Where'd you get an attorney?"

"My mother met him at one of her poker games. You know, at the church." I told him how at that time in Queens, the diocese made up its deficits by holding all-night high-stakes poker games at Catholic grammar schools. The Irish cops wouldn't crack down on them, so the games metastasized, and soon filled up every parish in driving distance. And my mother attended so many, that to this day when I hear phrases like "St. Sebastian," "St. Rita," "Most Precious Blood," and "Corpus Christi," my first thought is: "Oh crap, another poker game. We'll be eating Spam again this week."

All this took place in the late days of the long-lived, much-loved, heretic Bishop Francis Mugavero—who died in 1991 with a spotless record: he'd never turned down an annulment.

I described how the cafeterias at schools from Astoria to Glendale filled up three nights per week—including Fridays in Lent. On one of these sacred evenings, when the priest who sold the chips started handing out bologna sandwiches, my mother rebuked him: "It's bad enough you're having this game two days before Palm Sunday," she rasped.

"And bad enough that I'm here. But now you're serving us meat?" So the pastor stood up and gave every poker player in the room a "special dispensation" to eat his sandwiches. I described these lunchrooms filled with addicted housewives, compliant cops, and shady gents of Mediterranean background with pointy loafers. The middle-aged attorney was fascinated.

"Were they…Mafiosos?"

I shrugged. "Or wanna-bes. All I know is that whenever they used profanity, my mother would reprimand them: '*Hey! Watch yer mouth! You're in the presence of a lady.*'

"They'd stare at her, swallow…then apologize. They realized what they were dealing with."

He must have decided that I offered Yale something…distinctive. He gave me the highest possible interview score, which is what got me in.[1]

elected Pope John Paul II and his key staff—including Cardinal Joseph Ratzinger, the future Pope Benedict XVI—know the seriousness of the pastoral situation throughout the West.

Groups were organized to sponsor celebrations of the old Latin Mass, which had been banned around the world—contrary to the will of the bishops of Vatican II. Catholics loyal to old-fashioned Catholicism—which was still the Church's official teaching—rallied around Mother Angelica in Alabama, who started a global TV network on a shoestring, even as the U.S. bishops were wasting tens of millions on their own failed endeavor at Catholic media—then trying to suppress and expropriate her network. When a bishops' representative demanded that she accord airtime to any bishop, regardless of his doctrinal views, implicitly threatening that she might otherwise be removed from control of EWTN, Mother Angelica responded famously, "I'll blow the damn thing up before you get your hands on it!"[2]

In America, the campaign of dissenting priests, nuns, and bishops culminated with the Call to Action conference in 1976, which its leading advocate, John Francis Cardinal Dearden of Detroit, described as "an assembly of the American Catholic community." This gathering of twenty-four hundred radical Catholic activists was composed of "people deeply involved with the life of the institutional Church and *appointed by their bishops*" (emphasis added). The conference approved "progressive resolutions, ones calling for, among other things, the ordination of women and married men, female altar servers, and the right and responsibility of married couples to form their own consciences on the issue of artificial birth control."[3] This was the mess created by the bishops appointed by the author of *Humanae Vitae*—a pope so scarred by the experience of Italian fascism in his youth that he never outgrew his suspicion of conservatives. And the worldwide episcopacy was the Augean Stable that Paul VI's successor St. John Paul II spent much of his pontificate trying to clean up.

With mixed success. Early on in his pontificate, Pope St. John Paul II attempted to rein in the excesses of the U.S. Bishops' Conference, even conducting an official investigation into the flagrant heterodoxy of Archbishop Raymond Hunthausen of Seattle—which led him to appoint Donald Wuerl, then seen as a doctrinal conservative, as a kind of watchdog coadjutor bishop for three years. But there was little precedent for actually removing bishops from office, and John Paul II faced the danger that American bishops might defy him and cut off the vital "Peter's Pence" collection from U.S. Mass-goers that provided much of the Vatican's operating budget, which was under strain at the time from the aid being funneled to Poland's Solidarity movement. So John Paul II appeared to settle into a pattern of trying to replace flamboyant liberals with quiet, reliable conservatives or moderates. Because by long Church tradition his choice of candidates was limited to men whom other U.S. bishops recommended—usually a list of three candidates, called the "terna," for each position—John Paul II was constrained in his alternatives, and he sometimes made grave mistakes, such as the appointment of stealth radical Roger Mahony to the hugely important Archdiocese of Los Angeles.

Frozen out of once solidly Catholic colleges and universities, where theology departments were quickly degenerating into pale copies of their counterparts at liberal Protestant seminaries, orthodox Catholics started their own institutions to serve as rallying points and examples of traditional Catholic education. Standouts among this group of little schools are the rigorously Thomistic Thomas Aquinas College in California, Christendom College in Virginia (bastion of Catholic homeschoolers and source of many interns for GOP lawmakers), and the revived and re-Catholicized Franciscan University of Steubenville in Ohio.

John Paul II managed to appoint some heroically faithful bishops, such John O'Connor of New York and Francis George of Chicago, along with many mediocre but less destructive prelates who replaced the outright dissenters who had reigned under Paul VI. Some of those bishops cleaned up the seminaries in their dioceses, many of which had become "pink palaces" that routinely rejected faithful Catholic candidates and were rife with unrepentant homosexuality.

John Paul II (at the strong encouragement of Cardinal Ratzinger) overrode the dogged resistance of liberal bishops worldwide and promulgated the *Catechism of the Catholic Church*, the first comprehensive doctrinal document to appear since Vatican II. For the first time, lay

★ ★ ★
If You Strike at the King…

It was Mahony's heretical (Lutheran, actually) preaching on the Eucharist that led Mother Angelica to criticize him on television. He in turn went to Rome and attempted to have her officially silenced. He failed—and the attempt helped make her a folk hero among embattled faithful Catholics.

★ ★ ★

Bishops Can "Grow in Office" Too

A pope can vet his appointments carefully, trying to select as bishops only those who agree with orthodox Catholic doctrine. But men can change, or hide their opinions. They can "grow in office," as judges who slide to the left on the bench over the years are said to do, in response to popular pressure. Religious orders can gradually fill up with men who don't express their real opinions until they're in positions of power, when it's too late to replace them—as happened with the Jesuits and many other orders as well.[4]

Catholics had an authority to which they could appeal when their pastor pretended that Vatican II had "overturned" or "nuanced" out of existence some crucial doctrinal or moral teaching. Now they had black letter law on their side, and the brute fact of the *Catechism* was enormously encouraging to faithful who had been trapped—sometimes for decades—under the authority of bishops who flouted Church teaching.

Tradition, Tradition!

A tiny but fervent and dedicated group of Catholics did not accept the texts of Vatican II as an orthodox set of documents being grossly abused by radicals. Led by Marcel Lefebvre, the highly successful missionary archbishop of Dakar, Senegal, the "traditionalists" rejected *Dignitatis Humanae*, the Vatican II document on religious liberty, as a serious departure from what popes had previously said about the proper relations of church and state.

Conservative Catholics who supported Vatican II countered that the previous Church policy, which had encouraged Catholic states to suppress, even persecute, "heretical" Christians, could not be traced back to the New Testament or the apostles, but had only emerged after Constantine's conversion. Nor had it ever been taught infallibly. Hence it was subject to revision.

Furthermore—as non-traditionalist orthodox Catholics who accept the Vatican argue—the new teaching has now had the support of four popes since Vatican II and been codified in the *Catechism of the Catholic Church*. To argue

(a) that the Church's previous policy of persecution is an essential truth of the Faith, and (b) that so many popes have erred so gravely, teaching heresy throughout the lifetime of most Catholics today, raises serious issues about papal authority. Since not one bishop in communion with Rome teaches the older theory, to assert that it is the authentic Catholic doctrine on church and state suggests that a crucial element of the Faith has essentially died out within the institutional Church—something for which there is literally no historical precedent. If this were true, it would cast grave doubt on the doctrine that the Church is "indefectible,"that it can never fail completely, and will always convey its essential saving truths to the faithful. To boil this complex question down in simple terms, it seems that neither the old policy of persecution nor the new embrace of religious freedom rises to the level of Catholic doctrine, and hence neither one forms part of the Church's Ordinary Magisterium—which by definition is the consensus of what popes and councils have agreed upon over the centuries. Since Vatican II, it seems logical to conclude that church-state relations are not part of that consensus.

Having lobbied unsuccessfully for bishops at Vatican II to vote down *Dignitatis Humanae*, in 1970, Archbishop Lefebvre founded a priestly society, the Society of St. Pius X (SSPX). This group took as its defining charism the preservation of Catholic doctrine and practice in their pre-conciliar forms. Its priests wore traditional garb such as cassocks and birettas—which most other clergy had cast aside after the council—and refused to celebrate the new, retooled vernacular liturgy that was now being said "facing the people." Instead, Lefebvre and his priests reverted to the pre-conciliar liturgy that had been codified at the Council of Trent, and hence is typically called the Tridentine Mass.

As Lefebvre noted, the new, post-conciliar liturgy had been crafted with intra-Christian ecumenism in mind, with the help of Protestant observers, and many of the changes brought the Catholic liturgy closer to Anglican and Lutheran liturgical forms. After initially accepting this liturgy out of obedience, Lefebvre decided that the new liturgy, while sacramentally valid, represented a false compromise with heretical views of the Eucharist. It was also, he noted correctly, so riddled with options and opportunities for improvisation that it was subject to gross abuse by pastors eager to provide their congregants with a more entertaining religious experience.[5]

The older liturgy, with its rigid rubrics and its use of a dead language, invited no such abuses—and if they did occur, the laity would probably fail to notice them in the ancient Latin. Lefebvre was correct that the liturgy that had resulted from Pope Paul VI's post-conciliar reform was quite different from what the bishops had called for in the Vatican II document on the liturgy, *Sacrosanctum Concilium*—which had not envisaged the total disappearance of Latin, the abandonment of Gregorian chant, or the turning of altars around to face the congregation.

★ ★ ★
That's Entertainment

Those of us who lived through the 1970s remember "clown masses" where the priest wore makeup and a rubber nose, and "home masses" with Pepsi and carrot cake instead of wine and bread, invalidating the sacrament.

The more progressive French bishops, whose seminaries were emptying while Lefebvre's were thronging with seminarians who had fled liberal dioceses, intervened with Pope Paul VI, who ordered Lefebvre to disband the Society and cease ordaining priests. Lefebvre refused, citing the necessity to preserve the Church's doctrinal and liturgical traditions, and opened an independent seminary in Econe, Switzerland, which began to send its priests all over the world to serve the many thousands of Catholics who felt alienated by the radical change in worship.

Repeated efforts by Pope John Paul II, encouraged by Cardinal Joseph Ratzinger, to heal the breach between the SSPX and the Vatican foundered on Archbishop Lefebvre's distrust of a Church bureaucracy that cracked down on the slightest conservative deviation while allowing

Three Books You're Not Supposed to Read

For a deeper understanding of the traditionalist movement, there is no better source than the trilogy *Liturgical Revolution*, written by its most eloquent proponent, the Welsh Catholic convert Michael Davies. The first volume, *Cranmer's Godly Order*, analyzes the changes made to the traditional Catholic liturgy during the Reformation by the founders of the Anglican Church and shows how post–Vatican II liturgical texts follow along similar lines. The second, *Pope John's Council*,

argues for the older Catholic understanding of the role of the state in supporting the true religion and shows how American bishops were instrumental in lobbying for religious liberty. And Volume III, *Pope Paul's New Mass*, goes into great detail on what Davies sees as theological deficiencies of the new liturgy, which he regards as responsible for the decline in Eucharistic reverence and the loss of an orthodox Catholic understanding of the sacrament among ordinary Catholic laymen.

and even enabling the practices of flagrantly heterodox bishops and theologians. In 1981, fearing that his death would deprive his order of the power to ordain new priests, Lefebvre took the radical step of ordaining four new bishops to carry on the SSPX's mission, thereby incurring an automatic excommunication. The Vatican reached out to priests within the SSPX who disapproved of this step and allowed them to form the Fraternity of St. Peter, the first of several priestly societies in communion with the pope that would be permitted to preserve the traditional liturgy. These priestly societies have grown, even as negotiations have continued between Archbishop Lefebvre's successors and the Vatican. In 2007, Pope Benedict XVI took the additional step of issuing the motu proprio (a document issued on the pope's own initiative) *Summorum Pontificum* (*Of the Supreme Pontiffs*), which extended permission for the celebration of the traditional liturgy, ruling that the old Latin Mass that (with very few changes) had prevailed in the Western Church since circa 500 AD had not ever been effectively banned.

How the Catholic Church Became a Subculture

Before the doctrinal tumult of the 1960s, almost every sociological Catholic was also, insofar as he gave the matter any thought, a doctrinally orthodox Catholic. That doesn't mean that the Church was packed with saints, of course. Human nature was always as flawed and fallible as it remains today. But Catholics of every level of religious practice, however their lives might diverge from the Church's teachings, pretty much acknowledged what those teachings were. The disobedient realized that they were sinners—or fancied themselves "realists"—rather than becoming doctrinal dissenters.

Some questions of human behavior are best mapped on a bell curve, but the spectrum of faith looks much more like an umbrella leaning against a wall—a slow rising incline with a sharp upwards curve at the top. The people down at the tip of the umbrella are those least interested and informed on questions of faith, while those up in the handle are the most devoutly doctrinal. So in 1930, down at the umbrella's tip you might find mafia hit men, prostitutes, thieves, and quasi-Catholic adherents of voodoo or Santeria. Moving up, you'd see the level of knowledge and interest gradually increase, until it suddenly spiked: up in the handle you'd find the tiny minority of saintly mystics, fearless missionaries—and self-righteous bigots and Jew-baiting cranks. In between, you'd find all the ordinary people you might expect to populate a Church intended to serve and save the great mass of humanity, the people Chaucer pictured as pilgrims to Canterbury. All these people along the umbrella differed in their levels of commitment, but their creed was the same.

But with the controversy over birth control, the handle came off the umbrella. With the mass rejection of the natural law teaching presented in *Humanae Vitae,* the only people who technically remained orthodox believing Catholics were to be found in that fragment deeply interested in and consciously committed to orthodoxy. There were saintly, self-sacrificing priests and laymen who suffered for their beliefs—and self-congratulating

Pharisees who preened themselves on being part of the "saving remnant." There were working class people who accepted the discipline of remaining open to life or the ascetical practice of Natural Family Planning—and there were "white trash" Catholics who used the Church's teaching as a pretext for going on public assistance (See chapter twelve).

It's a very mixed bag. And a small one. A good friend of mine who works for one of America's largest Catholic publishers reported to me the results of some very pricey market research his company had undertaken to determine the actual size of the "orthodox Catholic market." Many thousands of dollars later, his company learned that if you count Catholics who go to Mass more than once a week, or who spend a single dollar on Catholic books or other media, or volunteer for any parish activity, the grand total for the United States of America is no higher than 1.2 million. That's less than 5 percent of the Catholic population. There are more active Mennonites in Pennsylvania and more Hasidic Jews in Brooklyn than there are "orthodox" Catholics in the entire United States.

That is the whole Catholic market. No wonder there isn't enough revenue to go around. All the quarrels between traditionalists and just plain conservatives, between crypto-socialist lovers of Dorothy Day and free market fans of John Courtney Murray, are fights for pieces of this tiny pie. A pop tart, really.

And pop tarts aren't health food. It isn't normal for the Church to consist just of saints and zealots, ascetical future "blesseds," and Inquisition re-enactors. Faith is meant to be yeast that yields a hearty loaf of bread. But since 1968 there has been nothing left to leaven, and we find ourselves eating yeast. (My apologies to English readers who love their Marmite.) The last time I was at the Catholic Marketing Network, which includes all the

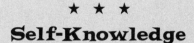

★ ★ ★
Self-Knowledge

Al Capone was, and knew himself to be, a Catholic murderer. He did not proclaim himself a "dissenter" on the "life issue," and align himself with friendly Jesuits whom he found more "open-minded" about the commandment he chose to break. Capone did not found an advocacy group called "Catholics for Free-Fire Zones."

★ ★ ★

Let Both Grow Together until the Harvest

Is this Church of the Umbrella Handle, with its much smaller set of human types, the smaller, purer Church of which Joseph Ratzinger spoke when he warned that "The Church will become small and will have to start afresh more or less from the beginning. She will no longer be able to inhabit many of the edifices she built in prosperity"?[6] Or is it the subset of modern Pharisees tainted by "Promethean neo-Pelagianism" against whom Pope Francis has warned?[7] Of course, it is both, and the wheat is irretrievably mixed up with the tares. But one thing is certain: it is as inbred as a coalition of captive cheetahs, with all the dangers of deformity and disease that that implies.

leading companies in the orthodox Catholic market, most of the attendees seemed to be people who had bought their own booths—so the whole day was spent watching vendors try to sell each other their stuff. "I'll trade you three copies of *The Secret of the Rosary* for one of those 3-D Divine Mercy holograms."

Man cannot live on yeast alone, and the Church cannot weather the storm with only the handle of the umbrella. We need to encounter a broader range of humanity than can be found in that doctrine-conscious 5 percent—which I'm sure is no odder or more dysfunctional than it has always been throughout Church history. But we used to have the whole umbrella.

The undeniable weirdness, bitterness, crankiness, and general mediocrity that pervade the orthodox Catholic subculture are the direct result of having few people to choose from. Right off the bat, at least 95 percent of potential applicants for any position have disqualified themselves for doctrinal reasons, because they can't wrap their minds around *Humanae Vitae*. Beyond that, it's such a pleasant surprise to find a fellow orthodox Catholic ("You mean that you're 100 percent full-blooded Latvian, too?") that it's tempting not to ask too many more questions—for instance, about the person's qualifications, talent, or temperament.

If he checks off the same doctrinal boxes, we accept him as a fellow Party member, and bend over backwards to think the best of him—at least until we get in an argument with him over liturgy, doctrine, or economics. Then we spend all our time combating his errors, convinced that we are somehow helping to turn the tide of history, when in fact we're just making waves in the kiddie pool.

The Rest of Us

What's the answer? We need that other 95 percent. And given that the key issue on which most dissent hinges today is contraception, we need to do a much better job conveying the Church's position on that fraught subject to ordinary people.

It's a hard sell already, because the argument hinges on rediscovering and accepting that there is teleology in nature—that bodies and organs have purposes, not merely "functions" dictated by evolution. But that argument can be made, and we might start by boning up on how what Aristotle called "final causes" pervade the natural world.

Next we can show people how, without some notion of natural law, there is no coherent case for human rights—much less for legal rights, or filigrees like anti-discrimination laws. Finally, we can point to the miserable outcomes for children whose parents treat their sexual powers as toys. The statistics on the children of divorce and single parenthood are eloquent on that topic, and political scientist Charles Murray documents these painful outcomes in grim detail in *Coming Apart* (Crown Forum, 2013).

All of these truths can be argued without any reference to Jesus or the Church. They depend not on revelation but on nature. And it is only by moving people toward a healthier sense of human nature that we can win them back to the mainstream of the Church—and thereby make the Church itself a healthier, more natural environment.

A Book You're Not Supposed to Read

For the best arguments on the teleology in nature, see Edward Feser's *The Last Superstition* (South Bend: St. Augustine Press, 2010).

I'm not saying that better arguments for natural law and *Humanae Vitae* will help make orthodox Catholics out of everyone—even though that's precisely whom the Church is meant to encompass, from drug dealers to crooks on Wall Street. But we have to start somewhere.

The Church as righteous subculture is unappealing to nearly everyone—including the kids who grow up inside it, who despite all those years of homeschooling and chapel veils frequently flee for what look like saner pastures. We need to stop treating people who don't "get" the Church's teaching on contraception as if they were clones of Judas, or heretics like Arius (whom St. Nicholas rightly slapped). They are people who don't understand a complex intellectual argument based on the remote implications of natural law reasoning, which is based on an older view of nature that modern science has not so much disproved as simply dismissed. Given the massive implications of this Church teaching for their personal lives, they aren't willing simply to take the argument on authority. So arguing from authority won't convince them; it will simply discredit the authority.

Many Catholics oppose abortion, and treasure the sacraments, and love their spouses, and even have decent-sized families—all of it without understanding or accepting *Humanae Vitae*. Millions of psychologically normal, hard-working, well-meaning people have blundered into dissent, and ended up in the same camp with bitter heretics like Charles Curran, over this single issue. Then dissent on that single issue softened them up to drift away from the Church on other issues as well.

We shouldn't count these people out of the Church as we would those who willfully accept abortion or polyamory. We need to listen to their real questions and objections and do a much better job of explaining ourselves. Or else that's who we'll go right on talking to—ourselves.

CHAPTER 7

The Church and the Free Market

As we've seen, thousands of articulate and highly educated Catholics who had built their lives around the mission of spreading the Faith and transforming the world via its teachings suddenly turned against that Faith and those teachings—on critical issues where the Church had staked its authority. What were such people to do with themselves? Where would they spend the energy and commitment that had led them to take lifelong vows? What would laymen who still identified as Catholic, but followed pastors who had radically redefined what being Catholic actually meant, do now? As we have seen, the past forty years have answered such questions definitively: these people would cling to, exaggerate, and distort those aspects of Catholic teaching that still appealed to them—specifically, those which didn't seem to impinge on the Sexual Revolution. In other words, like secularized Jews and mainline Protestants, they would focus on aiding the poor, and using big government to do it. They would take aspirations that popes had expressed—for world peace, for greater equality, for more cooperation over competition—and inflate them into absolute mandates of Catholic morality, which could only be attained via cooperation with the political Left and its programs. And they would prove every bit as dogmatic

Did you know?

★ The first major papal statement on economics defended private property

★ Money is not the root of all evil

★ Pope Francis's attack on "absolute market freedom" is a war on a straw man

★ You can't be a faithful Catholic and a socialist

★ St. Thomas Aquinas favored the market theory of value (versus the labor theory of value, which Marx relied on)

about their new moral agenda as they once had been about the Church's actual dogmas and doctrines. The second part of this book, which starts here, explores this new dogmatism and explains how and where it departs from authoritative Catholic teaching.

One extremely stubborn myth about the Catholic Church is that its teachings are fundamentally hostile to business, private property, the profit motive, and other critical elements in the free market economy. You can't really blame clueless secular reporters, who wouldn't know the Holy Trinity from a Hopi Indian, for getting such issues wrong. But plenty of our bishops, and a few of our popes, have vented private opinions that suggest the very same thing—even though if you really do the reading, you'll find out that the Church's teachings favor all these wholesome things, so long as they're not abused.

It's the job of pastors to warn us against our all-too-human tendency to misuse the things God gave us, but sometimes they get carried away and seem to condemn those things in themselves, or the human drive to want them. That's how you end up with preachers who seem to be condemning sex itself, or business itself, or political and economic freedom—since each of these good things is frequently abused. But only a Gnostic who thought that God had massively screwed up when He created the universe could really believe that such basic goods are evil. The most evil, destructive political systems in history were dreamed up by idealists who found the real world tainted and foul compared to the one that they saw in their daydreams. Those systems were put into practice by power-hungry ideologues, and their death toll is in the hundreds of millions (and counting).

Catholicism or Socialism: Pick One

Every single thing in the universe was created good by God, including the impulse to create, to improve, to innovate, and to accumulate a legacy to pass on to one's children. The Bible at times seems almost obsessed with the question of legacy—think of Jacob's battle with Esau, and Jesus' parable of the Prodigal Son. Private property is not some crass Republican construct designed to let Wall Street tycoons hoard all the good things of the earth. Instead, as Pope Leo XIII taught, it is a fundamental human right that flows from our human dignity: "For, every man has by nature the right to possess property as his own. This is one of the chief points of distinction between man and the animal creation.... [Because] man alone among the animal creation is endowed with reason—it must be within his right to possess things not merely for temporary and momentary use, as other living things do, but to have and to hold them in stable and permanent possession."[1] In other words, natural law grants us the right not just to consume things the way wild animals surviving from one moment to the next do, but to own property so that we can plan for the future, maintain our families, and even, in Leo's words, "keep up becomingly" in our "condition in life."[2]

Leo XIII's defense of private property in *Rerum Novarum* (*Of New Things*), the first major papal statement on economics, is remarkably close to John Locke's argument in his two *Treatises of Civil Government*—documents that were key to the American founding. In fact, the scholars who helped Leo draft that landmark encyclical looked to Locke for their understanding of how to distinguish private property from the wild goods of nature.[3] Here is the key point on which Leo and Locke agree: man turns the "commons" of the created world, which belong to no one, into private property by mixing them with his own "labor of brain and hands."[4] Hence a writer takes words that belong to everyone and no one, and freely uses his labor

★ ★ ★

We Seek First the Kingdom of Heaven, Not Marx's Classless Society

Given the language in *Rerum Novarum* about keeping up our condition in life, intellectuals should not be forced to work in the fields producing grain, nor ballet dancers to abandon their inessential profession and go dig wells for the thirsty.

to create something new that rightly belongs to him. Every free act of human labor at any job, however manual or tedious, is an exercise of human dignity, and to unjustly take away the fruits of that labor is to make the worker a slave. That applies not just to authors but to ditch diggers, farmers, entrepreneurs, even investors—who are risking their own accumulated labor in the form of money on a project that might create new jobs for thousands of other people. As Leo XIII warned, "The right to possess private property is derived from nature, not from man; and the State has the right to control its use in the interests of the public good alone, but by no means to absorb it altogether. The State would therefore be unjust and cruel if under the name of taxation it were to deprive the private owner of more than is fair."[5]

We can certainly argue about how much is "fair," but the fundamental principle is that property should be private because man is more than an animal to be led and controlled and fed from a common trough. We should regard attempts by politicians to raise taxes and buy the votes of one group of people by taking the property of some other people as a near occasion of sin.

The urge each of us feels to work and be productive is part of the way God made us. Because of the Fall, we often experience work itself as a form of suffering, but Thomas Aquinas pointed out that even in the Garden of Eden, Adam was busy at work both physical (tending the plants) and intellectual (naming the beasts).[6] Why do we work? Well, most of the time we do it in order to gain something for ourselves or those we love—most typically our families. Because we are physical creatures that live in the flesh and need food, clean water, decent housing, transportation from place to place, medical care, and a host of other frankly material things and services, most of the time the gain we seek from work is material.

Money Is Not the Root of All Evil

That material gain comes in the form of money, which we use as a marker of value and trade for the things that we need or want. Some Christians cluelessly misread St. Paul's statement that "the love of money is the root of all evils" (1 Timothy 6:10) as implying that money itself is evil. But Paul was referring to an all-consuming lust for money that amounts to the deadly sin of greed. A comparable love of sex would add up to lust—but that doesn't mean sex is evil in itself.[7]

Money is the language of human cooperation. It saves us from having to barter for everything we need—to hunt down someone who needs exactly what we're good at making, who makes precisely the thing that we happen to need at the moment. ("I'll trade you three handwritten copies of a book on the Catholic Church for that pepperoni pizza. Do you know anyone who makes Q-tips—and needs such a book?") What is more, because the currencies of different countries are mutually exchangeable, money is a universal language, with banks as the Star Trek-style pan-galactic translators.

Even Franciscans and Dominicans, whose orders were founded to practice a holy form of poverty, had to overcome their initial resistance to carrying

Leo XIII vs. Socialism

"Lured, in fine, by the greed of present goods, which is 'the root of all evils which some coveting have erred from the faith,' [socialists] assail the right of property sanctioned by natural law; and by a scheme of horrible wickedness, while they seem desirous of caring for the needs and satisfying the desires of all men, they strive to seize and hold in common whatever has been acquired either by title of lawful inheritance, or by labor of brain and hands, or by thrift in one's mode of life.... [The Church] knows that stealing and robbery were forbidden in so special a manner by God, the author and defender of right, that thieves and despoilers, no less than adulterers and idolaters, are shut out from the Kingdom of Heaven."

—*Quod Apostolici Muneris*

A Book You're Not Supposed to Read

Tea Party Catholic (Crossroad, 2014) by scholar Samuel Gregg is a lively, carefully documented, and very readable look at how Catholic principles were instrumental in the founding of a free (and free market) republic, the United States of America. Gregg shows how Catholic signer of the Declaration of Independence Charles Carroll exerted a major influence on the founding, and how principles of liberty are critical to promoting a just society.

money[8]—because their vows didn't exempt them from the physical needs that come with being a mammal that lives on the earth. In a similar way, while they preached about the special holiness of vowed virginity within a religious order, such friars had to recognize that sex and fruitful marriage are also holy.[9] Without them, we wouldn't have any new nuns or monks! Likewise, without prosperous, hard-working people out for profit, no one would have any coins to drop in the friar's begging bowl.

Unfortunately, not all clerics are willing to recognize such basic human realities. In 2015 the prominent Italian cardinal Edoardo Menichelli was using rhetoric that is all too common on the Catholic Left when he announced that the Catholic Church, under Pope Francis, was launching "a fight against capitalism similar to the one against communism under Pope St. John Paul II." As the progressive Catholic news site *Crux* reported:

> Echoing Pope Francis, Menichelli said that if money is the center of the universe, the human person loses meaning and society becomes a desert of values.
>
> "If economy is reduced to finances, it kills," Menichelli said. "We need to start from those who are last to return dignity to the people [and to] eliminate injustices...."
>
> The prelate said that the social dimension is an integral part of the faith, and quoted Francis's apostolic exhortation, *Evangelii Gaudium*, in which the pontiff warned against ideologies that defend absolute market freedom and financial speculation.[10]

This is a straw man: there is not a single nation on the face of the earth that maintains "absolute market freedom," with no regulation of wages or safety conditions. Nor is there a major political party in any developed country that favors such a system. But Pope Francis appears to harbor a fervent belief in this scarecrow, which he trots out to give rhetorical color and force to his regular endorsements of leftist economics. Faithful Catholics were shocked in July 2015 when Francis, visiting Bolivia and meeting with its far-left president, Evo Morales, was presented with what reporters called a "Communist crucifix" that featured Christ's body on top of a hammer and sickle. The artwork had been designed by a leftist Bolivian Jesuit who had died in a government crackdown and whom Francis had come to honor. Initial reports that the pope had objected to the gift were later debunked by the Vatican itself, and in his meeting with Morales the pope praised the eco-populist president and offered "words of encouragement in support of your work." Then the pope went to attend a conference of leftist activists from around the world,

Apples to Oranges

John Paul II had direct, personal experience of communism. Neither Cardinal Menichelli nor Pope Francis has ever lived under its tyranny—nor in anything like a free economy, either: both Italy's and Argentina's economies are prime examples of "crony capitalism," a system in which powerful private interests use government intervention to shackle the market and fleece consumers through a mishmash of cronyism, subsidies, nepotism, and corruption. Actually, those two countries are so far gone in this direction that it would be more accurate to describe their systems as "crony socialism." In such a system, entrenched business interests wield populist rhetoric and backroom connections to boost prices and crush competitors—often in collusion with Marxist-controlled labor unions. Judging "capitalism" by your experience with such an economy is about as fair as evaluating democratic socialism based on Ceausescu's Romania.

the World Meeting of Popular Movements, where Francis "used language remarkably similar to that used by other leftist populist Latin American politicians."[11]

Even more upsetting was Francis's decision to allow socialist presidential candidate Bernie Sanders to address a major political and economic conference at the Vatican in April 2016. Coming as it did at the height of the campaign season, just before the Democratic primary in New York where many Catholic voters live, it looked like a quasi-endorsement of Sanders—who favors legal partial birth abortion, same-sex marriage, and a host of other practices that the Church calls intrinsically evil, but who seems to share Francis's personal view of economics.

Well-meaning Catholics sometimes dig back in the writings of the Church Fathers and find statements that, taken out of context, seem to deny that working hard and seeking to make a profit are morally legitimate. The popular orthodox Catholic radio host Al Kresta cites numerous socialist-sounding quotes from ancient saints in his otherwise quite useful book *Dangers to the Faith*.[12] The problem with citing celibate monks from the fourth century on the topic of modern economics is that those good men lived and worked in an ancient pre-capitalist economy where nearly all wealth was agricultural, and mostly wrung from the sweat of foreign slaves captured in Rome's wars of conquest. Economic and technological innovation were nearly unknown at the time. The master-slave economy in the ancient world was as close as life comes to a zero-sum game. To the early Church Fathers, Leo XIII's phrase "labor of brain," applied to anything but sheer intellectual work such as writing philosophical dialogues, would have been nearly incomprehensible—or else it would have suggested dishonest dealing. Trade had been stigmatized as vulgar by nearly every classical philosopher—a prejudice most Christians breathed in with the ancient air. So in their time and place, it made some sense to see wealth as the fruit of theft. But history didn't end there.

★ ★ ★

Conquest Conquers Trade

Catholic historian Christopher Dawson once wrote that any thought for the economic future—such as investing money or even saving it—was incompatible with Christianity. So was leaving an inheritance for one's children. Dawson even averred that the conquistadors who plundered Mexico were more admirable than merchants engaged in honest trade.[13]

It would take the very Christian civilization that the early Christians were building on the ruins of the classical pagan empires to establish the dignity of labor—which the ancients despised as worthy only of inferior human beings born to be slaves—and remake society so that human beings became *vital resources* whose rational efforts to earn their daily bread might also leave the world a richer place for their children. Indeed, they might accumulate by "labor of brain" enough of a surplus to redistribute it through investment, creating opportunities for other human beings to better their lots as well. In doing that, in being good and honest capitalists, we are imitating the "good and faithful servant" whom Jesus praised in the parable of the talents, increasing the general share of wealth, and tapping human potential. But as Rodney Stark documents in *The Victory of Reason*, it would be some six or seven hundred years from the Incarnation before Christian monks pioneered agricultural improvements that would double, then triple, production, and create the first "capital" for capitalists to invest.[14] These were by and large Benedictines, whose motto—"Ora et Labora," ("Work and Pray")—encapsulates the Christian respect for labor that was the monks' first and most crucial contribution to the rise of capitalism.

Thus, in the modern economy whose foundations Christians established in the Middle Ages, private property does more than allow us to feed our families. Property rights also protect from unjust seizure the capital we need to invest in ways that create productive opportunities for others as well as security for ourselves. Providing for those who cannot help themselves is our obligation as Christians—not something the state should require of obedient citizens under the compulsion of the law. The proper

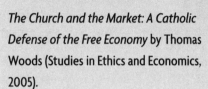

A Book You're Not Supposed to Read

The Church and the Market: A Catholic Defense of the Free Economy by Thomas Woods (Studies in Ethics and Economics, 2005).

penalty if we don't exercise charity is not federal prison but perdition. Giving to the poor is a command of faith, binding on those who believe, and we cannot fulfill it by voting to raise our own taxes—or those of our wealthier neighbors, whom we view with an eye full of Envy (and their property with Covetousness).

It can be hard for those who have never seen a free economy operate to believe that a society with transparent rules and honest, limited government can really exist—much less, that such societies typically prosper and improve the prospects for every class, especially the poor. Such colors are invisible to those born in deeply unfree economies, where the economic math is confined to zero-sum equations: if one man becomes a bit richer than others, it must be because he has stolen from the poor. In conditions of crony capitalism, outright socialism, or feudalism, that's usually the case. And yet some early modern Catholic thinkers, most of them Spanish priests and scholastic philosophers, were able to see past the flaws and injustices of the semi-feudal economy in which they lived and grasp the fundamental principles by which a free economy might work.

These Catholic philosophers writing during the Renaissance avoided the worst mistakes of nineteenth-century thinkers such as Marx—a fact that makes it all the more tragic that so many modern churchmen like Cardinal Menichelli slide into crude Marxist mistakes when they speak about economics.

A Book You're Not Supposed to Read

In *Faith and Liberty: The Economic Thought of the Late-Scholastics* (Lexington, 2003), Alejandro A. Chafuen, a Catholic free market economist from Argentina, unearths the keen economic insights of the Spanish Thomists of the School of Salamanca, such as Martín de Azpilcueta (1493–1586), Diego de Covarubias y Leyva (1512–1577), and Luis de Molina (1535–1600). Chafuen shows how these thinkers applied St. Thomas Aquinas's keen methods of analysis to the emerging issues of a dawning market economy—giving sound theological rationales for such necessary innovations as interest-bearing investments.

Economics for Catholics Who Are Bad at Math

The economy is not like a monastery or a convent—where everyone has made a conscious decision to renounce his private pursuits and embrace the evangelical counsels of poverty, chastity, and obedience. There, and only there, property is organized "from each according to his ability, to each according to his need" (a principle that Karl Marx wanted to apply to society as a whole—with truly disastrous results).

This arrangement works and is spiritually fruitful in a monastery because, and only because, it is voluntary. Each person has renounced the primary project of ordinary mammals—reproduction—and willingly surrendered the fruits of his labor to serve a common good, as determined by a superior whom he obeys (excepting sin) as the voice of God. This calling is sacred and comparatively rare. The Church does not expect the vast majority of human beings to enter monastic life; in fact, for those who are not called to this radical inversion of natural human instincts, such a life would be a kind of hell. Every political attempt to organize society as if it were a monastery must end in a brutal dictatorship. And it always does.

When, as we shall see, Leo XIII and his successors condemned every form of socialism, they were recognizing that forcibly taking from people the property, fertility, and liberty that monks and nuns willingly give up indeed amounts to a diabolical parody of the good.[15] Let's give those popes credit for being prophets: long before the gulag, and the famines and purges that decimated Russia, China, North Korea, and Cambodia had demonstrated the true evil of socialism, these theologically educated men saw it. The popes were relying on more than logic; they also had the lessons of history—in the form of the crackpot millenarian movements that had erupted in late medieval Europe, composed of outraged peasants and self-appointed messiahs who began as penitents trying to ward off the plague by scourging themselves and ended as armed mobs massacring Jews and merchants and creating short-lived tyrannies that tried to abolish liberty,

A Book You're Not Supposed to Read

The Pursuit of the Millennium (Oxford University Press, 1970) by historian Norman Cohn paints vivid, appalling pictures of medieval end-of-the-world movements, which the author sees as the forerunners of revolutionary socialism. Citing Gospel quotes out of context and preying on the often legitimate grievances of peasants toiling under feudalism, the leaders of these movements claimed that private property was evil and must be redistributed by force. They seized the goods of merchants, enslaved peasants and townsfolk in forced labor schemes, and in many other ways anticipated the catastrophes and cruelties of twentieth-century communism.

property, and the family—and the clear principles of the moral law written in both revelation and on the human heart.

The Just Price Is the Market Price—as Thomas Aquinas Taught

Given that prices are the essential "data" by which consumers inform producers how much of something to make, they are at the very heart of human cooperation. It seemed only natural to thinkers like Marx that we should value objects based on how much work and thought had gone into them. But this theory does a poor job of explaining the actual prices that emerge in an open market; some items that require comparatively little effort to create (let's say, suddenly fashionable hats) in fact command higher prices than the fruit of enormous labor (for instance, brilliant but difficult novels). To compare apples with apples, a cheaply made but well-written comedy film like the brilliant *Office Space* may outsell a hugely expensive, carefully researched historical drama like *Heaven's Gate.* While those of us on the outside may cry injustice, such outcomes are merely the fruit of *adults making their own decisions* about which products they really want.

The "labor theory of value" is not what St. Thomas Aquinas taught. As Samuel Gregg documents in his fascinating study of Catholic teaching on banking, *For God and Profit*:

Though influenced by Aristotle, Aquinas rejected "the Philosopher's" view that those involved in commerce would become obsessed with their own riches and unconcerned with the common good. Instead Aquinas held that it was entirely possible for people to engage in commerce, and with correct intentions such as the desire to help the needy or take care of one's family.

Aquinas invested considerable effort in examining how one determined the justice of a given commercial transaction, how one measured the value of a good, and what constituted a just price. In his view, it was normally the case that the measure of something's value is the price it would presently fetch "in the market" [*secundum commune forum*].[16]

Aquinas's insight, forgotten by materialists like Marx in the nineteenth century, would be rediscovered in the twentieth by the economists of the Austrian school. Instead of looking at the economy as a vast, mysterious machine intended to build up the wealth of an abstraction (such as the nation, or the race), the Austrians started small, like the Spanish scholastics—with the factors that influence each one of us in his daily decisions about what products to buy, where and how to work, and how much to save or invest.

An economic system that refuses to acknowledge how human beings express their moment-to-moment preferences will massively fail to help them achieve their goals. Applied consistently, such a system will yield only famines and tyranny; cobbled together piecemeal, as in the programs of European socialists and left-wing Catholics, such a system grows an ever-larger apparatus of government, hiring ever more managers to tamp down the chaos created by its irrationality and waste. The more holes you drill in the bottom of the boat, the more sailors you need to bail, as Pope St. John Paul II observed in his masterful critique of welfare-state socialism,

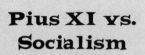

Pius XI vs. Socialism

"Whether considered as a doctrine, or an historical fact, or a movement, Socialism, if it remains truly Socialism…cannot be reconciled with the teachings of the Catholic Church because its concept of society itself is utterly foreign to Christian truth."

—*Quadragesimo Anno*

Centesimus Annus. Following up on the work of Pope Pius XI in *Quadragesimo Anno*, John Paul II reiterated the Church's firm embrace of subsidiarity. This principle is so central to Catholic social and economic thought that it deserves a section all its own.

Subsidiarity: The Catholic Church's Tea Party Principle

In 1931, when every enlightened thinker in the West seemed to favor expanding the government's control over the lives of individuals in the name of "rational planning," one man stood against the raging tide of bureaucratic statism and social pseudo-science. In *Quadragesimo Anno* (*In the Fortieth Year*), Pius XI laid down a permanent roadblock that should have stopped any Catholic from supporting Soviet Communism, National Socialism, or even the vast expansion of federal control over consumers and producers that Franklin Roosevelt (partly inspired, he once admitted, by Mussolini)[17] was promoting in the United States as the New Deal. Facing governments that were trying to absorb Catholic schools, nationalize major business, set wages and prices for every industry, and make each individual citizen dependent not on his family, friends, or even local government but on the centralized national state, Pius wrote, "Just as it is gravely wrong to take from individuals what they can accomplish by their own initiative and industry and give it to the community, so also it is an injustice and at the same time a grave evil and disturbance of right order to assign to a greater and higher association what lesser and subordinate organizations can do. For every social activity ought of its very nature to furnish help to the members of the body social, and never destroy and absorb them."[18]

In practice, Jason Scott Jones and I explained in *The Race to Save Our Century*, subsidiarity demands that:

> …social problems be resolved, whenever possible, by free individuals working together as families, charities, churches, or other units of "civil society." Only when it is obviously clear that a vital good, or a norm of justice, cannot be maintained without the use of government force are we even permitted to call in the police. And wherever possible, the person we call should be the sheriff—not the FBI or the United Nations. In other words, subsidiarity dictates that any problem addressed by the state should be resolved at the local level, by the relevant town or county. Only issues that cannot be fixed this way should be referred to the next highest level of power, the state or province. If a problem eludes the power and expertise of New York or Manitoba, only then should it be referred to the federal government. Issues that reach beyond even what national governments can resolve must be addressed by the United Nations or through treaties.[19]

How many social problems really meet this criterion? Some do: it took federal intervention to force desegregation and grant African Americans their rights as U.S. citizens. Controlling America's borders is the federal government's job—and one it's failing at so spectacularly that

★ ★ ★
Is the Catholic Church for States' Rights?

To the extent that "states' rights" is simply code for segregation or slavery—the putative "right" of a majority population to hold a minority in bondage or perpetual second-class citizenship on the grounds of race—and that's certainly what the phrase has meant at some times in America's past, then of course faithful Catholics can't be in favor. But to the extent that "states' rights" actually means that more local units of government (states) shouldn't have to surrender all their authority to a larger unit (the national government), then it follows from Church teaching on subsidiarity.

Pius XII vs. Socialism

[The Church insists on] "the protection of the individual and the family against a current threatening to bring about a total socialization which in the end would make the specter of the 'Leviathan' become a shocking reality. The Church will fight this battle to the end, for it is a question of supreme values: the dignity of man and the salvation of souls."

—the pope's September 14, 1952 radio message

hard-hit states such as Texas are actually trying to step up and plug the gaps, then getting slapped down by federal courts. But most problems don't meet this standard. The next time your local bishop calls for another expensive federal program, you might want to send him a note asking him how many private, local, and state solutions have yet been tried.

As Catholics and as rational human beings, we believe that freedom is better than coercion, and small-scale local solutions are better than ambitious national programs, except in cases where a problem simply cannot be solved by private or local action. Big central governments tend to impose blunt, one-size-fits all programs that trample on people's rights; ignore real differences between life in, say, New York City and rural Idaho; and empower unaccountable bureaucrats to trample the rights of citizens.

The most obvious recent example is Obamacare, and the Obama administration's mandate that religious employers help their workers buy contraceptives, including abortifacients such as the "morning after pill." When Obamacare was proposed, it received broad support from naïve religious leaders because it rectified a supposed injustice: unequal access to health care in America. Conservative critics, many of them Catholics and other Christians, warned that federalizing health care violated subsidiarity. And the Obama administration's aggression on this subject proves that conservatives were right. Obamacare poses a grave threat to the right of employers—including religious employers, such as Hobby Lobby and the Little Sisters of the Poor—to follow their consciences and make their own free decisions on how to spend their own money, time, and talents. The Democrats know that letting religious employers opt out of paying for abortifacients won't "force" working women into pregnancy. They are fighting on principle, the principle that no citizen's conscience can be permitted to trump federal policy. If the mandarins in Washington, D.C., decide that a practice is in the best interest of the masses, then the masses will comply. They must be forced to be free.

Our new battle is not with overt Marxist tyranny, but with something more subtle—an irreligious government that wants to agglomerate ever more power over our lives in the name of making things fairer and keeping people happier, of smoothing over our differences and soothing our fragile egos. If two men want to get married, then it is the Supreme Court's job to protect their "dignity" and open the way for them—and the state's job to punish those florists, caterers, and preachers who won't cooperate. If an employee wants the abortion pill (and in five years, if the Democrats win, you can count on it, a sex change operation), then Mt. Zion Baptist or Our Lady of Sorrows will have to pay for it. There is no logical stopping point for this kind of radical secularism and statism. It is an ideology, which means that its appetite only grows the more that it feeds.

Because our government is by its very nature secular, the larger the sphere of government action, the less freedom there is for Christians—full stop. The only free spaces for conscientious action by believers are those that we carve out by cutting the state down to size. Like kudzu, this invasive species won't give up, but will keep growing back, trying to smother us. So keep your weed-whacker fueled.

Solidarity: More than an Anti-Communist Labor Union

If you can't be a socialist of any kind as a Catholic, you can't be a Randian either. Ayn Rand's philosophy of absolute individualism and rejection of charity is directly contrary to the plain words of Jesus Christ all through the Gospels. The second key principle of any genuinely Catholic economics is *solidarity*, the obligation each of us owes to other members of the human family. (It was this profound Catholic principle that inspired the Polish labor organization led by Lech Walesa that helped bring down communism in Poland, and then throughout Europe.) None of us is actually self-made—both in the obvious sense that God created the world and our parents pro-created us, but also because our own successes would not be possible without the heritage of our ancestors, the civic order that our country's founders helped to establish, and the vast cultural heritage that informs us as human beings. Therefore the Church teaches, quite sensibly, that we owe a certain debt to the rest of society—and it's one that we can't pay back, so we must pay it forward. We must share the goods of the world and devote some of our time and talent (if only in the form of money) to helping those who genuinely cannot care for themselves.

As the *Catechism of the Catholic Church* explains the matter:

> On coming into the world, man is not equipped with everything he needs for developing his bodily and spiritual life. He needs others. Differences appear tied to age, physical abilities, intellectual or moral aptitudes, the benefits derived from social commerce, and the distribution of wealth. The "talents" are not distributed equally.... (1936)
>
> These differences belong to God's plan, who wills that each receive what he needs from others, and that those endowed with particular "talents" share the benefits with those who need them. These differences encourage and often oblige persons to practice generosity, kindness, and sharing of goods; they foster the mutual enrichment of cultures....(1937)

Solidarity is manifested in the first place by the distribution of goods and remuneration for work. It also presupposes the effort for a more just social order where tensions are better able to be reduced and conflicts more readily settled by negotiation. (1940)

Socio-economic problems can be resolved only with the help of all the forms of solidarity: solidarity of the poor among themselves, between rich and poor, of workers among themselves, between employers and employees in a business, solidarity among nations and peoples. International solidarity is a requirement of the moral order; world peace depends in part upon this. (1941)

Solidarity suggests that there should be a basic safety net for those who cannot support themselves and their families. But subsidiarity insists that this goal must be accomplished as much as possible by private and church-based charity, and then by local governments. Only those people whose cases fall through the cracks and simply cannot be helped by those means should be addressed by a state-level program. And it's hard to imagine any cases at all that ought to be handled by a federal-level program. In fact, as Pope Pius XI taught, to shift the power to deal with poverty problems away from the private sector, and away from your town or county, to the hands of federal bureaucrats is "an injustice and at the same time a grave evil and disturbance of right order."

The next time someone tells you that the Church requires you to vote for big federal poverty programs, remind him of that.

The enormous mechanism of federal programs that currently try—without much success—to aid America's poor in fact gets in the way of private initiatives. We see that vividly in the case of the Little Sisters of the Poor: a group of unpaid volunteers using privately raised money to care for indigent sick people is threatened with massive fines and closure by a federal government

John XXIII vs. Socialism

"[N]o Catholic could subscribe even to moderate Socialism. The reason is that Socialism is founded on a doctrine of human society which is bounded by time and takes no account of any objective other than that of material well-being. Since, therefore, it proposes a form of social organization which aims solely at production, it places too severe a restraint on human liberty, at the same time flouting the true notion of social authority."

—Mater et Magistra

that insists they must dispense the abortion pill. This is not just some eccentric act on the part of a left-wing administration. It is part of the progressive program, which sees the federal government—and the secular, anti-Christian ideology that drives it—as the right first responder to every social problem. Churches and private organizations, and more conservative local governments, are obstacles to this program. They must be forced to knuckle under and serve as obedient federal contractors, or else be cleared out of the way.

Solidarity Perverted

Very few Christians of any variety are tempted by absolute individualism of the Ayn Rand sort, which disclaims any obligation on the part of the strong, the smart, and the lucky to help the less fortunate. Sadly, too many Catholics on the Left are willing to cast aside the warnings of many popes against the evils of socialism, the grave dangers to the church and the family of overweening secular government power, and even the obvious failures of socialist systems to achieve either justice or lasting prosperity.

"Liberation Theology" is the name of the revolutionary socialist ideology adopted by a number of Latin American clerics. We learned in 2015 from Mihai Pacepa, a former communist spymaster, that Liberation Theology was at least in part the creation of Soviet espionage agents who saw the Catholic peasants of Latin America as vulnerable to Marxist recruitment through gullible, idealistic, or power-hungry clergy. As Pacepa confessed:

[I]n 1968 the KGB-created Christian Peace Conference, supported by the world-wide World Peace Council, was able to maneuver a group of leftist South American bishops into holding a Conference of Latin American Bishops at Medellin, Colombia. The Conference's official task was to ameliorate poverty. Its undeclared goal was to recognize a new religious movement encouraging the poor to rebel against the "institutionalized violence of poverty," and to recommend the new movement to the World Council of Churches for official approval.

The Medellin Conference achieved both goals. It also bought the KGB-born name "Liberation Theology."[20]

In subsequent years, hundreds of priests, nuns, and lay workers used their positions of influence over ordinary people to instruct them in a new, revolutionary reading of the Gospel. When the Marxist Sandinistas came to power in Nicaragua, Liberation Theology priests worked closely with the government—one was even the foreign minister in the revolutionary government—over the objections of Pope St. John Paul II.

Liberation Theology treats Jesus as a proto-revolutionary who came to save the poor from social injustice. It sees the Kingdom of God as the earthly paradise that the poor will construct on the ruins of sinful capitalism. The Church serves the role that the Party plays in more mainstream Marxism, the vanguard of the sacred class chosen by History (oops, "Jesus") to overturn the wicked "structures of sin," and put the Sermon on the Mount into action at the point of a bayonet. The meek shall inherit the earth, once the Party has rounded up all the non-meek into gulags and confiscated their land—the way the Soviets saved Ukraine from greedy farmers in the 1930s (and caused an artificial famine that killed some four million people).

For decades, Marxist idealists around the world had been willing to conspire, betray their country, go to prison, die—and wherever they came

★ ★ ★

Pope Francis vs. Communism

"'The Marxist ideology is wrong,'" he told Italian Vatican analyst Andrea Tornielli in a late 2013 interview when questioned about his economic views.

"In an interview [in 2014] with the Roman daily *Il Messagero*, he said that while [sic] concern for the poor is a mark of the Gospel and Church tradition, rather than an invention of communism. 'I must say that communists have stolen our flag. The flag of the poor is Christian,' he said, recalling the Beatitudes and the story of the Final Judgment in Matthew 25."[21]

to power, to kill their fellow men by the tens of millions, and imprison millions more, to force Marx's kingdom to come. That daydream became a nightmare on every patch of earth where it was tried, as any refugee from Vietnam, Cuba, Cambodia, North Korea, or Eastern Europe will tell you. History, it is perfectly clear, is not inexorably driven to produce a dictatorship of the proletariat. It took Soviet tanks to remind the workers of Hungary and Poland of what was good for them. It demanded concrete walls and barbed wire to stop the common people from fleeing "people's" regimes by the millions to live instead in wicked capitalist lands where they would be exploited. The sordid failure of materialist Marxism to fulfill any of its messianic promises posed a problem for people who were still, for their own reasons, drawn to revolutionary fantasies that entailed gaining power, confiscating other people's property, and silencing them by force. What to do, if you still find reality intolerable, and crave a revolution?

You turn to magic. You twist people's faith in Christ into the self-confidence of a conquering social class. You drag down their hope for heaven, and rope it to wishes for cheaper gas and more cassavas. Perversely, as Marxism by natural means began to collapse all around the world, liberation theologians tried to revive it by calling it Christian.

Latin Americans faced many tragic inequities in the 1960s and 70s, when Liberation Theology arrived on the scene with the KGB's assistance. Millions of people lived under dictators, working in fields for the descendants of conquistadors who had stolen most of the land. But the problem with such countries wasn't too much capitalism, private property rights that were too robust, too much freedom of thought, or the rule of law. It was too little of all those things. The Peruvian economist Hernando de Soto is a leader in the movement to give the poor around the world (and especially in Latin America) what they really need and deserve: recognition of their property rights over the homes, businesses, and farms that they have scraped together through

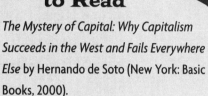

A Book You're Not Supposed to Read

The Mystery of Capital: Why Capitalism Succeeds in the West and Fails Everywhere Else by Hernando de Soto (New York: Basic Books, 2000).

hard work and thrifty living. Without legal protection for their property rights, which hundreds of millions are still denied by unresponsive governments, every farmer and business owner is at the mercy of corrupt bureaucrats, wealthy competitors, and well-connected bullies—who can use the power of the state to steal the poor's dreams. Changing that tragic situation really would be liberating, and it is exactly what is called for by Catholic theology.

But What about Dorothy Day?

One of the favorite icons of left-wing Catholics—and one of the four Americans Pope Francis held up as an example during his 2015 speech before Congress—was Catholic poverty activist Dorothy Day (1897–1980). New York's Cardinal Timothy Dolan is a big booster of her "cause" for canonization.

Like Planned Parenthood founder Margaret Sanger, Dorothy Day was appalled by urban poverty, in an era when there was no effective safety net for the jobless and sick. But instead of Sanger's top-down eugenics solution—reduce poverty by culling the poor—Day sought to better the conditions and wages of workers so that they could support their families in dignity. Like Sanger, Day began her adult life as a sexually "liberated" secular intellectual. But the experience of having an abortion changed Day profoundly, turning her into a lifelong opponent of that cruel procedure. Having spent her formative years as a full-on supporter of the Communist Party, Day found her way to faith.

Those aspects of Dorothy Day's story are inspiring. But there is much else that is distinctive about the thought of Dorothy Day—and much of it is troubling.

The movement that Day founded upon her conversion, the Catholic Worker, is held up by many today as an alternative to both socialism and capitalism. Those who think that the Catholic Church prescribes its own "third way" like to cite Dorothy Day's moralizing statements about economics. That crucial topic was something that Day learned about only third-hand, through her reading of Peter Maurin, an eccentric autodidact whose homemade economic ideas in turn were mostly drawn from G. K. Chesterton and Hilaire Belloc's "distributism."

Distributism is a speculative (that is, never-been-tried) economic system that proposes that the government break up large businesses and agribusinesses into tiny mom-and-pop shops and subsistence farms, then heavily regulate every sector of the economy to make sure that no large (that is, successful) businesses or farms emerge ever again. We must do this in service of "true freedom," so that none of us need be "wage slaves"—that is, employees. Instead, with the help of federal agencies that make it illegal to operate or shop at wicked, exploitative chains like Hobby Lobby, In-N-Out Burger, or Chick-Fil-A, we will restore the kind of economic utopia enjoyed in the Middle Ages before the wicked, pro-capitalist Reformation spoiled everything.[22] Perhaps this quotation from Day will make the Distributist program clearer: "We believe in widespread private property, the de-proletarianizing of our American people. We believe in the individual owning the means of production, the land and his tools. We are opposed to the 'finance capitalism' so justly criticized and condemned by Karl Marx but we believe there can be a Christian capitalism as there can be a Christian Communism."

The problem is, that "widespread private property" that Distributists crave can only be widely spread by the heavy hand of government coercion, with the threat of police and prison terms backing a confiscation and redistribution by the state.

The greatest stain on Dorothy Day's putative sanctity was her lifelong love affair with the radical Left. We can see evidence of this passion in the editorials she penned for the newspaper she founded, *the Catholic Worker*, and in her autobiography, *The Long Loneliness* (1952). That book recounts the journey of a young, idealistic Christian into communism, then back out again.

Some very dark threads run through Day's life and opinions, beginning even before her embrace of socialism and carrying on long past her acceptance of Christianity. These threads connect her to other figures who have embraced revolutionary movements, left and right, and they profoundly disfigure her witness.

Early on in her memoir, Dorothy Day remarks that even before she had encountered truly poor people, she had a visceral distaste for the middle class, for the staid and "comfortable" people she met in church, whom she saw as part of a system of exploitation and injustice. At the same time, she was drawn to society's misfits and outcasts, to those who were oppressed

★ ★ ★

The Church Offers No "Third Way"

Pope St. John Paul II bluntly denied the notion that there is some unique Catholic ideology of economics and government. He wrote, "The Church's social doctrine is not a 'third way' between liberal capitalism and Marxist collectivism, nor even a possible alternative to other solutions.... Nor is it an ideology, but rather the accurate formulation of the results of a careful reflection on the complex realities of human existence, in society and in the international order, in the light of faith and of the Church's tradition.... It therefore belongs to the field, not of ideology, but of theology and particularly of moral theology."[23]

by circumstances, and to those who willfully flouted social conventions. With a youthful self-righteousness, she threw herself almost indiscriminately into radical causes, at times taking an overtly masochistic delight in the sufferings she endured.

It was inevitable that such a self-dramatizing political dilettante would find herself entwined in organizations led (openly or secretly) by communists—themselves expert at locating real injustices and exploiting them, as for example in the segregated American South. As her memoir expresses eloquently, in the midst of all this political and organizational energy, Day felt a deep spiritual void that sent her along many byways and that finally landed her inside the Catholic Church. But she never overcame or even seemed to question her initial repugnance at people of property, at middle class citizens who owned their businesses and strove to better themselves and their families.

The communist movement that Day was serving was even then viciously persecuting the small landowners of Russia, especially in the Ukraine, driving them off the land and confiscating all their food, then deporting those who survived the terror famine to exile in the gulag. Uncounted millions died for the crime of having tried to accumulate some wealth for their families—or even just for "hoarding" food so that their families might survive. After Stalin's alliance with Hitler soured and the Soviet Union conquered Eastern Europe, the communist movement would go on to savagely persecute the middle class in every country it controlled—from Hungary to Korea, China to Cuba.

Indeed, we could usefully compare the communist hatred of property owners to the Nazi hatred of Jews, each partly fueled by the deadly sin of Envy. Although Day renounced the methods of Marxism, adopting a kind of anarchism that led her even to condemn the New Deal as too bureaucratic and impersonal, she never renounced her disdain for the middle class or the profit motive.

Nor did Day fully distance herself from communist sympathizers and activists, as one might expect a penitent Christian convert to do. In fact, throughout the mortal struggle the West waged from 1945 on against an aggressive communist empire now armed with nuclear weapons, Day counseled pacifism and called for the West to dismantle its nuclear weapons, unilaterally if need be.

When the United Nations intervened in 1950 to help the infant nation of South Korea fight off a savage, unprovoked invasion by the Stalinist puppet regime in Pyongyang, Day opposed American military aid to the beleaguered South Koreans.[24] We can see today, in the freezing, starving, terrorized lives of North Koreans, what would have been the fate of the South Koreans—and of the Europeans—had Americans been convinced by Day's plea for "peace." Perhaps that should count for something, when we consider the prospect of elevating Day as an example for every Christian. Of course, Day had previously opposed the U.S. defending itself against the Japanese and the Nazis after Pearl Harbor, so perhaps we should chalk up her stance in the Cold War to consistent, if delusional and irresponsible, pacifism.[25]

"God Bless Castro"

Except that Day wasn't consistent in her pacifism. Not entirely. Discussing Fidel Castro's savage attacks on the Catholic Church during the Cuban revolution, she wrote of the situation in 1961 that "the church is functioning as normally as it can in our materialist civilization." So things in communist Cuba weren't much worse than they were in, say, Chicago. Discussing Castro's armed takeover, seizure of private property, and imposition of a Leninist one-party state, she commented,

> We are certainly not Marxist socialists nor do we believe in violent revolution. Yet we do believe that it is better to revolt, to fight,

as Castro did with his handful of men, he worked in the fields with the cane workers and thus gained them to his army—than to do nothing.

We are on the side of the revolution. We believe there must be new concepts of property, which is proper to man, and that the new concept is not so new. There is a Christian communism and a Christian capitalism as Peter Maurin pointed out. We believe in farming communes and cooperatives and will be happy to see how they work out in Cuba. We are in correspondence with friends in Cuba who will send us word as to what is happening in religious circles and in the schools. We have been invited to visit by a young woman who works in the National Library in Havana and we hope some time we will be able to go. We are happy to hear that all the young people who belong to the sodality of our Lady in the U.S. are praying for Cuba and we too join in prayer that the pruning of the mystical vine will enable it to bear much fruit. God Bless the priests and people of Cuba. God bless Castro and all those who are seeing Christ in the poor. God bless all those who are seeking the brotherhood of man because in loving their brothers they love God even though they deny Him.[26]

Day wrote of North Vietnamese communist leader Ho Chi Minh, whose regime was equally as tyrannical and bloodthirsty as Castro's, that if the Catholic Worker could have "gained the privilege of giving hospitality to a Ho Chi Minh, with what respect and interest we would have served him, as a man of vision, as a patriot, a rebel against foreign invaders."[27]

One cannot help but wonder what people would make of a person who was driven by rabid patriotism to join the Nazi movement, and who then broke with it, but never denounced its supporters or reformed her attitude toward Jews, and who greeted the invasion of Poland with a call for pacifism and disarmament. Some might question how deep that convert's conversion had gone.

Day embraced the Christian tradition of lauding voluntary poverty and serving the poor—which has led many to compare her to St. Francis of Assisi. But there is one crucial contrast that needs to be pointed out. One of Francis's early struggles was with an irrational fear and hatred of lepers. Indeed, upon his conversion, that sentiment was something that so shamed him that he made a special point of serving and treating lepers, even kissing their wounds.

Had Dorothy Day's trajectory closely followed his, we might expect that she would have repented her long-time involvement in a movement that hunted and murdered middle class people and property owners by the millions in a similar dramatic way. She might have mortified her ancient hatred by serving the despised bourgeoisie. Indeed, the most penitential, and therefore the most saintly, thing that Dorothy Day could have done would have been to choke down her disgust and minister to hard-working families in the suburbs. She should have joined Opus Dei.

CHAPTER 8

Amnesty Equals Abortion

Did you know?

★ The U.S. already takes in more than a million immigrants a year

★ An overwhelming majority of self-identified Catholic immigrants vote for pro-choice Democrats

★ The *Catechism of the Catholic Church* puts significant conditions on our obligation to accept immigrants

★ The U.S. bishops received more than $85 million in federal dollars for refugee resettlement in a single year

If there is a single issue on which public perception of Catholic teaching is most at odds with reality, it is immigration. And we can't blame the secular media. There has been a concerted attempt by Catholic leaders in the U.S. to corral public opinion among Catholic voters behind support for America's longtime policy of permitting large-scale, unskilled immigration into the U.S.—even as our nation's manufacturing jobs disappear or are outsourced, wages stay flat or shrink, and budget deficits threaten to crush our grandchildren under a mountain of debt to pay for a social safety net that has morphed into a cozy multigenerational hammock. Before we address the moral arguments about immigration, let me point out that Americans already "welcome"—to quote the language with which the bishops continually hector us—*more than a million legal immigrants per year.*[1]

The Church's Teaching, Distorted by Our Shepherds

Prominent U.S. bishops have tried hard to create the impression that there is a Catholic position or even an official Church teaching mandating that the United States should admit large numbers of immigrants and give them generous public benefits. Sadly, Pope Francis himself, the U.S. Bishops' conference, and even the American bishops deemed "conservative" on doctrinal issues have for their own reasons chosen to present the Church's teaching on immigration in a grossly imbalanced fashion—hiding under a bushel the complex, nuanced, and profoundly sensible reflections that actually bind faithful Catholics: namely, the teaching offered in the *Catechism of the Catholic Church*. Instead of the broad and plausible principles laid out in that Magisterial document, we hear from churchmen at every level, from Rome on down, a series of moralizing, sentimental, one-sided, and unjust assertions about this issue, which sometimes seem lifted straight from the political playbook of the multiculturalist, anti-Western radical Left. These clerical statements even make bold to judge the motives and denounce the moral character of opponents of mass immigration, while airbrushing the profound challenges and real threats that immigration can pose to the common good of countries, especially to the poorest citizens of those countries. At their worst, these statements violate not just charity but justice, and cross the line from detraction into slander.

The best known of these statements in recent years is probably Pope Francis's flippant comments about 2016 Republican presidential candidate Donald Trump, in which the pope said baldly that anyone who wished to build a wall to contain illegal immigrants was "not a Christian." For a pope to judge the personal faith commitment of a Protestant over such a debatable issue shocked U.S. public opinion, to the

---

★ ★ ★

Not a Great Track Record

The American bishops' lobbying on immigration today is reminiscent of their political activism in the 1980s, when they produced one policy statement after another endorsing larger government, higher welfare payments, more regulation of business, and the decrease of U.S. defense spending.[2] Thankfully, none of the bishops' quixotic policies were implemented—or else the U.S. might already have gone bankrupt, and the Soviet Union might still exist.

---

point where pro-immigration Catholic presidential candidates such as Governor Jeb Bush and Senator Marco Rubio felt the need to rush to Trump's defense. Bush later complained that Pope Francis's intervention helped Trump win the nomination.[3]

But the pope's statement was nothing new. In 2008, newly appointed Los Angeles archbishop José Gómez (himself a Mexican immigrant), addressing the Missouri Catholic Conference on the subject of immigration, compared Catholics who oppose the mass illegal influx of millions of unskilled workers to Julian the Apostate, the neo-pagan Roman emperor who tried to stamp out Christianity. "We must defend the immigrant if we are to be worthy of the name Catholic," Gomez said.[4]

In 2015, Archbishop Charles Chaput gave a speech on immigration that tracked exactly with the positions of the Democratic Party and radical Mexican nationalist groups such as La Raza. Chaput defended birthright citizenship for children of illegals, opposed any deportations of illegal immigrants, and even condemned attempts to refine America's criteria for legal immigration to focus on skilled immigrants, rather than relatives of recently amnestied illegals. Chaput warned that opponents of immigration play on "on our worst fears and resentments" and that policies such as detaining

Good Catholics and Good Citizens

We do not have the right to favor immigration just because many of the immigrants seeking entrance to the U.S. are Catholics and we feel a spiritual kinship with them. To do that would be blatantly unfair to our non-Catholic fellow citizens, whose ancestors admitted our Catholic forefathers on the understanding that we would be loyal citizens, not secret agents working for our fellow Catholics around the world regardless of the best interest of Americans. We cannot flush the natural virtue of patriotism down the toilet of religious tribalism—unless we want to prove that the nineteenth-century Know-Nothings were right to try to keep our ancestors out. Happily, the anti-Catholics are wrong. The Church does not teach theocracy, nor does it urge us to tribalism. Instead, it draws on natural law (not divine revelation, in this case) to offer brief and sane criteria for principled policy. We may not, without sin, use our neighbors' tax money and employ the guns and the jails of the state to promote our own group at the expense of others—or to enforce laws based solely on verses from the Bible or quotes from Our Lady of Fatima.

★ ★ ★

The Democrats' Loyal Allies

One side effect of the bishops' venture into legislative politics is to damage and divide the coalition of pro-life and pro-family voters. Well-meaning Protestants who stand side by side with the Church in trying to halt the gross crime of abortion are simply flummoxed by the time and money that churchmen spend helping liberal Democrats on every other issue. The most vocal pro-life Protestants in the current Congress (and many of the Catholics) oppose the proposed amnesty bill for illegal immigrants and wonder why the Church has thrown its weight behind a bill that is favored by the Left partly because amnesty will create so many new Democrat voters.

families where one or more members were illegal aliens—a crucial tool for any enforcement of America's immigration laws—were "needless and inhumane."[5] One could fill half this book with boilerplate statements like these from U.S. bishops, pastors, and Church bureaucrats—and the pro-choice, anti-marriage Democrat politicians who delight in quoting them on the campaign trail. Pope Francis himself offers fodder for this kind of politicking, as the Huffington Post reported: "During a Wednesday speech on income equality, Obama remarked, 'Across the developed world, inequality has increased. Some of you may have seen just last week, the pope himself spoke about this at eloquent length.'

"He went on to quote a line from Pope Francis' apostolic exhortation 'Evangelii Gaudium,' asking, 'How can it be that it is not a news item when an elderly homeless person dies of exposure, but it is news when the stock market loses two points?'

"Obama called the growing income gap the 'defining challenge of our time,' along with the increasing difficulty of upward economic mobility, AP reported."[6]

But more shocking are Pope Francis's callous statements welcoming the millions of Muslim immigrants who have come to Europe in waves of mass migration, many of them as refugees from the civil war in Syria, or the various conflicts in their native African countries, and his dismissal of the concerns of Europeans whose lives have been upended by the influx. Those who follow the news will be well aware of the thousands of radical Muslims who dwell in self-enclosed enclaves across Western Europe. One out of four residents of Brussels under age twenty is of "Islamic origin."[7] The colonization of formerly Christian Europe has proceeded very quickly, aided and abetted by generous social welfare programs that offer immigrants a comfortable life in Germany or England for the price of showing up. Muslim immigrants and their children have been behind most of the terrorist attacks in Europe, from the 2016 bombing in Brussels to the 2015 slaughter in Paris and the 2014 butchery of journalists at the magazine *Charlie Hebdo*. It was Muslim immigrants who conducted the wave of public gang-rapes that shocked Germany on New Year's Eve 2015–16, and dozens of European-born Muslims have been apprehended en route to volunteering for the murder squads of ISIS.

But Pope Francis has repeatedly and explicitly condemned any attempt to stop the influx of Muslim migrants. The pope's statements on the immigration issue have been one-sided and moralistic in the extreme, far different in tone and content from the official Church teaching as codified in the *Catechism*, and starkly at odds with many centuries of Catholic practice. Francis's most sweeping and theologically unfounded statement on the subject was probably his 2013 speech at Lampedusa, a town in impoverished Sicily that is inundated annually with hundreds of thousands of economic migrants from Africa, who by that time outnumbered citizens. In that speech, he compared those economic migrants who drowned in the Mediterranean while trying to reach and settle illegally in Italy to Abel and Western "indifference" to their fates to the mindset of Cain—who, as Bible buffs will remember, actually murdered his brother. The pope waxed lyrical and sentimental, saying,

> I would like to ask.... Has any one of us wept because of this situation and others like it? Has any one of us grieved for the

death of these brothers and sisters? Has any one of us wept for these persons who were on the boat? For the young mothers carrying their babies? For these men who were looking for a means of supporting their families? We are a society which has forgotten how to weep, how to experience compassion—"suffering with" others: the globalization of indifference has taken from us the ability to weep! In the Gospel we have heard the crying, the wailing, the great lamentation: "Rachel weeps for her children...because they are no more." Herod sowed death to protect his own comfort, his own soap bubble. And so it continues. ... Let us ask the Lord to remove the part of Herod that lurks in our hearts; let us ask the Lord for the grace to weep over our indifference, to weep over the cruelty of our world, of our own hearts, and of all those who in anonymity make social and economic decisions which open the door to tragic situations like this. Has any one wept? Today has anyone wept in our world?[8]

That's right, he compared Europeans (worried, financially strapped, and sometimes physically brutalized by the migrants) to King Herod, who slaughtered the infants of Bethlehem in an effort to murder Jesus.

And German Chancellor Angela Merkel listened. Instead of enforcing international law, under which refugees must be accepted by the "first safe country" that they reach, which in the case of those fleeing the Syrian civil war was NATO member Turkey—a comparatively prosperous Muslim country where they could have been easily integrated, and one which bore some responsibility for the war in the refugees' native land—under Merkel's leadership Germany followed the advice of the pope, and the dictates of post-Christian, post-Western multiculturalism. With high-minded abandon she accepted more than a million Syrian migrants, forcing much of Europe to follow suit. The results have been an unmitigated catastrophe, as hundreds of thousands of military-age Muslim males, mostly unaccompanied by the "women and children" that leftist media and church bulletins love to highlight, have flocked to Western European countries.[9]

Already hard-pressed public welfare systems are cracking under the strain of hundreds of thousands of foreigners whose ancestors never paid into them. (Such welfare is widely regarded among Islamists as *jizya*, the tribute that non-Muslims ought to be paying Muslims anyway, according to the Koran.) Countries such as Spain and Germany and Italy where youth unemployment is already at staggering levels are being flooded with low-skill workers who don't speak the local language. Governments are responding not by reconsidering the wisdom of their refugee policies, but by cracking down on the free speech rights of Europeans who question it. Water cannons in the streets of Cologne were turned on the demonstrators who responded to the rape mob. Christmas trees and carnivals, crucifixes and classical statues are disappearing from public spaces, lest they offend the puritanical sensibilities of the intolerant newcomers.[10] The president of a German university in Hamburg has proposed that every young German be required to learn Arabic to prepare for the "multicultural" society which that country's government has imposed on them.[11]

And things may well get even worse. As the British newspaper *the Telegraph* reported, "jihadists hope to flood [Libya] with militiamen from Syria and Iraq, who will then sail across the Mediterranean posing as migrants on people trafficking vessels, according to plans seen by Quilliam, the British anti-extremist group. The fighters would then run amok in southern European cities and also try to attack maritime shipping."[12]

Are Europeans who take such documented threats seriously really like Cain or Herod in any way? It is frankly demagogic to say so. It is true that the threat of ISIS emerged only after Pope Francis's homily, but he has at no point retracted or corrected his unbalanced statements on immigration; if anything, he has doubled down, even using the papal plane in 2016 to transport Muslim migrants from Lesbos, Greece, to Italy—while leaving Christian refugees behind. As *The Daily Mail* reported, "A Christian brother and sister from Syria say they have been 'let down' by the Pope after he left them behind in a Lesbos refugee camp despite promises they would be given a new life in Italy. Roula and Malek Abo say they were two of the lucky 'chosen 12' refugees selected by the Vatican to be taken from the desperate camp and housed in Rome. But what seemed like the chance of a lifetime was cruelly snatched away when they were told the following day they couldn't go. Instead three Muslim families were taken."[13]

What the Church Actually Teaches on Immigration

Whatever Pope Francis's inner feelings or personal opinion, the Church has a settled teaching on immigration, which he does not have the authority to simply alter as he sees fit. As we have seen, the Magisterium of the Church is not some magical power which offers every pope new, unprecedented insights on the best, fairest, wisest, or even most moral policy on every issue. Instead, the Magisterium is the office by which the pope and bishops pass along, unaltered, the teaching of Jesus that was given to the apostles. So if a pope were to say something quite new, out of continuity with what the Church taught and practiced in past centuries, it's hard to see how it can be considered part of the Magisterium, which teaches "only that which has been handed on.... it draws from this one deposit of faith everything which it presents for belief as divinely revealed."[14] Thus the pope does not have the power to announce that the Church now supports the abolition of private property, or the practice of polygamy—because it is obvious that Jesus never said it, or one of the apostles or early bishops would have certainly mentioned it.

Likewise, the Church is not free to demand of every nation on earth the abolition of borders and the elimination of citizenship. If these were teachings of Christ, passed on to the apostles, there would have been some evidence of that fact in the early Church, in previous centuries of Catholic practice, and in statements by popes from centuries past. There is no such support for this position in Church tradition, and in fact the Church's official *Catechism* is quite at odds with the pope's statements.

This is the Catholic Church's official teaching on immigration, from the *Catechism*:

> The more prosperous nations are obliged, to the extent they are able, to welcome the foreigner in search of the security and the means of livelihood which he cannot find in his country of origin. Public authorities should see to it that the natural right is respected that places a guest under the protection of those who receive him.
>
> Political authorities, for the sake of the common good for which they are responsible, may make the exercise of the right to immigrate subject to various juridical conditions, especially with regard to the immigrants' duties toward their country of adoption. Immigrants are obliged to respect with gratitude the material and spiritual heritage of the country that receives them, to obey its laws and to assist in carrying civic burdens.[15]

Notice that while there is an obligation to accept immigrants, it comes with some important limitations. Even the "more prosperous nations" are obliged to accept migrants only "to the extent they are able." The government can put conditions on the right to immigrate. And the immigrants, too, have obligations to the country that accepts them—including the obligation to

★ ★ ★

Because Apparently It Doesn't Go without Saying: Immigration Hawks Are Not Murderers

Those of us who, after serious reflection, come up with an answer different from the pope's about the optimum number of migrants for our country to admit while remaining consistent with the common good ought not to be falsely branded as "dissenters" or "apostates," compared to Cain or Herod, or charged with any of a long list of other made-up hate crimes that are routinely adduced by leftist activists and well-meaning but addled Catholics who have internalized leftist arguments.

obey its laws. Those are the basic principles, and Catholic laymen are free—indeed, we are obliged—to use our own judgment in applying them in our own country and context, just as we apply "just war" teaching to particular conflicts our nation faces. While we listen to the advice of popes and bishops on this prudential matter, which requires judging the particular circumstances of our own concrete situation, we know that they can be wrong, as some medieval popes were wrong to call crusades against Christian heretics or to wage war on neighboring cities. Let us parse the key points made in the *Catechism* and see how the proper application of this Church teaching can be discussed in a civil manner.

"To the Extent They Are Able"

We are obliged to accept immigrants only to the extent we are able—a statement broad enough that we could argue over its application indefinitely. Theoretically, it is physically possible for the entire population of the world to fit into the state of Texas, with several feet of wiggle room to spare. Does that mean that the U.S. is able to accept the entire world? Clearly not, because, even for bare survival, people need more than room to stand and wave their arms—starting with food, clothing, and shelter. And fostering the common good requires more than ensuring bare physical survival. There are countless economic, environmental, cultural, fiscal, and other factors that determine how many immigrants we are actually able to accept. All those points are things we must determine by rational argument, setting our national priorities by democratic vote.

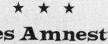

Does Amnesty Equal Abortion?

Why does virtually every recent immigrant group—including pro-life Hispanic Catholics[16] and socially "conservative Muslims"—rally to the pro-choice, anti-marriage Democrats? Could it be that voting in their ethnic and economic self-interest trumps the sanctity of life and of the family for them?

There is no secret "Catholic answer" to these questions, though natural law principles can and should be invoked in our discussions of the matter. Such arguments are prudential, and the Church does not pretend to have the competence to answer them; if it did, we should simply ask Pope Francis to use his infallible authority to draw up the U.S. budget every year.

How many unskilled immigrants is the U.S. able to accept from Latin America without unjustly endangering the interests of low-skill American workers—whose wages have been static for two generations?[17] What should we say to working families who pay taxes to support the 50 percent of immigrant households receiving welfare? (If you look at just Latin American immigrant households, that number shoots up to 73 percent.)[18] To how many Muslim economic migrants can Europe offer asylum and cradle-to-grave welfare benefits without unjustly harming its tens of millions of unemployed native citizens? How many potential jihadists is Europe able to safely welcome so that they may attend radical, Saudi-funded mosques that preach the need for sharia in London, Brussels, and Rome? And in the zero-sum contest between unborn American babies and Mexican-American voters who overwhelmingly support the pro-choice Democrat Party, who is really "the least of these"?

There's no principle in Catholic teaching, or in the natural moral law, that requires you to keep taking more people into your lifeboat until it sinks. So it's reasonable to ask whether the very prosperity that makes immigrants flock to the U.S.—and gives us, as one of the "more prosperous nations," a (limited) obligation to accept migrants—could be destroyed by the mass immigration of people whose votes will erode the strong private property rights and other economic freedoms that made America rich in the first place. The United States has by and large preserved the rule of law and protected property rights in a context of limited government. Are we obliged to accept unlimited numbers of new citizens who carry with them very different expectations—whose voting patterns show that they favor a big government that does not respect property rights but instead massively redistributes wealth away from those who earn it? As Mark Kirkorian notes in *National Review*:

> Conservative immigration romantics imagine [immigrants] to be natural Republicans, having a right-winger inside just waiting to burst out, if only they're welcomed with open arms. Unfortunately, a mountain of survey research gives us no reason to believe that to be the case. Put simply, immigrants and their adult children are disproportionately big-government liberals who vote heavily Democrat because that party's policies accord with their own views and interests....
>
> The 2008 National Annenberg Election Survey found that 62 percent of immigrants supported government health insurance,

as opposed to 45 percent of the native-born. The 2010 Cooperative Congressional Election Study found 58 percent of immigrants supported affirmative action, versus 35 percent of natives. The Pew Research Center found in 2011 that Hispanics (mainly immigrants or the children of immigrants) had the most negative view of capitalism of any group polled—more negative even than self-identified supporters of Occupy Wall Street. Pew also found that 75 percent of Hispanics preferred a larger government providing more services to a small one providing fewer; the figure for the public at large was just 41 percent.[19]

We must discuss such questions using a cost-benefit analysis, looking both at the common good and at how a given policy affects our *poorest fellow citizens*. Wait, can we really say that? Isn't it "xenophobic" and "discriminatory" for Americans to privilege poor Americans over poor Mexicans, Iraqis, or Somalis? Aren't those "foreigners" equally made in the image and likeness of God?

Of course they are. But just as we owe family members more than we owe strangers, we owe more to fellow citizens—whose ancestors paid taxes to build our roads and fought in our country's wars, who may even have been American slaves—than we do to the residents of foreign countries.

In some ways a country is like a club where members pay dues and take on certain duties in return for certain privileges. To flood such a club with non-members and offer them every

★ ★ ★
Who Is My Neighbor?

Jesus had twelve apostles He singled out from hundreds of disciples, an inner circle of three He took up the mountain for the Transfiguration and to pray with Him in the Garden of Gethsemane, and one "disciple He loved," to whom He entrusted His Mother as He hung on the Cross. The belief that we have equal obligations to every single person in the world is communism, not Christianity.

privilege members have earned is simply unjust to the other members. It is up to the members to vote on whom they will admit and how many. And one of our key criteria as Catholics must be, "How does this influx affect the American poor?" Given the U.S. birth dearth and the collapse of public schools (in part under the weight of mandatory bilingualism), we must also ask, "How does it affect working families who are striving to educate their children?"

Other people deserve our consideration as well. If the Church's "preferential option for the poor" means that middle class people (and ethnic majorities, and even prosperous elites) have no moral claims whatsoever—and may simply be exploited with abandon—then it is no option at all. It is neither justice nor mercy but simple resentment, an ideological stick for Liberation theologians to beat the bourgeoisie.

Even if working class people are not as needy as would-be migrants, working class people have rights and claims under justice, too. So do *middle class people living in the suburbs.* So do the rich, even. Pope Leo XIII taught that, while we are all called to acts of charity, we are not commanded by the Gospel to give away so much that we sink from one social class to another.[20] Religious vocations aside, the rich are not required to turn themselves into paupers. America need not—in fact, it should not—join the Developing World. That would do no one any favors, least of all the poor.

If an American today wants to offer properly Christian aid to an immigrant, the existing law offers him an ideal way to do that: he may sponsor a legal immigrant, promise not to allow that immigrant to become a "public charge," then honor that promise by providing the migrant with financial support until he gets on his feet. To do all that at one's own expense is truly to "welcome the stranger." As to those (including churchmen) who shunt that responsibility onto the taxpayers, then "announce it with trumpets, as the hypocrites do" (Matthew 6:2)…they already have their reward.

"Immigrants Are Obliged to Respect with Gratitude the Material and Spiritual Heritage of the Country That Receives Them"

We could also argue for years about what exactly immigrants' obligation to respect the heritage of the countries they immigrate to entails. But surely it includes a certain degree of assimilation: namely, learning the English language and switching their loyalty from their nation of origin to the U.S. When tens of thousands of recent immigrants, both legal and illegal, march through the streets chanting foreign slogans and waving foreign flags,[21] that raises legitimate fears among Americans that the immigrants are not willing to keep up their side of the bargain. It doesn't help when immigrants go to their former nations' consulates to vote in their elections, or when they vote as ethnic blocs in our elections for larger government programs to tax the wealth of native-born citizens to fund programs from which the immigrants disproportionately benefit.

For a change of pace, our bishops should address the fierce nationalism that motivates so many immigrant organizations, driving them to lobby incessantly for the private interests of their own racial groups. Is the tribal groupthink practiced by Chicano organizations such as MEChA not a form of racism? If not, why not? Just because many members of the race involved are poor? The "preferential option for the poor" does not give poor people a free pass to indulge in racial resentment—and to act as if it does is to dehumanize the poor. To hold one group to a lower moral standard is patronizing and suggests that they are forever slow-witted children or loveable, mischievous pets.

"To Obey Its Laws and to Assist in Carrying Civic Burdens"

If we are indeed to treat immigrants as fully human, equal moral adults, then we won't wax hysterical when they face the consequences of breaking

★ ★ ★
That Which Is Caesar's

If Caesar has the right to mint currency and collect taxes—and we have this on pretty high authority—then he's probably also in charge of granting citizenship.

the law. If I snuck into Mexico and used false identity papers to gain financial benefits from its citizens, I know I might end up in a jail cell. I wouldn't expect a Mexican parish to hide me.

Indeed, as Michelle Malkin observes, Mexico maintains quite strict immigration laws and policies, aimed at restricting the influx of Central Americans:

> The Mexican government will bar foreigners if they upset "the equilibrium of the national demographics." If outsiders do not enhance the country's "economic or national interests" or are "not found to be physically or mentally healthy," they are not welcome. Neither are those who show "contempt against national sovereignty or security." They must not be economic burdens on society and must have clean criminal histories. Those seeking to obtain Mexican citizenship must show a birth certificate, provide a bank statement proving economic independence, pass an exam and prove they can provide their own health care.

> Illegal entry into the country is equivalent to a felony punishable by two years' imprisonment. Document fraud is subject to fine and imprisonment; so is alien marriage fraud. Evading deportation is a serious crime; illegal re-entry after deportation is punishable by ten years' imprisonment. Foreigners may be kicked out of the country without due process....[22]

Like the U.S., Mexico has its structures and its legal codes, and except where they are grossly unjust, we are expected to obey them when we're in that country.

Those who have not obeyed U.S. immigration laws have forfeited any strict claim in justice to remain on American soil. Under strict justice, the U.S. government would be completely within its rights to deport every illegal immigrant in America. The fact that a law is poorly enforced does not mean that we are free to violate it, demand that the state later give us amnesty, and sign up for social programs we barely paid taxes to support. Whether or not a mass removal of illegal immigrants is prudent or politically plausible is a separate question, of course. At the very least, as we search for a prudent policy for dealing with the ill-effects of poor law enforcement—the presence of more than eleven million illegal residents in the United States[23]—we must make sure that such poor enforcement does not continue. But at the moment the multiculturalist Left and cheap-labor Right are fighting every truly effective policy for securing our country's borders tooth and nail, demanding amnesty first and enforcement later. And our bishops are egging them on.

Furthermore, it is not even true that massive, unregulated immigration necessarily benefits *the immigrants themselves.* As Jason Jones and I pointed out at Fox News in 2014:

> [T]housands of helpless immigrant children now haunt emergency shelters throughout the American Southwest—having been lured here by rumors of an imminent amnesty. And their presence is being used to promote just such an amnesty.
>
> That goes far to proving the point of many amnesty opponents: That without a firm lockdown of the U.S. border, any path to citizenship that is granted to current resident illegal immigrants will serve as a powerful magnet to millions more.
>
> In other words, there is nothing "one-time" about the amnesty proposals currently stalled in Congress; as our borders currently stand, with our lax laws that let employers get away with exploiting

illegal workers, with our broken system for identifying people who overstay visas, any amnesty we passed would in fact amount to welcome mat for millions more immigrants who wished to enter America.

Millions of newly legalized workers, now protected by workplace laws and entitled to health insurance, would be promptly replaced by millions more illegal immigrants, who hoped for another amnesty down the road.

Such an outcome would suit the most callous of Americans: those who profit from the status quo, who prefer that millions of immigrants remain in the shadow economy, where their labor can be extracted without the protection of workplace safety laws…

There is a better way. We must answer the current crisis with sincere efforts at humanitarian help, and a firm commitment to return these children to their native countries and their families.

Only an absolute certainty that a hazardous journey to America would be completely futile will turn off the magnet that is drawing parents to abandon their children across our border.

If we do anything less, we are essentially offering free advertising to the ruthless *coyotes* (human traffickers) who promise parents that they will safely deliver their children on U.S. soil— but in fact, put their lives in danger.[24]

When we inflict radical changes on our society, or tolerate a collapse of civic order at our borders, we should ask ourselves whether we are being faithful stewards of the prosperous, free societies for which our ancestors struggled, fought, and sometimes died. Perhaps instead we are squandering our inheritance for the sake of that happy frisson we experience when we do or say something supporting "openness," "tolerance," and "social justice."

We are purchasing moral approval with social capital stolen from our children and grandchildren. We are feathering our own cozy nests, while making life even more wretched for our own nations' native poor—whose ancestors did fight and die, alongside ours, for their descendants' stakes in the nation. We are stealing the precious gifts of freedom and order from our least-advantaged fellow citizens—the blue collar workers, the unemployed, the troubled war veterans—in order to salve our confused consciences, and feed our self-esteem.

Mass Immigration as a Mode of Conquest and Plunder

It is true that traditionally, Christians are rightly sympathetic to the plight of refugees who are fleeing persecution, and even of economic migrants wishing to find new opportunities where work and thrift pay off and private property is protected by the law. We look back to Bible verses such as "Welcome the stranger," and listen to Jesus' many calls for compassion toward the vulnerable. From these authorities we learn that the plight of dislocated people entitles them to our compassion, within the firm bounds of prudence and fairness to the citizens of our own communities.

But the situation of modern mass immigration, in an age of democracy and welfare states, is something almost unprecedented in human history. It is our assumption today that newcomers to a country—or at least their children—will gain full citizenship and the right to vote. They also gain, almost immediately, access to generous social welfare programs that citizens of our countries created to help the least fortunate members of our own community—descendants of slaves, war veterans, hard-working citizens who have fallen down on their luck. If an immigrant group grows large enough, it can even use the state to confiscate the wealth of native-born citizens, and restrict their religious liberty, through purely democratic methods. What does all this mean? That large immigrant groups organized in cohesive political movements today can enjoy most of the spoils that in past centuries would have come to a conquering army. What else does an armed invader seek but control over the government and wealth of a country?

When large numbers of Sunni Muslims attempted to colonize much of Europe in the sixteenth and seventeenth centuries, Christians energetically organized to prevent them from doing so—as students of history will remember from the Battle of Lepanto and the sieges of Vienna. Now the Islamic world is employing a different tactic for expansion. Instead of sending armies waving banners, it sends armies of "refugees" waving asylum claims—marching them straight through Turkey into the heart of once-Christian Europe.

★ ★ ★

Conquest by Ballot

If accepted into Europe, Muslim migrants will someday gain the rights of citizens—the power to vote in laws that fit their values instead of ours. We have seen those values in action from Saudi Arabia to Pakistan. Their fruit is honor killings of women, executions of homosexuals, and the death penalty for "apostasy" from or "blasphemy" against Islam. There are already plenty of countries where people can live if they wish to be ruled by sharia. Why should we inflict that illiberal creed on our children? Is that what Christ called us to do?

Traditionally nations made up of Christians have in fact policed their borders, limited the franchise to citizens, and directed public welfare first to those who had contributed something to their societies. A medieval Spaniard who emigrated to the Holy Roman Empire, or a Frenchman who went to England, had no guarantee of a vote, and no chance to use the state to redistribute the native citizens' wealth in his own direction. Millions of persecuted Jews flocked to the tolerant medieval Kingdom of Poland. But there was never any question that they might exercise the political power to make Poland an officially Jewish state, much less that they would lobby the government to redistribute Polish citizens' wealth to their own pockets. If there had been such a prospect, the Kingdom of Poland would have had to consider much more carefully the wisdom of admitting them, and the Church would have backed Poland up.

How do we know this? Because in repeated historical instances where a mass influx of people would have had either effect, the Church stood four-square behind governments that resisted. Christian Roman emperors fought against the mass influx of barbarians throughout the fourth century, an influx that most historians now agree was not so much an attempt at armed conquest as a mass migration of peoples who wished to share in the wealth and political benefits enjoyed by Roman citizens.[25] No pope ever condemned those emperors or forbade Christian soldiers from using deadly force to stop the Visigoths, Ostrogoths, and Vandals from entering the empire. When Attila led the nation of the Huns into Italy circa 452 in search of political power and treasure, Pope Leo rode out personally to meet Attila and persuade him—through who knows what means, perhaps supernatural threats—to march his people away from Rome. When the Arabs began their incursion into Spain in the eighth century, again in hopes of gaining political power and wealth, the Church led resistance efforts among local Christians, and it played a major role in the seven-hundred-year crusade to expel the Arabs at last. When the Ottoman Empire flooded the Balkans with Muslims in the sixteenth and seventeenth centuries, it was the Church and Christian monarchs that led the effort to defeat them; one priest, Saint John of Capistrano, was canonized specifically for his efforts to organize Christian armies to stop this Muslim influx.

Some might object to such historical comparisons by pointing out that in each of the cases above the newcomers arrived in the form of armies threatening violence—which meant that Christian governments were obliged to respond with force. That much is true. The Hunnic, Visigoth, Arab, and Turkish influxes into Europe were led by soldiers—because there were no other means available at the time to take over the political structure and wealth of a country, except by open conquest. No one had yet pioneered the idea that millions of people with aggressively alien values would simply walk through a country's borders unopposed and demand to share political power and redistribute the wealth!

Apologies. The above is not quite accurate. There was one energetic group whose leaders in fact did come up with such a strategy for taking over foreign nations, imposing its political and religious views on them, and confiscating their property. But for centuries it never had much opportunity to put this plan into practice, because few nations were willing to open their borders and be colonized—until recently, of course. Can you guess which world religion has as one of its precepts the obligation to emigrate, with the specific intent of transforming other nations and seizing their wealth? (A quick hint: it isn't the Quakers.)

That's right, we're talking Islam here. Leading Muslim authorities consider *hijra* (emigration) one of the pillars of Islamic expansion, a critical means of accomplishing the mission that all orthodox Muslims consider God-given and sacred: the conquest of every country on earth by Muslims, and the conversion or subjugation of all non-Muslims to Islam. Here is Egyptian cleric Yusuf Qaradawi, chairman of the International Union of Muslim Scholars, and—thanks to the Internet—one of the most influential Muslim scholars in the world, on the duty of Muslims to conquer Western countries without firing a shot: "Islam will return to Europe. Islam entered Europe twice and left it...Perhaps the next conquest, Allah willing, will be by means of preaching and ideology. The conquest need not necessarily be by the sword... [The conquest of Mecca] was not by the sword or by war, but by a [Hudabiyya] treaty, and by peace...Perhaps we will conquer these lands without armies."[26]

The Center for Security Policy confirms that this strategy is already in effect around the world, including in the United States: "As practiced today, the hijra strategy is an important part of a covert, *pre*-violent 'civilization jihad' pursued by the Muslim Brotherhood. The UN High Commission on

Amnesty Equals Abortion

Refugees—which, like the rest of the United Nations, is dominated by the dictates of the Islamic supremacist organization known as the Organization of Islamic Cooperation (OIC)—is complicit in the process of bringing Muslim refugees to America. Interestingly, no Muslim refugees are ever resettled in wealthy, low-population density Islamic countries like Saudi Arabia."[27]

While their agenda is quite different and starkly secular, there are vocal Latino activists who regard immigration into the United States as a means of "reconquista"—reversing the conquest of the U.S. Southwestern states from Mexico in the nineteenth century.[28] And even activists who are not committed to the literal reconquest of California and Texas by Mexico seem eager to appropriate our wealth—including at least one Catholic cardinal. Harshly anti-American (and anti-Semitic)[29] Catholic cardinal Oscar Rodriguez Maradiaga of Honduras serves as a member of Pope Francis's "Gang of Eight" inner circle. An outspoken opponent of America's attempts to control illegal immigration, Maradiaga called for the "globalization"—that is, the redistribution—of wealth from wealthier North Americans to less wealthy Latin Americans in an address at the University of Dallas in 2014. In that same speech, he praised long-time Fidel Castro ally Jean Ziegler and spoke of the need to dismantle "neoliberal dictatorships that rule democracies," such as the United States, whose governments, he argued, serve not their people but the "world dictatorship of finance capital."[30]

May Catholics in America reject the plans of foreign nationalists and leftists to remake U.S. institutions in the image of Latin American socialism, and confiscate our wealth via transfer payments to recent immigrants and ever-growing government? Is it legitimate for us to reject attempts by Islamists to form a critical mass in our countries and impose sharia law on us? The answer to both questions is yes. St. John Paul II wrote eloquently in *Memory and Identity* that nations have the right to preserve their own cultures and independence—remembering how German colonization by immigrants over previous centuries had primed his homeland for oppression and invasion.[31]

Now millions of Americans of every race feel that our own beloved country faces similar dangers, and Europeans are dealing with more than one million Muslim colonists. We must exercise the virtue of prudence in the service of our duty of patriotism to answer these dangers to the common good.

Visible and Invisible

There are diverse reasons that too many Catholics are complicit in the bait-and-switch on immigration. Let's start with the most creditable motives. The great Catholic libertarian economist Frédéric Bastiat—whom Leo XIII lauded upon his death—wrote a famous essay that explains much of what goes wrong inside the heads of high-minded progressives and sentimental Christians when faced with a social problem. In his essay "That Which Is Seen, and That Which Is Never Seen," Bastiat identifies the "broken window" fallacy. A compassionate politician or clergyman meets a glassmaker who's out of work, and gets a bright idea on how to free this poor man from unemployment—by strolling through the town with a stick and breaking all the windows. Then he stands by happily watching as the glassmaker goes to work and collects his pay. The glassbreaker walks home with a spring in his step, having done his Christian duty.

Now what is the problem with that strategy? It fixates on *what is seen*—the newly employed glassmaker—and completely ignores *what is not seen*: the other potential uses of the money that was wasted fixing the window. Once you have smashed the window, you can see with your own two eyes the friendly glassmaker who's happy to earn some money fixing the thing; what you'll never see is the person who might have been hired to plant the garden if the window hadn't been broken, or the roses that never grew there. In just the same way, well-meaning "progressives" habitually fixate on immediate problems, grab the nearest blunt instrument to solve them—and refuse to think of the pain they unjustly impose on innocent third parties.

So Pope Francis can congratulate himself, and earn praise from sympathetic secular media, for inviting a million Muslims into Europe. That will assuage everyone's bad conscience over highly publicized drownings in the Mediterranean. No one will come back later to question the pope when radical Muslims blow up a theater or rape hundreds of women, or (once they are sufficiently numerous) vote to legalize polygamy and honor killing. No one will hold him responsible, or even notice his contribution to the situation, when millions of Europeans strain under crushing taxes, or cannot find jobs, or fear for their physical safety, thanks to the terrorist enclaves that the leader of Christendom has helped to establish in their neighborhoods.

Window-smashing Catholics actually make a virtue out of their rejection of prudence and planning, dismissing any concern about harm to innocent third parties as utilitarian or Pharisaical efforts to compromise the Gospel—as Pope Francis did in his remarks at Lampedusa.

Migrants' stories pervade European and American media, and European governments scramble not merely to save them from drowning but to hear their asylum pleas and arrange resettlement and generous government benefits for them. These immigrants have been *seen*. It seems to occur to no one that such actions invariably increase the numbers of such asylum- and benefit-seekers—launching still more rickety boats onto the Mediterranean, still more clans of intolerant Muslims on the hijra into Europe.

Whose stories will never be broadcast, will go forever *unseen*? The millions who suffer from the predictable side-effects of admitting millions of low-skill migrants who cling to a savagely intolerant religion into a crowded, high-tech continent with stifling socialist economies that do not produce new jobs. Also *unseen* are the thousands of Christians who have fled savage Muslim persecution, who now languish in camps without access to schools or the right to work. Unlike Muslims, they have no safe refuge in the Middle East, and they cannot gain passage to Europe. These are the genuine refugees, who left their homelands not for better jobs or welfare payments but one step ahead of the killing squads of ISIS. As of this writing, *only one European country*, Slovakia, has offered these Christians preferential treatment over Muslim economic migrants—and the EU and the UN sharply condemned Slovakia for this sane policy.

The real nature of mass immigration also remains *unseen,* because Europeans are too timid and beaten down by multiculturalism and politicized Christianity to look it in the face, and call it for what it is: a slow-motion conquest.

Cash Cows and Canon Fodder

But no honest account of Catholic attitudes on immigration in America can overlook the issue of institutional self-interest. Unlike the situation in Europe, where Church leaders' embrace of a massive Muslim influx is so clearly self-destructive as to resemble Ayn Rand's caricature of "altruism," in the U.S., Catholic leaders gain enormously in the short term from the influx of millions of Latin Americans. It is these migrants who refill the emptying pews in our parishes—where schools and CCD programs, preaching, and other forms of evangelization are manifestly failing to pass along the Faith. In 2015, the Pew Study reported that a shocking 41 percent of adult American Catholics leave the Church at some point, most never to return: "Both the mainline and historically black Protestant traditions have lost more members than they have gained through religious switching, but within Christianity the greatest net losses, by far, have been experienced by Catholics. Nearly one-third of American adults (31.7%) say they were raised Catholic. Among that group, fully 41% no longer identify with Catholicism. This means that 12.9% of American adults are former Catholics, while just 2% of U.S. adults have converted to Catholicism from another religious tradition. No other religious group in the survey has such a lopsided ratio of losses to gains."[32]

In other words, the native-born American Church is bleeding members, and Catholics would be diminishing quickly as a share of the U.S. population, were it not for a constant influx of Catholic immigrants. According to a subsequent report by Pew,

> [M]ore than a quarter of U.S. Catholic adults (27%) were born outside the country, compared with 15% of U.S. adults overall; most of these Catholic immigrants (22% of all U.S. Catholics) are from elsewhere in the Americas.
>
> As of 2014, an additional 15% of Catholic Americans have at least one foreign-born parent. That leaves 57% of Catholics who were born in the U.S. to two native-born parents. By comparison, nearly three-quarters (74%) of American adults overall were born in the country to two U.S.-born parents....
>
> The median age of Catholic adults in the U.S. is 49 years old—four years older than it was in 2007. Catholics are significantly older than members of non-Christian faiths (40) and people who are not affiliated with any religion (36).
>
> Just 17% of Catholic adults are under the age of 30, compared with 22% of U.S. adults, 35% of religious "nones" and 44% of U.S. Muslims.[33]

Without the mass immigration of Catholics who have not yet been subjected to the acid of our secular culture and the tepidness of our local church institutions, the Catholic Church in America would look much more like the Episcopal or Methodist church: a shrinking, aging organization with diminishing influence. But those new Catholic recruits are by no means sure to continue warming our parish pews. *First Things* has reported (citing Pew statistics): "Roughly one-third of Catholic adults in the U.S. are Latino, but just over half (55 percent) of Latino adults here are Catholics.

As recently as 2010, that figure stood at two-thirds...Close to one in four Latinos were raised Catholic but have since become (for the most part) Protestant or unaffiliated. Among Hispanics ages eighteen to twenty-nine, just 45 percent are Catholic, and that number could keep dropping as they age: Almost four in ten of these young adults say they 'could imagine leaving the Catholic Church someday.'"[34]

Aside from temporarily bolstering the statistics for Mass attendance, and creating the perception that our bishops represent a strong and stable religious organization, the influx of Catholic migrants also provides a significant source of revenue, through the tens of millions of dollars that Catholic agencies such as Catholic Charities and the various diocesan immigration outreaches receive from the taxpayer in the form of federal contracts—especially in the area of resettling "refugees." The *Washington Times* reported, "The Church and related Catholic charities and schools have collected more than $1.6 billion since 2012 in U.S. contracts and grants in a far-reaching relationship that spans from school lunches for grammar school students to contracts across the globe to care for the poor and needy at the expense of Uncle Sam, a *Washington Times* review of federal spending records shows.... Catholic Charities USA, the largest charitable organization run by the church, receives about 65 percent of its annual budget from state and federal governments, making it an arm of the federal welfare state, said Brian Anderson, a researcher with the Manhattan Institute."[35]

According to the 2014 Annual Report for the U.S. Conference of Catholic Bishops Migration Fund, church agencies received $85,506,950 in federal money for refugee resettlement—accounting for 97 percent of their budget.[36] Much of that money is disbursed helping immigrants, of course. But a significant percentage of it goes to overhead and salaries, and the entire enterprise of the Church acting as a spigot for federal money allows the bishops to present the Church as a much more significant source of private charity

As Innocent as Serpents, as Wise as Doves

It may seem puzzling that the Church's historic teaching on immigration—codified in the *Catechism*—is so widely obscured by Church officials, from the highest level to the lowest. But don't be too scandalized. This sort of thing has happened before. From the early Church on, Christians looked at slavery as an evil we had inherited from the pagans, an institution that we should hem in, try to make less inhumane, and wherever possible abolish. And indeed, by the late Middle Ages there were virtually no slaves in Christian Europe—even as the Arab slave trade kidnapped hundreds of thousands of Europeans and Africans and sold them into bondage. But the discovery of America opened vast new opportunities for powerful monarchs in Spain and Portugal to build up overseas empires—which wouldn't have grown as quickly or as rich without the use of slaves. And with the Reformation, the Church lost most of its power over even Catholic monarchs, who now could threaten a scolding pope that they would pull a "Henry VIII" and break with Rome, taking their countries out of the Church. So popes looked the other way as these mighty secular rulers exploited every loophole they could find in the Church's condemnations of slavery, and it took until 1888 for a pope to finally plug those loopholes, decades after most of the world had outlawed the practice anyway. We're seeing something similar today, as big businesses profit from cheap immigrant labor; leftist politicians bid for the votes of the poor with promises of big government programs; and Church leaders, who garner prestige and money from the phenomenon of mass immigration, collude in obscuring the genuine Christian position on the subject.

than in fact it is. When it comes to helping immigrants, it is much more accurate to describe the American Church as a federal contractor, which lobbies annually for increases to its budget.

Secure the borders, and two things happen: Catholic parishes will be forced to sink or swim, to evangelize and catechize the children of American Catholics, without the constant human subsidy of millions of Catholics who haven't yet been confused and alienated by the state of the American Catholic Church. And bishops will see their budgets shrink by tens of millions of dollars, as "charities" have to rely on the willing donations of laymen, instead of tax money that has been collected from Americans by force and handed over to the bishops. Both developments would be healthy for the American Church, and for America.

CHAPTER 9

Is the Catholic Church a Global Gun-Free Zone?

Every heresy starts with at least a tiny mustard seed of truth. However great a distortion it is to say that Christianity preaches pacifism, non-violence, and passive surrender to the aggressions of other cultures, faiths, and ideologies, that notion begins with something real. There is a stark difference between Christianity and the religions that have surrounded it for most of its history. To put it another way: would we need a whole chapter of a book to refute the idea that Islam is a pacifist religion? Hardly. It won't take that long. In fact, let's go ahead and do it.

The self-styled prophet Muhammad began by preaching his distinctive religion, which many scholars see as cobbled-together bits of Judaism and extreme Arian Christianity (which denies Jesus' divinity), two creeds that were common in the region of Arabia where he grew up, all filtered through an intense tribal nationalism. The Arabs had been disorganized, dispossessed, and frequently governed by foreign rulers for many centuries, practicing either fractured and primitive forms of paganism, or faiths that came to them from other nations—such as Christianity and Judaism. Muhammad's creed, by contrast, told them that Arabs were in fact the people of God, that God's own Word had been written in their own language before

Did you know?

★ The *Catechism of the Catholic Church* teaches that you have a right to defend yourself

★ St. Thomas Aquinas called the defense of others "not only a right but a grave duty"

★ You can't be a Catholic and a pacifist

★ Pius XII supported the speedy execution of Nazi war criminals

★ The Crusades were by and large just wars

all eternity and dwelt alongside Him in heaven. No translation of the Koran from Arabic into any other language is even considered authentic by true believers, merely a paraphrase. The holy place where all must come to pray would be in Mecca, not Jerusalem, and the whole Arab peninsula must be purged of every other religion. After a decade or so of preaching this message with little success in Mecca itself, Muhammad fled to Medina, where warring clans turned to him as a peacemaker—and a political savior. He began to reign over Medina as a theocratic king.[1]

Suddenly, the constant stream of messages that Muhammad claimed to be hearing from the Angel Gabriel took on a quite different tenor. While he had been weak and almost friendless, God had told him to preach tolerance and peaceful coexistence with other religions. Once he had at his disposal significant wealth and an army keen for commerce raids and conquest, Muhammad began hearing messages of quite another sort. These later messages, he would explain to his followers, "abrogated" the first set of teachings: the God in whom he believed was perfectly free to change his mind. (Indeed, the Islamic concept of Allah leaves Him quite unbound by reason, logic, self-consistency, or even the duty to keep His promises—only His Will is sovereign, and it's quite free to prove capricious.)

It was at this point that the Islamic faith we have come to know and love took the shape it has kept ever since: it's a creed of conquest that claims the whole non-Muslim world consists of sinful rebels against Allah who deserve to be subjugated by force and either converted or killed—though reluctant exceptions are offered in principle (quite often ignored in practice) for other monotheists such as Jews and Christians. Those peoples are damned to hell in the next life, but in this one they may be left to live in peace, provided they accept absolute subjugation to the authority of Muslims, defer to them in every sphere of life, refrain from making converts or advertising their faith, and pay a special, heavy tax.

Muhammad put this creed into practice, leading armies into battle, raiding caravans to raise money, and after massacring unbelievers who resisted his offer of faith or subjugation, taking women and girls as sex slaves. To this day, Muslim men are restricted to "only" four permanent wives, but are free to keep as many captured concubines as they can kidnap in wars fought for Islam. This doctrine is used today by ISIS in Iraq and Syria to justify the sex slavery of hundreds of non-Muslim women and girls. Unfortunately, Muslims consider Muhammad as the "perfect example" of human behavior, which means that virtually everything he did is worthy of imitation. Since he married a nine-year-old, that means that strict Muslim countries make it legal for their men to do the same—as Iran did in 1979 after its Islamic Revolution.

The example set by Jesus is...different, to put it mildly. Jesus responded to religious authorities who challenged His authority by engaging them in debate. He preached that we must go beyond the Old Testament's call for proportional justice ("an eye for an eye"), and that when insulted with a slap we should "turn the other cheek." He ordered us to "love your enemy" and "pray for those who persecute you." He told His disciples that when they preached His message and were rejected, they should just quietly leave town. When gendarmes of the corrupt Temple establishment had Him arrested, He forbade His disciples to fight them, even healing the single Temple guard an apostle had rashly wounded. Insulted and beaten by guards, He spoke not a word of rebuke. From the Cross He did not denounce His persecutors, but called on His Father to forgive them, because they knew not what they were doing.

Don't Try to Compete with Jesus

Jesus issued a powerful challenge to our natural (but fallen) instinct to avenge every slight, humiliate our enemies, treasure grievances, and wait

★ ★ ★

Jesus the Innocent Scapegoat

The brilliant anthropologist and literary critic René Girard was converted from fashionable atheism back to Catholicism by reflecting on Jesus' life and finding in His willing self-sacrifice a potent rebuke to the dark social phenomenon Girard had seen in every culture he had studied: in times of social crisis, when a city or tribe is fragmenting violently into factions, what usually heals the breach and restores communal order is finding a scapegoat—a perfectly innocent victim or group of victims who can be blamed for causing the crisis, then expelled or sacrificed. On top of Jesus' theological mission of redemption, Girard saw in the Gospels the seeds for social redemption as well: Jesus' innocence and meekness and the forgiveness he offered his tormentors are a stark reminder to every society afterward of the evil of scapegoat politics. Every time a medieval Christian mob expelled the Jews from a town or city, the true message of the gospel should have burned a hole in their consciences. To learn more about Girard's fascinating reading of Jesus's life, see *The Scapegoat* (Johns Hopkins University, 1989).

for a chance for vengeance—in other words, to follow the advice of Niccolo Machiavelli, whose politics manual *The Prince* was essentially a self-help book from the anti-Christ. But the contrast between Jesus and Muhammad can be taken much too far, particularly if we pluck Christ's statements out of their proper context and misunderstand His mission in a way that turns out to be perversely self-aggrandizing.

Because here's the thing: Jesus is not meant to serve as our example in every single way. We are not called on to overturn the existing interpretation of sacred scriptures, for one thing. (Imagine if every Catholic showed up at the Vatican and preached, "The Church says unto you X, but I tell you Y!") Nor is each of us a prophet preaching a brand new covenant between God and man. Few of us miraculously heal the sick, give sight to the blind, or dispense forgiveness to sinners on our own authority. As bad as some liberal Catholic parish Masses can be, we don't have the right to rampage through the sanctuary, overturning the altar and scattering the liturgical dancers. (Resist the temptation, okay?) Most of us are not even called to poverty, chastity, and obedience—as the apostles were, on whom monks and nuns model their very special and rare vocations. Most important of all, not one of us is called to be a pure sacrificial victim, going willingly to our deaths at the hands of unjust authorities so that our suffering can make reparation to the Father for the sins of all mankind. Really. No matter how righteous and altruistic you're feeling at the moment, Jesus has been there, and done that.

While Jesus called on us to carry our daily crosses, He did not threaten to nail us all up to them. The infinitesimally small percentage of Christians who face the stark choice between renouncing Jesus or dying as martyrs are in some ways emulating Jesus, but even they fall far short: their deaths do not forgive sins, though they can offer their sufferings in union with Christ's for the sake of other sinners. We are not sacrificial lambs going peacefully to the slaughter out of obedience to the Father for the sake of man's redemption. And martyrdom isn't God's plan for the human race—or else He would have told us so. A few Christians in the early Church, during the Roman persecution, got it into their heads that it was virtuous to seek out martyrdom and turned themselves in to the pagan procurators to claim a glorious Christ-like death. The Church Father St. Gregory of Nazianzus condemned them for their rashness.[2]

The Church does not teach that we are to simply surrender our lives to anyone who attacks us. The *Catechism of the Catholic Church*, relying on St. Thomas Aquinas, defends the lethal use of force for the "legitimate defense of persons and societies": "Love toward oneself remains a fundamental principle of morality. Therefore it is legitimate to insist on respect for one's own right to life. Someone who defends his life is not guilty of

★ ★ ★

Jesus Uses Force

Remember that the Temple in Jerusalem was the holiest place on earth. But it was controlled by the Sadducees, a faction whose agenda was less than holy—far worse than what the Pharisees were preaching. The Sadducees had inherited control over the Temple and made a lucrative business out of selling animals for sacrifice and converting "unholy" Roman money into kosher Jewish money that could be accepted for offerings. The same Sadducees rejected most of the Old Testament, denied a life after death, and collaborated willingly with the pagan Romans. When Jesus saw what they had done to His "Father's house," He didn't turn the other cheek. Instead, "Making a whip of cords, he drove them all out of the temple, sheep, and oxen; and poured out the coins of the money changers and overthrew their tables; And he told those who sold the pigeons, Take these things away; you shall not make my Father's house an house of trade. And His disciples remembered that it was written,'Zeal for thy house will consume me."(Jn. 2: 13–22)

murder even if he is forced to deal his aggressor a lethal blow: 'If a man in self-defense uses more than necessary violence, it will be unlawful: whereas if he repels force with moderation, his defense will be lawful. . . . Nor is it necessary for salvation that a man omit the act of moderate self-defense to avoid killing the other man, since one is bound to take more care of one's own life than of another's.'"[3]

Nor are we expected—or even permitted—to leave innocent third parties defenseless at the hands of violent aggressors. As St. Thomas points out in another passage quoted in the *Catechism*: "Legitimate defense can be not only a right but a grave duty for one who is responsible for the lives of others. The defense of the common good requires that an unjust aggressor be rendered unable to cause harm."[4] We are called to use force, if need be at the risk of our own lives, to protect others. That responsibility has motivated Christian policemen, soldiers, and spies over the centuries.

To demonstrate that Jesus' call to accept mistreatment rather than retaliate is not a mandate for Gandhi-style non-violence, let us look rationally at the various levels of self-defense, starting with the personal and ending with the geopolitical. We will go from gun rights, to the death penalty, to war.

Gun Rights Are Human Rights

It's unfortunate, but the U.S. bishops have come down on the wrong side of gun rights, taking a position that flies in the face of natural law—the moral code that binds all human beings, even pagans. The news service controlled by the bishops, Catholic News Service, announced in 2011,

> The Catholic Church's position on gun control is not easy to find; there are dozens of speeches and talks and a few documents that call for much tighter regulation of the global arms trade, but what about private gun ownership?
>
> The answer is resoundingly clear: Firearms in the hands of civilians should be strictly limited and eventually completely eliminated.[5]

But you won't find that statement in a headline or a document subheading. It's almost hidden in a footnote in a document on crime by the U.S. bishops' conference and it's mentioned in passing in dozens of official Vatican texts on the global arms trade.

The most direct statement comes in the bishops' "Responsibility, Rehabilitation and Restoration: A Catholic Perspective on Crime and Criminal Justice" from November 2000: "As bishops, we support measures that control the sale and use of firearms and make them safer—especially efforts that prevent their unsupervised use by children or anyone other than the owner—and we reiterate our call for sensible regulation of handguns."

That's followed by a footnote stating, "However, we believe that in the long run and with few exceptions—i.e. police officers, military use—handguns should be eliminated from our society."

Here the bishops have exceeded their authority and frankly promoted a teaching with no basis in Catholic doctrine. Fortunately, Pope St. John Paul

II, a.k.a the Great (and this is only one of many reasons he is Great) made it crystal clear that there is no magisterium of the USCCB. For a teaching of the bishops' conference to have authority, it must be either taught unanimously by all the bishops (in which case each of them is exercising his individual teaching authority over his diocese), or else ratified by the pope: "In order that the doctrinal declarations of the Conference of Bishops.... may constitute authentic magisterium and be published in the name of the Conference itself, they must be unanimously approved by the Bishops who are members, or receive the *recognitio* of the Apostolic See if approved in plenary assembly by at least two thirds of the Bishops belonging to the Conference and having a deliberative vote."[6] In fact there is no magisterial teaching explicitly on gun rights, but the implications of Church teaching on self-defense for the gun issue are clear, as we can see from the *Catechism of the Catholic Church* and the passages of Aquinas already cited.

Legitimate defense can be not only a right but also a grave duty for one who is responsible for the lives of others. The defense of the common good requires that an unjust aggressor be rendered unable to cause harm. For this reason, those who legitimately hold authority also have the right to use arms to repel aggressors against the civil community entrusted to their responsibility.[7]

As Jason Scott Jones said in *Legatus*, the magazine for Catholic CEOs,

> ... [T]here will always be situations where citizens must defend themselves and their families against immediate threats from criminals. That is their inalienable right, and for the state to deprive them of that right would be intrinsically evil. No situation justifies doing what is intrinsically evil. Therefore, no argument of public policy, no appeal to some "seamless garment" or sentimentalized version of Christian non-violence, could ever justify preventing citizens from protecting themselves from violence.

In seeking the common good, of course, we see that rights hang in tension. We must preserve public order and make sure that one person's attempt to exercise his rights and protect his human dignity does not infringe on someone else's rights and dignity. Someone who wishes to protect his property from trespassing children, for instance, may surround it with [a] fence, but not a lethal electric fence. Our efforts to defend our rights must be proportional to the threat and must not directly or through negligence harm the innocent.

Therefore, the state has good reason to regulate the level of lethal force available to private citizens, to make sure that it is proportional to the threats they may face. This means that there is no "one-size-fits-all" firearms regulation appropriate to all people everywhere. Christians living in the lawless parts of Syria, for instance, may well have to own and operate military-grade weapons to protect their families from the depredations of ISIS. For U.S. citizens, such weapons would be totally disproportionate.

In many American cities, violent crime is a constant threat to citizens' well being—not only to their safety and that of their children, but to the fruits of their hard work. The home, the car, the possessions that a member of the working poor has managed to accumulate might have taken him many years to acquire and could prove impossible to replace. But short of full-on surveillance, there is no way for the state to provide such citizens adequate protection.

★ ★ ★

It's Happened Before

Gun control is not the first subject on which a nation's bishops have been wrong. Remember when Henry VIII split off from Rome? The number of English bishops who opposed the king was exactly one: St. John Fisher, who was later executed for standing up for the truth. We must be willing to do the same when our bishops try to take away fundamental rights that God has granted us—such as the right to defend our families against violence.

189

★ ★ ★

Gabriel Possenti:
A Patron Saint for the Second Amendment

Did you know that there was a patron saint for gun owners, marksmen, and snipers? Well, the Vatican hasn't named him as such yet, but there's a very strong candidate: St. Gabriel Possenti (1838–1862), canonized by Pope Benedict XV in 1920. Gabriel experienced a conversion from a worldly, sinful life and entered the seminary of the Passionist Order at age eighteen. He died of tuberculosis at age twenty-three, before he could even be ordained. But aside from a life of exemplary love for Christ, there's a story told of Gabriel about a moment of heroism that appeals to Americans in particular.

As the Saint Gabriel Possenti Society tells the tale, Gabriel's "marksmanship and proficiency with handguns single-handedly saved the village of Isola, Italy from a band of 20 terrorists in 1860." In 1860, civil war raged through Italy as the army of the violently anti-Catholic Garibaldi tried to conquer Rome from the pope. Garibaldi's soldiers poured into Isola. They set fires, plundered the stores, and were dragging off a peasant girl to rape her. Gabriel quickly got permission from the rector

of the seminary and ran to face down the soldiers. They looked at the unarmed young man in his habit and laughed—until Gabriel grabbed the gun of one would-be rapist. He ordered him to let the girl go, and for good measure grabbed another soldier's gun. The soldier released the girl, who ran for safety. More soldiers gathered, and Gabriel saw that he was in mortal danger from these men, who routinely pillaged churches and fanatically hated priests. "At that moment a small lizard ran across the road between Possenti and the soldiers. When the lizard briefly paused, Possenti took careful aim and struck the lizard with one shot. Turning his two handguns on the approaching soldiers, Possenti commanded them to drop their weapons. Having seen his handiwork with a pistol, the soldiers complied. Possenti ordered them to put out the fires they had set, and upon finishing, marched the whole lot out of town, ordering them never to return. The grateful townspeople escorted Possenti in triumphant procession back to the seminary, thereafter referring to him as 'the Savior of Isola.'"[8]

So these citizens must be allowed to arm themselves in a proportionate manner.[9]

Eternal Vigilance Is the Price of Liberty

Violent crime is not the only threat that citizens face. Sadly, our very own governments can turn from protectors into persecutors. R. J. Rummel is a scholar of genocide and other forms of mass murder by the state. His landmark work *Death by Government* documents the devastating effects of organized violence against helpless civilian populations. According to Rummel, some 262 million people were killed intentionally by their own governments during the twentieth century—not including casualties of war.[10]

In 2015 presidential candidate Dr. Ben Carson became the target of media scorn when he alluded to government violence, pointing out that the Nazis could have been resisted more effectively had Europe's Jews not been disarmed by their own governments before the Nazis took over their respective countries. Because they had no means of resistance, Jews and millions of other victims were forced into passivity—a fact confirmed by survivor accounts and recent accounts of Nazi genocide such as Timothy Snyder's *Bloodlands* and Mark Mazower's *Hitler's Empire*. The latter documents precisely how much resistance the Nazis encountered as they tried to implement Hitler's delusional racial anti-utopia—which aimed at turning all of Eastern Europe into a depopulated frontier where surviving Slavs were illiterate helots of German colonists and Jews were a vanished race. The answer is: surprisingly little resistance, in almost any country that they occupied, with a few glaring exceptions.

What did those countries where the Nazis saw armed resistance have in common? The resistance forces had access to private weapons. Polish resistance forces such as the Home Army had stored caches of military-grade weapons before the country's final surrender. Jewish militias in the Warsaw ghetto also obtained weapons, sometimes from other sympathetic Poles. In Yugoslavia, Ukraine, Belarus, and the parts of Western Russia that saw serious partisan activity, the resisters were also armed with leftover military weapons or smuggled arms from Stalin. French resistance forces had stock-piled caches of arms, and received more via airdrops from Britain.

And of course, the Holocaust could never have been implemented had the Nazis not come to power in Germany in the first place, meeting little resistance as they overturned key protections of Germany's constitution. It is here that the issue of private gun ownership was even more critical. In *Gun Control in the Third Reich* Stephen Halbrook has performed a detailed analysis of the role of gun control laws in the Nazis' seizure of absolute power. He shows how crucial Nazi officials such as Josef Goeb-bels were intent on disarming private citizens, especially those in groups that the Nazis considered their worst political enemies. Halbrook cites statement after statement from Nazi leaders about the urgency of confis-cating private weapons from the Iron Front (a Social Democrat militia), from communist groups, from Catholic conservatives, and from individual law-abiding Jews.

The build-up to the first national Nazi pogrom, the brutal *Kristallnacht*, saw a frenzied effort on the part of the Nazis to track down all the registered firearms owners of Jewish descent and seize their weapons so that there could be no real resistance when storm troopers attacked Jewish businesses and burned historic synagogues.

And the Nazis' job was an easy one, because virtually all of Germany's Jews who owned any guns had dutifully registered them years before, in compliance with the laws of the Weimar Republic—which was trying to disarm extremist groups. As Halbrook writes,

> The decree also provided that in times of unrest, the guns could
> be confiscated. The government gullibly neglected to consider
> that only law-abiding citizens would register, while political

extremists and criminals would not. However, it did warn that the gun-registration records must be carefully stored so they would not fall into the hands of extremists.

The ultimate extremist group, led by Adolf Hitler, seized power just a year later, in 1933. The Nazis immediately used the firearms-registration records to identify, disarm and attack "enemies of the state."[11]

Anti-gun activists claim that it is absurd to suggest that firearms in private hands could be used to resist a totalitarian government. In fact, the opposite is the case. There is no single example of a country where firearm ownership was widespread among the general population that has developed into a totalitarian state, except after a wide-scale civil war (as in Russia) or foreign conquest (as in Poland). Governments moving in an authoritarian direction typically seize private firearms long before they dare to suppress other civil liberties. Conquerors disarm the conquered. (Upon occupying France, the Nazis gave the French twenty-four hours to turn in their weapons, on penalty of death.) Even within our own history, Jim Crow laws included restrictions on black citizens' owning guns, which they could have used for self-defense against lynch mobs, unjust police, and the Ku Klux Klan.

The issue of gun rights turns, finally, on a question about human nature. Are common citizens like you and me responsible adults made in the image of God, with the primary right and responsibility of caring for ourselves and our dependents? Or are we dim-witted, passive sheep who must look to our protectors in the government for food, protection, and guidance in our everyday decisions? May we defend ourselves and our loved ones when confronted with threats of violence, or is it our duty to surrender passively, then wait for the police to come tag our bodies? Are we free citizens with human dignity and responsibilities, or lambs awaiting the slaughter?

The Death Penalty:
Confusing Mercy with Mushiness

Should the terrorists who murder civilians in California, Florida, or Paris die for their crimes? Should Oklahoma City bomber Timothy McVeigh have been executed? Did abortionist butcher Kermit Gosnell of Philadelphia deserve execution instead of imprisonment? Or, on the other hand, should the U.S. have tried to capture Osama bin Laden alive and bring him to the U.S. for a years-long public trial, with the goal of imprisoning and rehabilitating him?

All these questions turn on just one issue: whether or not the death penalty—prescribed in the Old Testament and practiced by nearly every Christian society for some two thousand years, affirmed and endorsed by popes (who employed their own executioner until 1870, and kept the death penalty on Vatican City's law books until 1969)[12]—is in fact evil and sinful.

There is a growing movement to convince Christians that two thousand years of almost universal teaching was deeply wrong, that we must now completely renounce the use of execution as a punishment for crime. This movement is dangerously wrong-headed, and it plays into some of the most poisonous trends in today's secular society. It is no accident that most of the politicians and activists who oppose the death penalty around the world also favor legal abortion. In fact, both positions grow from the same profound rejection of justice, sometimes in the name of what's mislabeled "mercy." In truth, what often hides behind that label is a jaded, cynical shrug at the eternal realities of good and evil, a lazy hedonist craving for life in a Brave New World.

Christians see human life as a cosmic drama of good and evil, where we must sometimes sacrifice our happiness or even our lives to bear witness to the gospel, or to save the innocent. Our sins are a serious business that can merit eternal death in the next life, or a lethal injection in this one. To the modern liberal, such talk makes us sound like drama queens—which is why Hollywood moralist Michael Moore was willing to label *American Sniper* hero Chris Kyle a murderer. (Kyle was the U.S. Army sniper with the most successful kills in American history, having shot 120 legitimate military targets and saved countless civilian and U.S. servicemen's lives.)

Distinguishing Kyle's combat heroism from the slaughters committed by ISIS terrorists requires that we accept a good bit of the Judeo-Christian worldview, particularly the part about "innocence" and "guilt," two concepts that make many liberals profoundly uncomfortable. The modern secularist views life not as a drama but as a farce—a snuff farce, where the whole cast dies at the end. Think of wildly popular comedies in recent decades such as *Seinfeld, Curb Your Enthusiasm*, and *Louie.* What makes them so darkly funny is the fact that all the characters' best efforts come to nothing, and nothing ever changes. So the shows make us laugh while confirming the grim truth that secular viewers always suspected: given the wretched fact of our mortality, it's hardly worth breaking a sweat.

Given that for the liberal life is a farce, it also becomes a math problem: how do we maximize the limited number of pleasurable moments that we can enjoy before we plunge like a match into Darwin's toilet? Part of getting the equation right entails respecting the "right" of other people to grab their own share of happy moments, too. If we don't, they might not let us enjoy ours, either. Besides, thinking of ourselves as fair-minded people makes us feel good, so it's worth it.

But to make this system work in a world of limited resources, we must choose *which people* have the right to enjoy themselves, and who is most likely to take advantage of it. The unborn are helpless, dependent, and cannot speak for themselves. And recognizing their right to life might seriously cut down the number of happy moments for the rest of us—just think what an end to abortion would mean for our sex lives. The handicapped and the gravely ill are unlikely to enjoy themselves very much, and caring for them costs us money and time that we could otherwise spend on enjoying ourselves, so we must factor them, too, out of the equation.

None of these life-and-death decisions has the slightest connection to innocence or guilt. Those antiquated concepts are holdovers from the religious view of life, which causes unhappiness by making us question ourselves and judge other people's choices to enjoy themselves in the way they see fit. A justice system based on the modern liberal moral code does not imprison people to punish them for crimes; it identifies primates whose behavior is causing social problems by diminishing the happy moments quota. So a thief or a killer is not a "criminal" meriting punishment so much as a buzzkill who's hogging the bong and ruining the party. Have the bouncer remove him, but put him someplace comfortable. Give him a cell with satellite TV porn and lots of Prozac. Maybe the dude will calm down and we can let him back in later.

If life is a drama with eternal stakes, people will act like red-blooded Americans (or medieval Christians). They will pray, fight, breed, blame, judge, and execute. If life is a party, they will waste their energy on none of these things. They will live like twenty-first-century Belgians, in whose nation executions are unheard of, euthanasia has become a leading cause of death and is now being performed on children, the army is unionized, and the Muslims are taking over, one cradle at a time.

It would be tragic if Christians and other pro-lifers accidentally advanced the culture of death by opposing all capital punishment, dissolving

A Book You're Not Supposed to Read

As Jewish moralist David Goldman writes in his stark, profound book *Why Civilizations Die*, the secular person has no rational reason (and too few instinctual promptings) to join the army, raise a family, or develop difficult virtues, since all his efforts will amount to is dust in the wind. So it's no surprise that in the countries where the churches are empty, so are the kindergartens. In most of those countries, abortion is widely practiced, and the death penalty is completely forbidden. Is all of that an accident?

Christian notions of justice and mercy in the stew of sentiments, lusts, and confusions that we call the modern liberal "mind."

Why Some Christians Oppose the Death Penalty—but Shouldn't

Why would pro-life Christians join secular pro-choice leftists in a drive to eliminate capital punishment? There are a number of plausible motives. Let's leave aside the cynical reasons, such as a craving for approval from an implacably anti-Christian society, and move on to the pure ones.

- *"It Will Help Us Fight Abortion!"*

There are pro-life Catholics (like the worthy Princeton philosopher Robert George) who think that rejecting capital punishment will show the depth of their commitment to human life as an absolute and unconditional good. They hope that this extreme, outrageous gesture will convince their opponents to come on board and reject the cost-saving, ruthless expedients of abortion and euthanasia. Pro-lifers have tried this tactic rhetorically, and it leads exactly nowhere. Try it yourself: the next time you get in a discussion with a pro-choice person who cites the death penalty to prove that conservatives are inconsistent, say to him, "Fine. I think the death penalty is justified, but I'm not particularly attached to it. Let's trade: I'm willing to eliminate executions, if you will ban abortions. I'm willing to spare the guilty, if you will spare the innocent." Chances are, he won't take the deal. That's because, as Jason Scott Jones writes,

> The typical critic of capital punishment in America is the fashionable urban liberal for whom the death penalty is not a profound moral question, deeply connected to the modern contempt

for life. No, it's one of those tacky, "red state," redneck things like gun rights, pickup trucks, country music, and going to church. That is, it is something you ritually reject in order to mark off your status as a progressive sophisticate. Like GMOs or NASCAR or homophobia.

These lifestyle anti-deathers never follow the issue closely. You won't find them visiting prisoners on death row, or even writing them letters. They aren't involved in crusades like the Innocence Project, or in efforts at stomping out the national epidemic of prison rape. They don't help groups like Prison Fellowship, which try to bring hope and healing to convicted criminals. No, the men and women on death row in America are merely abstractions to them, little plastic pawns they move around on the chessboard of their minds—as wispy and insignificant as nameless unborn children. [The people] who wax passionate over mimosas about the evil of capital punishment are always, to a person, pro-choice when it comes to abortion.[13]

Legal abortion is indispensable to these people's way of life. They're not about to trade it for the abolition of capital punishment, which they don't really care about all that much.

- *"The Death Penalty Is Often Abused"*

The other reasonable motive for objecting to capital punishment is fact-based: it is often abused. Some countries, such as Saudi Arabia and China, execute criminals for offenses that do not remotely call for capital punishment, if any punishment at all. Here at home, each year seems to turn up another innocent man sitting on death row, for the "crime" of having employed an inadequate attorney—often an unqualified public defender appointed by the court. Such cases rightly appall us, and could certainly justify a moratorium on ordinary criminal executions until our system is fixed.

But abuses do not prove that capital punishment is intrinsically unjust, any more than the imprisonment of innocent people proves that we need to throw open all the penitentiaries, just in case. The abuse of an institution doesn't disqualify it from being used rightly and justly. The same U.S. Army that expelled American Indians also marched south and freed the slaves. The death penalty could be reserved for exemplary criminals whose guilt is beyond all question, such as terrorists and traitors, but it must be maintained in law as the ultimate means of enforcing justice.

Yes, we must spare the innocent. The execution of an innocent man, like his imprisonment, casts a stain on the whole system of justice—which performs a central and sacred civilizational duty: to render retribution against those who violate the inalienable rights of others and to protect the innocent from exploitation by human predators. As the *Catechism of the Catholic Church* teaches, "The efforts of the state to curb the spread of behavior harmful to people's rights and to the basic rules of civil society correspond to the requirement of safeguarding the common good. Legitimate public authority has the right and duty to inflict punishment proportionate to the gravity of the offense. Punishment has the primary aim of redressing the disorder introduced by the offense. When it is willingly accepted by the guilty party, it assumes the value of expiation" (2266).

This is the perennial teaching of the Church. In an article on "Catholicism and Capital Punishment" in *First Things,* Avery Cardinal Dulles cites the "nearly unanimous" testimony of the Fathers and Doctors of the Church in favor of capital punishment, and he lists a wide range of Catholic authorities—St. Thomas Aquinas, popes from widely different eras, the Catechism of the Council of Trent, and saints from the modern era—in favor of the death penalty. Dulles points out that many Christian sects in the past have

★ ★ ★

The Good Thief Approved of Capital Punishment

Remember the Gospel account of the two thieves who hung on crosses to Jesus's left and right? Here's the passage from St. Luke:

"One of the criminals who were hanged railed at him, saying, 'Are you not the Christ? Save yourself and us!' But the other rebuked him, saying, 'Do you not fear God, since you are under the same sentence of condemnation? And we indeed justly; for we are receiving the due reward of our deeds; but this man has done nothing wrong.'

"And he said, 'Jesus, remember me when you come into your kingdom.'

"And he said to him, 'Truly, I say to you, today you will be with me in Paradise'" (Lk 23: 39–43).

Most readers overlook it, but the "good thief" here affirmed the justice of capital punishment, admitting that he and his colleague received the "due reward" of their deeds. That admission is as much a part of the thief's confession of faith as his plea to Jesus for mercy, and Christ doesn't contradict him. In fact, He promises the thief He will be in heaven. This is the Bible passage the *Catechism* cites in its defense of punishment, including capital punishment.

believed all capital punishment to be wrong—"the Waldensians, the Quakers, the Hutterites, and the Mennonites"—but never the Catholic Church, and that the "mounting opposition to the death penalty in Europe since the Enlightenment has gone hand in hand with a decline of faith in eternal life." On the other hand, he also explains that, "the classical tradition held that the State should not exercise this right [to execute criminals] when the evil effects outweigh the good effects."[14]

The God of the Happy Moments

To reduce the role of the state, as some Christian critics of the death penalty do, to the lone, lame goal of "protecting people," is to march seventy yards closer to the secular liberal "happy moments" theory of life. We would not execute or imprison people as punishment—that would be judgmental and vindictive. No, we will just put people away for our protection, and for their own, so they can get the help and rehabilitation that they need. In fact, some say, we should not even imprison people without parole, because then they would live without "hope"—redefined not as a Christian virtue focused on salvation in the next life, but rather the expectation of grabbing a few more happy moments in this one.

Critics of capital punishment (including, as we will see, St. John Paul II) who would allow for executions only as a last resort for the protection of society—where prisons are insecure, for instance—seem not to realize the ominous principle they're admitting. They're conceding that no one really deserves to die at the hands of the state in the name of justice, but they will allow the state to execute someone if he is a persistent danger to society. Thus his guilt is irrelevant to whether he lives or dies; that depends on the thickness of prison walls and whether the guards can be bribed.

Consider the logic of this position for a moment. Stephen Spielberg played it out in his anti-utopian film *Minority Report*, where criminals are captured and punished before they've even had the chance to complete their crimes, for the better protection of the innocent. If we can execute people not because they are guilty but only out of expediency, then why can't we imprison them for the very same reason? And why wait for them even to commit a crime? Much better to put them in therapeutic confinement the moment they are diagnosed with strong anti-social tendencies.

Before you scoff at that as science fiction, remember that states across the U.S. have already tried to enact "preventive detention" laws, holding sexual abusers captive after they've served their sentences in order to stop them from striking again. As genetics advances, and we learn more about "predator genes," do you really put it past the mad scientists who make up our country's bioethics as they go along—who have filled IVF centers' freezers with hundreds of thousands of embryos—to get behind preventive detention? Why not eugenic screening? The last thing Christians need to do is to encourage such madness by abandoning the clear, stark standard of justice as the only criterion for punishment.

If we will not execute terrorists whose guilt is plain as day, but instead leave them to sit in comfortable cells composing their memoirs and manifestos, we dishonor the lives they ended and degrade our very own. We embrace, whether we know it or not, the secular liberal consensus that life is cheap, so it needs to be fun, because nothing really matters.

St. John Paul II on Capital Punishment

Ever since St. Paul wrote, Christians have believed that death could rightly be inflicted as a penalty—not merely to stop a murderer from killing again, but *as an act of justice*. The Catechism of the Council of Trent (and few Reformers would have differed with Catholics on this point) called the civil magistrate "the legitimate avenger of crime."[15]

Pope St. John Paul II made history when he issued the encyclical *Evangelium Vitae*, then revised the Church's *Catechism* to match it—suggesting that the only proper use of capital punishment is for societal self-defense, in cases where even modern prisons could not safely contain a killer. The reason, according to the revised *Catechism*, is that bloodless punishments "better correspond to the concrete conditions of the common good and are more in conformity to the dignity of the human person."[16] Some scholars have seen this as a development of doctrine. Others, including Avery Cardinal Dulles, have disagreed, pointing out that John Paul was "coming to a prudential conclusion" rather than changing a doctrine of the Church.[17] And as Christopher Ferrara has noted, that prudential conclusion—John Paul's condemnation of capital punishment in modern societies on the basis of his judgment of "concrete conditions" (*Evangelium Vitae*)—may or may not be correct. That judgment rests outside the scope of papal authority. It deserves respect but does not demand "religious submission." And in fact, even in modern societies, "convicted murderers routinely kill each other in prison, or kill guards, or are paroled to claim more victims among the general population."[18]

In any case it's hard to see how a teaching that appears at such variance with previous, equally authoritative statements could be said to be binding in conscience on Catholics. Perhaps we can think of an encyclical that appears to teach something new as analogous to a district court's decision; until the Supreme Court (the Extraordinary Magisterium—exercised in an ecumenical council or by the pope teaching ex cathedra) weighs in, the question remains unsettled. *Humanae Vitae*, in contrast, reaffirmed millennia of previous teaching. Had it approved contraception rather than condemning it, the situation would be analogous to that brought about by *Evangelium Vitae*.

We should listen closely to death penalty reformers who point to the innocent men executed, the paucity of decent legal representation for the accused, and the racial imbalances among those put to death. This is all part of weighing good and bad effects in pursuit of the common good, as the Church has always taught we must. If the U.S. were largely to cease employing the death penalty until these outrages are fully addressed, that might mark

★ ★ ★

Not Perfectly Prudent

The pope is no more infallible in the concrete application of Church teaching on capital punishment than he is on just war. A pope can solemnly teach what makes a war just or unjust, but his opinion about any given war is just that—his opinion Not every crusade or war led by the pope in person (as Julius II memorably did; watch Rex Harrison play him on horseback wielding a sword in *The Agony and the Ecstasy*), was necessarily a just one. Infallibility does not guarantee that the popes will be correct in their prudential judgments about the actual conditions prevailing on the ground in society, but rather about the moral principles that must be applied to them.

progress for the sanctity of life—because it would be centered on sparing the innocent. (Though a better use of our energy might be to work to stop the routine, rampant rape of prisoners in America.) But when someone is manifestly guilty of heinous crimes of public import, crimes rightly deserving death, the rush to mercy may in fact entail a miscarriage of justice.

Consider Nuremburg. The Nazis executed for crimes against humanity could surely have been contained safely in prison and prevented from re-establishing National Socialism in Germany. By John Paul's standard, it would have better served the common good and the dignity of the human person for such men to spend the rest of their lives in humane prisons writing their memoirs, answering fan mail, and giving advice to aspiring activists who shared their goals. Is this really true? Would the world have been better served by reading Goering's prison memoirs? (He killed himself to cheat the executioner.)

Likewise, for a criminal abortionist like Kermit Gosnell to escape the executioner undermines our respect for justice. In the "concrete conditions" of life in America in 2013, the unborn are treated as worse than chattel—literally worse than cattle, actually, since those are killed more humanely. Embryos are kept frozen in limbo for our convenience, and through stem cell research are cannibalized for parts. Late-term abortions, such as Gosnell routinely performed, are legal in most states—and President Barack Obama, as an Illinois state senator, refused to rule out the killing of babies who survived this gruesome process.

Sending the most hardened murderers off to watch cable TV and share the weight room with embezzlers and drug users makes a mockery of justice. It shows profound disrespect to their victims, and the next victims of our culture of death. In cases as grave as these, where notorious criminals commit appalling crimes that still go mostly unpunished, true justice and genuine mercy demand the hangman.

The Church's Timeless Teaching on Self-Defense Assailed by Peaceniks at the Vatican

The Catholic Church has never taught that pacifism is the appropriate response to conflict. St. John Paul II, who had seen his native country devastated by World War II—which killed one out of every four people in Poland—knew better than to let the memory of such horrors cloud his judgment here. The *Catechism of the Catholic Church*, issued on his watch, rephrased the Church's ancient teaching on just war as follows:

> The strict conditions for legitimate defense by military force require rigorous consideration. The gravity of such a decision makes it subject to rigorous conditions of moral legitimacy. At one and the same time:

> - the damage inflicted by the aggressor on the nation or community of nations must be lasting, grave, and certain;
> - all other means of putting an end to it must have been shown to be impractical or ineffective;
> - there must be serious prospects of success;
> - the use of arms must not produce evils and disorders graver than the evil to be eliminated. The power of modern means of destruction weighs very heavily in evaluating this condition

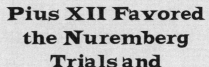

★ ★ ★
Pius XII Favored the Nuremberg Trials and Executions

Father George Rutler, the noted Catholic author, reports, "Pope Pius XII was so eager for vindictive penalties that he lent the help of a Jesuit archivist to assist the prosecutors at the Nuremberg trials. He personally told the chief United States prosecutor, Robert Jackson: 'Not only do we approve of the trial, but we desire that the guilty be punished as quickly as possible.'"[19]

These are the traditional elements enumerated in what is called the "just war" doctrine. The evaluation of these conditions for moral legitimacy belongs to the prudential judgment of those who have responsibility for the common good.[20]

Not everyone is satisfied with the Church's teaching, of course. As we've seen, Dorothy Day and her Catholic Worker movement rejected it, calling on the U.S. not to respond militarily to Pearl Harbor. If Day is indeed named a saint, count on pacifist radicals to use this as "evidence" that the Church's tradition has been wrong for almost two thousand years.

Already, activists are trying to rope the Vatican into the movement for self-disarmament. In April 2016, the Vatican's Council for Peace and Justice sponsored an international conference that spread confusion about the Church's actual teaching on just war and peace. Gathering pacifists of every denomination, the "Non-Violence and Just Peace" conference concluded with a call on the Church to "no longer use or teach 'just war theory.'" While there was no good reason for the Vatican to host such a conference at all, at least we can console ourselves that Cardinal Peter Turkson, president of the Peace and Justice Commission, gave a talk reiterating the Church's just war teaching. Evangelical Christian writer Mark Tooley rebuked the conference's leaders for their facile refusal to engage the harsh facts of life for millions of threatened people around the world. As he wrote in *The Detroit News*, "What would...Catholic peaceniks suggest for Iraqi and Syrian villages protected by American air power from ISIS brutality, or Nigerians needing armed protection from Boko Haram as their daughters are kidnapped and young men slaughtered? What forms of creative nonviolence should they instead pursue?"[21]

Still, there are some high-minded people who shake their heads at such objections, insisting that true Christian faith is blind to pragmatic outcomes and faithful despite the consequences—which is true as far as it goes. In certain extreme situations we must be willing to die rather than compromise our principles. But is fighting defensive wars against totalitarian

★ ★ ★

Joan of Arc: A Soldier Saint

You already know the outlines of her story. Joan of Arc (1412–31) was a peasant girl who experienced private visions of Saint Margaret, Saint Catherine, and the Archangel Michael, commanding her to do the seemingly impossible: raise up an army and expel the English invaders who were devastating her country. She obeyed the visions and by a series of apparent miracles was able to rally the defeated, divided French. Joan won decisive victories that made it possible for the French to regain the city of Rheims and crown a true, French-born king. Later on she was captured and subjected to a rigged heresy trial by the English.

Because she refused to deny the divine origin of her military visions, Joan was burned alive at the stake. After her death, her parents appealed to the pope, who annulled the verdict of the biased jury. In 1920, Pope Benedict XV declared Joan a saint for her heroic witness to the faith—in her case, faith in divine visions that told her to wage a just defensive war. For an accurate and beautiful depiction of Joan's heroic, saintly actions, see the silent classic *The Passion of Joan of Arc*, which was based closely on the detailed transcripts of her trial.

movements really one of those situations? Could it be that the Church has blinded itself to the real message of Jesus for all these centuries, until Dorothy Day came along and read the gospel honestly?

To answer such questions, let's engage in a thought experiment. Imagine if the Vatican were to hold a conference for advocates of *universal celibacy*, hosting Christians who did for Jesus' words about being a "eunuch for the Kingdom of Heaven" what pacifists do with "turn the other cheek": ripped it out of context and made it a universal command for every Christian in every situation, instead of taking the Catholic approach, which would be to read that Bible verse—just like the "turn the other cheek" one—in light of two thousand years of tradition and the magisterial teachings of the Church. So just as every Christian must abstain from any violence, he must

★ ★ ★

Are Bombs to be Made by Angels?

The "Non-Violence and Just Peace" conference helped start rumors that Pope Francis may write an encyclical contradicting the established teaching on just war.[22] And from his off-the-cuff remarks there is some reason to think that Francis is closer to pacifism than any previous pope, at least in his private opinions. In a 2015 talk to young people in Turin, Italy, he suggested that armaments manufacturers and investors who "call themselves Christian" should not be trusted. On the other hand, in the very same talk, he complained about the tragedy of the Holocaust, saying, "The great powers had the pictures of the railway lines that the trains took to…Auschwitz…. Tell me, why didn't they bomb them?"[23] But just whom would the pope have trusted to make those bombs?

also give up sex, marriage, and children. What would we think?

Don't sell the idea short. If implemented consistently, *eunuchism* would solve every problem in the Church in just seventy short years. We'd have no more issues with worldly, self-satisfied Christians—nor with wild-eyed radicals. We could stop wasting money building Christian schools and expanding church facilities. We could take the billions we saved on diapers and tuition and share it with the global poor. Just think of all the hospitals and sustainable organic farming collectives we could fund in Iran or Pakistan, if we simply accepted this "radical gospel imperative" and renounced the selfish, fallen, animal urge to breed and feed our own biological offspring. Jesus never did that. Why should we?

At last, after our forebears in the Faith allowed themselves to compromise the Gospel for two thousand years, our generation of eunuchists would finally have seen its full message clearly. What a wondrous, God-given privilege. How very special we would be, as the first Christians in history to faithfully follow Jesus! We would earn the praise of environmental scientists, LGBT activists, and virtually every NGO at the United Nations, and deep, heartfelt encouragement from our friends in the Muslim community. The chorus of approval would be almost literally deafening, as a grateful world waved us good-bye.

If Christian leaders, with the encouragement of the Vatican, advanced such a theory, what should be our reaction? Should we wade into detailed analysis of Scripture, and engage the eunuchists' theory— conceding that if their textual arguments proved convincing, we might have to accept their conclusion?

I bet that most of us wouldn't. We would reject this theory out of hand because its conclusions are clearly absurd, and we would treat the eunuchists like sadly addled eccentrics.

But we might feel a little uneasy. Some would accuse us of worldliness, of pragmatism or utilitarianism, because we allowed the practical outcome of an argument to stop us from engaging it. But in fact we'd be practicing sanity, and sound philosophy, and acting in the spirit of orthodox Christians for the past two thousand years. Here's why:

1. Neither pacifism nor eunuchism was understood by the early Church to be demanded by the Gospel. Catholic leaders have always accepted married couples, treated marriage as holy, and encouraged the rearing of families—asking only that couples be faithful. Likewise, since the early Church, the same leaders welcomed soldiers and allowed them to serve in various armies, asking only that they serve justly.[24] For that matter, Jesus Himself never told married couples to separate—or the soldiers he met to throw down their weapons—as He would surely have done if sexual intercourse or warfare was intrinsically evil. So either this teaching isn't Christian, or it's more Christian than Jesus.

2. Both eunuchism and pacifism are incompatible with human life. Eunuchism, if we succeeded in preaching it to every person on earth—as Jesus said we ought to preach the gospel—would

wipe out the human race, full stop, in one generation. So it cannot be good, since He wishes our race to prosper, because He loves us. If only Christians were convinced, then the Church would disappear and leave behind a pagan world. Christian pacifism would leave Christian nations defenseless from conquest and persecution at the hands of aggressive non-Christians. If its message of "non-resistance" to violence were practiced consistently, it would mean that we'd have no police either, and that parents should not defend their helpless children from murder or rape. If all people of good will converted to this way of thinking, then the world would be run by sociopaths and criminals—whom we will have always with us.

If someone approaches you with a theory about what Christianity "really" means—a theory curiously pleasing to the Church's enemies and persecutors—that negates our every God-given animal instinct, two thousand years of Christian practice, and the example of Jesus himself, what should you say? What if the widespread acceptance of that theory would wipe out Christianity, or even the human race? Do you really need to wade into that activist's shiny rationalizations? Do they deserve the patience two Christians might afford each other arguing over, say, the most effective strategies for helping the poor?

If ever there's a widespread upsurge of sinful militarism among Christians, it won't be stopped by plunging headlong into the opposite error. The great Catholic philosopher Elizabeth Anscombe—who damned the American bombing of Hiroshima as too indiscriminately destructive—saw pacifism as the handmaiden and enabler of ruthless, bloodthirsty warfare.[25] By dismantling the carefully thought-out, prayed-over rules that Christians have tried (not always successfully) to obey over many centuries, pacifism offers us a false and poisonous choice: be ready to watch invaders overrun your country and rape your daughters, or be ruthless enough to slaughter your enemies' children in their cradles. The true Christian will do neither.

But What about the Crusades?

On February 5, 2015, the day after the terrorists of ISIS had burned an "apostate" Jordanian pilot alive in a steel cage, President Barack Obama addressed Christian leaders at the National Prayer Breakfast. After duly condemning that outrage, he warned the assembled reverends, "And lest we get on our high horse and think this is unique to some other place, remember that during the Crusades and the Inquisition, people committed terrible deeds in the name of Christ." Much outrage ensued, as Obama went on to talk about slavery and segregation—two practices that some Christians engaged in, but that clearly had no religious motive whatsoever. But few in the media were much troubled over Obama's Crusades reference. It is pretty much established in our culture that the Crusades were a hideous, anti-Christian endeavor for which the Church should never stop apologizing—and which Muslims are justified in resenting to this day. (Indeed, Osama bin Laden and other Islamic terrorists routinely have used "Crusader" in propaganda broadcasts to refer to Western soldiers present in any Muslim country—even at the invitation of those countries' elected governments.)

It wasn't always so. For centuries, Catholics and Protestants alike looked back on the Crusades as a heroic if doomed attempt to liberate conquered

Catholics Aren't Supposed to Be Theocrats

The loud advocates of pacifism in Christian circles turn the real message of Christianity into a caricature that would (and should) repulse any sane person. In addition, it's a problem that they are willing to use their power as voting citizens to impose what they claim is exclusively the product of faith in Jesus—which is a supernatural gift to Christians, not a principle of the universally accessible natural law—on all of society, including non-believers who have no reason to consider Jesus' commands binding on them. Why not impose on them the message of Our Lady of Fatima, too, and mandate codes of modest dress for every citizen, regardless of religion?

nations from the yoke of intolerant Islam. And in large part that is exactly what they were. Go through the New Testament and look at the names of the cities where St. Paul planted churches: Corinth, Ephesus, Philippi. Read any history of the Church and see where the most critical councils of the Church took place: Nicaea, Carthage, Chalcedon, Constantinople. What do all those places have in common? They were evangelized by Christians and freely converted, and were later conquered by Muslims who, after the initial slaughters, imposed on Christians the crushing system of "dhimmitude," the religious equivalent of Jim Crow laws, with crushing punitive taxes that non-Muslims had to pay—with the eventual result of conversion of their populations to Islam.

Back when Americans had to study Western history, we used to know this, to understand that the Arab conquest of the Mediterranean—and of other lands such as India—was a classic example of brutal religious intolerance that amounted in many cases to genocide.[26] Catholics looked at the various Crusades launched over the centuries through the filter of "just war" teaching and judged that while some of those wars did not meet the Church's strict criteria, most of them did. Those just Crusades were waged to remove the yoke of a religious system that by any standard must be judged totalitarian, and to liberate ancient churches and peoples from the grip of their Arab conquerors—churches that today are under siege, like the Coptic Church in Egypt, or on the verge of extermination, like the Assyrian churches of Iraq. In an age when virtually every Islamic regime felt entitled to act much as ISIS acts today, wars launched to free their victims were likely to be just wars—provided they met the criteria the Church lays out, and were waged with due respect for civilian safety. That didn't always happen, alas.

We have always acknowledged that during the Crusades, out-of-control soldiers and bands of civilian volunteers committed appalling atrocities—of the kind that accompanied virtually every war in world history before the professionalization of armies in the eighteenth century. Catholics denounced those abuses—indeed, popes sometimes denounced them immediately after they happened, as in the Fourth Crusade, which targeted fellow Christians, for which its Venetian leaders were excommunicated by Pope Innocent III.[27] But there was nothing specifically "Crusadey" about those abuses. It's an ugly fact that medieval armies (Christian and Muslim, Frankish and Mongol) were poorly controlled by their officers and prone to abusing civilians. No one is shocked that Mongol or Arab armies butchered inhabitants of cities they conquered. We look with ambivalence at many incidents in the Crusades precisely because they violated the strict Christian just war standards—standards that orthodox Muslims didn't respect then and don't respect now, which would have disappeared from the world completely if Christians had been pacifists!

Much of the ugly reputation that the Crusades suffer today is the result of work by anti-Christian Enlightenment pamphleteers like Voltaire, who had an ideological ax to grind and wished to contrast supposed Christian "barbarism" with the occasional glimmer of tolerance they dug up from Muslim history. Perhaps the greatest damage to the honest historical record was done by novelist Sir Walter Scott, who idealized the Muslims and caricatured the Crusaders in his wildly popular novels.[28]

A Book You're Not Supposed to Read

In *The Decline of Eastern Christianity under Islam* (Fairleigh Dickinson, 1996), the Israeli scholar Bat Ye'or undertook painstaking research to reconstruct the long Christian histories of lands such as Syria, Iraq, and Egypt, and discover the means by which Muslim governments slowly ground down the Christian majority in each country, until most of the inhabitants converted to Islam. She documents the periodic massacres and the kidnapping of young boys for service in the army and girls for slavery in harems—noting that in the Balkans, up to one Christian child out of five was stolen. Ye'or also recounts the confiscatory taxes and the humiliating rituals of subservience to which non-Muslims had to submit, on pain of death. Most vivid, perhaps, was the "head tax" levied in Yemen—which every "unbeliever" had to offer while kneeling, and then be publicly smacked across the head.

A Book You're Not Supposed to Read

The Crusades, Christianity, and Islam by Jonathan Riley-Smith (Columbia University, 2008) is an honest account by a leading historian of the Crusades that stresses the religious nature of those wars—how Christians saw that they had a moral duty to rescue the oppressed victims of fierce religious intolerance from regimes that treated non-Muslims as practically subhuman. In other words, Osama bin Laden may have gotten just one thing right: the War on Terror is a lot like the Crusades—a just war against overpowering evil.

★ ★ ★ ★ ★ ★

A Conversation You're Not Supposed to Have

Why Not Use Violence against Abortionists?

Q: The kind of rhetoric and graphic images that you people use is bound to provoke this kind of violence.

A: Our rhetoric matches the facts. Each year, a million innocent children are murdered in America. Those pictures are of the victims. Does the reality of abortion trouble you? It ought to. Should we collude in sanitizing it? I won't.

Q: The way you people talk about abortion providers, I'm surprised that violent attacks don't happen more often.

A: Well, there are reasons that they don't.

Q: What are they? It seems to me that if you really believed your own words, if you thought that every Planned Parenthood clinic was no different from a Nazi extermination camp, you wouldn't be condemning people who attacked them. You'd be applauding them. Since you aren't, that means that you secretly agree with us. You know that fetuses don't have the same rights as their mothers, or else you'd favor fighting to protect the fetuses.

A: We do fight, within the law—just as abolitionists fought within the law to protect the rights of slaves.

Q: But why would you be satisfied with that, if you really, really believed that abortion is murder?

A: We don't "believe" that. We know it, as we know that people of different races are equally human. It's not a matter of opinion, or known only to Christians. It's the only rational conclusion to draw from the medical evidence.

Q: Fine, then you "know" that abortion is murder, but you're not willing to do anything about it.

A: We do quite a lot. You'll see us every Saturday morning praying outside clinics, you'll meet us on Capitol Hill, you'll spot us stuffing envelopes and thronging the Iowa Caucuses. The Center for Medical Progress used investigative journalism to unmask Planned Parenthood's organ trafficking.

Q: That's the kind of thing you do when

you want to balance the federal budget, or tweak immigration totals. But this is mass murder, according to you. If you saw your neighbor trying to kill his teenage daughter, you wouldn't picket his house with a sign. You'd run over there and use force to stop him.

A: That's true. But what if I lived in a country like Pakistan, where honor killings are tolerated, and the police turn a blind eye? In a country like that, if I intervened violently to stop an honor killing, the police might well shoot me. A mob might attack my family. So my only option would be to muster superior force, get a mob of people willing to fight against the other family and the police. In other words, to start a small-scale civil war.

Q: Well, sometimes civil war is justified. It took one to end slavery.

A: But notice who started that war—the *slaveowners*, when the law threatened to turn against them. They knew, in their guts, that slavery is wrong, just as you know that abortion is. They were in the habit of using violence against the innocent, flogging and raping slaves, and were ready to harness violence to defend their evil privilege. But so few

abolitionists used violence that we remember the names of those who did: John Brown, and his small band of followers, who tried to start a slave revolt.

Q: Would that slave revolt have been justified?

A: Its cause would have been just. But you need much more than a worthy cause to embark on something as grave and deadly as a war—especially a civil war.

Q: Oh yeah? What else do you need?

A: I'd follow Church teaching on the rigorous conditions necessary for a just war, which is always a last resort.

Q: So what are they?

A: Here you go:

1. The damage inflicted by the aggressor on the nation or community of nations must be lasting, grave, and certain

2. All other means of putting an end to it must have been shown to be impractical or ineffective

3. There must be serious prospects of success

4. The use of arms must not produce evils and disorders graver than the evil to be eliminated. The power of modern

★ ★ ★ ★ ★ ★

means of destruction weighs very heavily in evaluating this condition[1]

Q: **And you don't think that starting a civil war to end abortion meets those conditions?**

A: On number one, I'd say absolutely—a million children murdered every year. But number two is certainly arguable. Despite pro-choicers' use of an activist court to take abortion out of the hands of voters, we still do have the chance to replace Supreme Court justices who corrupt the Constitution, or we can try to amend it. Your side's anti-democratic effort to rule through the courts will fail, I believe, in the end.

But it's number three and number four that clinch the case. It's horrible to think about a civil war waged in America over any cause, even this one. I certainly can't pretend to say which side might win. More importantly, the destruction and death that would come in such a war might very well outweigh the evil of abortion. What would happen to our country's nuclear arsenal? Millions might die. Families would be torn apart. We would plunge our nation into poverty and ruin.

Q: **So that's why you're against vigilantes using force to stop abortion?**

A: Exactly. Not because abortion isn't murder, which it is. Not because violence is always wrong, because it isn't. But because clinic violence is *an act of civil war.* We have not exhausted all non-violent means of fighting this evil. The violent means might fail, and the destruction that they would cause would outweigh even the horror of a million dead children each year.

It's appalling that we even have to speak of such things in America. But that's not prolifers' fault. We're not the ones who favor mass killing in every city in America, who sell human beings dismembered to medical labs, and hide behind the courts because the voters aren't with us. We're not the side favoring violence, though it suits your side to accuse us of it. Psychologists have a name for that. It's "projection."

CHAPTER 10

Is the Church Anti-Science?

For centuries now, mainstream history and science textbooks have taken it for granted that the Church was one of greatest single forces that kept the "Dark Ages" dark by suppressing free inquiry, persecuting innovators, and keeping books (including the Bible) out of the hands of ordinary people. There is precious little truth in those stereotypes, which are mostly warmed-over piles of agitprop left lying around from the "Enlightenment"—a complex movement whose loudest and most success-ful self-publicists (such Voltaire and Diderot) were radically anti-Christian. But most of these self-proclaimed "*philosophes*" (wise guys) knew that they couldn't admit what they really thought about Christianity in general, so they focused on trashing the Catholic Church in particular, counting on hard feelings left over from the Reformation to convince Protestant readers that their beef wasn't with Jesus or the Bible, just the papacy. Far too many Protestants fell for that tactic and uncritically accepted frankly false notions of history—not realizing that the pig that they'd bought in a poke would lead them snuffling straight to secularism.

We will unpack those historical myths in this chapter. First, let's examine the assertion that Christian faith (especially Catholic faith) is incompatible

Did you know?

★ Catholic beliefs about creation do not contradict evolution

★ In the fifth cen-tury St. Augustine pointed out that the "days" of creation might not be literal twenty-four-hour days

★ The invention of the scientific method is a result of the Christian worldview

★ The pope has no more authority on "climate change" than on tomorrow's weather forecast

★ ★ ★
A Matter of Definition

In this chapter we'll use "science" in its popular contemporary sense, to cover only fields where hypotheses can be proved by empirical experiment—chemistry, physics, biology, and the like. That leaves out the shaky "social sciences," which rest on ideological assumptions and almost never prove anything, and the so-called "human sciences" such as history, which are really just liberal arts dressed up in fancy white lab coats.

with science. Leaving aside the vague impressions that linger in your mind from biased history books and Monty Python sketches, what would faith possibly have to fear from science?

On the face of it, the Christian faith doesn't even overlap with science, so there cannot be a conflict. None of the articles of faith that a Christian must accept can be tested by the kind of empirical experiments scientists do. The only such test we could dream up—short of a time machine that could take you back to Jesus' tomb on Easter morning—would be if someone found a corpse and claimed that it was Christ's. Perhaps if you found DNA on the Shroud of Turin, and took some from one of those Eucharistic hosts that had miraculously turned into flesh and blood (okay, but then how did *that* happen?), sequenced the genes, and compared them against the corpse's, the results might prove illuminating. But short of that, science just shoots off from faith in a diagonal direction. Christianity rests on a series of historical events, for which there's compelling evidence, and principally on the event of the Resurrection, to which there were eleven seemingly sane eyewitnesses who were willing to die rather than deny it. We have much less proof of which Roman senators murdered Julius Caesar.[1] Indeed, historians routinely build elaborate theories based on single fragments of parchment or gossipy, tendentious memoirs.

"But what about evolution?" someone will jump in and demand. Isn't that one place where science and the Catholic religion are in direct conflict? The answer is simply, "No." For centuries, science was unable to offer any insight at all about how the earth was populated by millions of different species, so even brilliant scientists such as Newton, Kepler, and yes, Galileo, leaned on the Book of Genesis for answers. Then as mostly Christian scientists, unhindered by any Church prohibitions on asking such questions, came up with natural explanations for things like fossils, some atheist scientists then stepped back and acted shocked—as if the Church had ever sold the Bible as a geology or biology textbook. Of course, it hadn't. Nevertheless, many believers found Charles Darwin's insights into the development of species unsettling. They had been using the magnificent design apparent in creation as proof of a Creator, and naturalistic explanations such as Darwin's seemed to knock out one leg of their apologetics. Some Protestants, in the absence of bishops, popes, or councils, had been resting on Biblical literalism—which Darwin indeed deflated. But the Catholic Church wasn't unduly troubled.

The Church did speak up to condemn some of the many fanciful, false, and even toxic speculations that ambitious thinkers quickly spun out from Darwin's theory of natural selection. Several popes insisted that no, you cannot use Darwin to justify atheism, nihilism, pantheism, or the "eugenic" sterilization of people who fail IQ tests (something that Darwin's nephew, Francis Galton, whom we have already met, used his family connections to promote). You also can't be a faithful Catholic and agree with the Nazis that Jews and "Aryans," blacks and whites are unrelated species that evolved separately as natural enemies.[2]

There is a very short list of things relevant to evolutionary debates that the Church takes from Genesis as essential to faith. Pius XII helpfully gave the complete list in the lucid encyclical *Humani Generis* (1950). We must believe that:

- "souls are immediately created by God" (36)
- all human beings are members of a single family, from a single set of human parents intentionally created by God (37)

★ ★ ★

Fourteen Centuries Before Darwin

As far back as St. Augustine, Christians have known that the Book of Genesis is not an attempt at a literal, scientific recounting of the means by which God made the world. Augustine himself, in the fifth century AD, had noted that the "days" mentioned in Genesis were probably not twenty-four-hour periods. As he wrote in *The City of God*, "What kind of days these were it is extremely difficult, or perhaps impossible for us to conceive, and how much more to say!"[3]

Augustine even warned Christians not make the Faith a laughingstock by insisting on a literal interpretation of Genesis that contradicts the facts people know: "It not infrequently happens that something about the earth, about the sky, about other elements of this world, about the motion and rotation or even the magnitude and distances of the stars, about definite eclipses of the sun and moon, about the passage of years and seasons, about the nature of animals, of fruits, of stones, and of other such things, may be known with the greatest certainty by reasoning or by experience, even by one who is not a Christian. It is too disgraceful and ruinous, though, and greatly to be avoided, that he should hear a Christian speaking so idiotically on these matters, and as if in accord with Christian writings, that he might say that he could scarcely keep from laughing when he saw how totally in error they are."[4]

The Bishop of Hippo also pointed out that the Bible was written to teach us the truths of the Faith, not what today we call scientific facts: "With the scriptures it is a matter of treating about the faith.... it was not the intention of the Spirit of God...to teach men anything that would not be of use to them for their salvation."[5]

- original sin refers to "a sin actually committed by an individual Adam and which, through generation, is passed on to all and is in everyone as his own" (37)

It is hard to see how biologists or geologists could prove, disprove, or even test any of these assertions. You would think that, if all science advocates wanted was the freedom to pursue their research unhindered by clerical meddling, such a statement would have satisfied them. But for far too many moderns, science has become a new religion all its own, whose authority bubbles up and overflows the narrow channels of disciplined experiment and responsible speculation. As we know from writings of his that were published only after his death, Charles Darwin himself was so troubled by the problem of evil that he wanted to disprove God's existence. It was essential to him, for personal and not scientific reasons, that natural selection *rule out entirely* the possibility that some divine design lay behind the process, or that man's sudden irruption was part of God's creative plan.

So Darwin wanted natural selection to leave no room at all for any divine purpose behind the processes of biology. But, as many critics of Darwinism and proponents of "Intelligent Design" like to point out, there are great big gaping holes in every version of materialistic Darwinism. The events we are trying to reconstruct took place long before any man ever walked the earth, and we cannot try to replicate them experimentally—taking millions of years to sit back and see if intelligent life randomly pops up somewhere else. Even if we could, how could we "prove" the absence of divine design? Why then do so many who claim that they are merely defending "science" from "dogmatic" Creationism insist that school textbooks (including kindergarten texts) explicitly assert what science cannot possibly know one way or the other: that evolution is a purely material process that happened randomly, with no guiding purpose or design? In other words, that we must choose between atheist materialism or a Christian version of *The Flintstones*?

Now it would be one thing if scientists simply wanted to make sure that we don't lazily stop doing research into the origins of life, sitting back and saying, "God did it. Stop funding science." But no one (outside, perhaps, the Islamic world) is advocating that. The ideologues who lean on evolutionary theory aren't worried that Catholics and Baptists want to shutter M.I.T, so much as they are committed to teaching a religion in competition with Christianity—materialism—and fighting to stomp out any heresy that challenges their materialist orthodoxy.

★ ★ ★

Pledge of Loyalty

For proof that some scientists value their belief in atheist materialism more than the scientific facts, read not some crazy blogger but Dr. Richard Lewontin, Alexander Agassiz Professor of Zoology and Professor of Biology at Harvard University and author of *The Genetic Basis of Evolutionary Change* and *Biology as Ideology*. Lewontin confessed his faith in the pages of the *New York Times Review of Books*:

> We take the side of science in spite of the patent absurdity of some of its constructs, in spite of its failure to fulfill many of its extravagant promises of health and life, in spite of the tolerance of the scientific community for unsubstantiated just-so stories, because we have a prior commitment, a commitment to materialism. It is not that the methods and institutions of science somehow compel us to accept a material explanation of the phenomenal world, but, on the contrary, that we are forced by our a priori adherence to material causes to create an apparatus of investigation and a set of concepts that produce material explanations, no matter how counter-intuitive, no matter how mystifying to the uninitiated. Moreover, that materialism is absolute, for we cannot allow a Divine Foot in the door.[6]

The Church doesn't reject science, including evolutionary science, but it rejects closed-minded Harvard dogmatism like that.

Did the Church Quash Education, Scientific Research, and Technological Development?

Before we get to the "Dark Ages," let's look at the ancient world—taking a quick overview of ancient Egypt, China, India, Greece, and Rome, the centers of pre-Christian civilization. What we will find in such cultures is extraordinary, so fascinating, in fact, that thousands of Western scholars have spent their lifetimes mining their riches without ever exhausting what the ancient philosophers, poets, and sages wrote. Read Will and Ariel Durant's admirable overviews of ancient civilizations just to whet your appetite for the vastness of what was created. No liberal arts education is complete without a study of Greek philosophy, myth, and literature and Roman rhetoric, history, and law. These pre-Christian achievements are vital contributions to the treasury of the human race, and we deepen and broaden our humanity by studying them respectfully.

There's just one thing that all of these civilizations lacked, something that wouldn't make its appearance until the Christian Middle Ages: experimental science that yields a reliable understanding of the material world and hence gives us technological advancements that better human life. Yes, there were careful and deeply insightful philosophical thinkers in the ancient world, and individual tinkerers whose curiosity drove them to test an invention or theory here and there. But no one ever followed up on the inventions of Archimedes, or systematically experimented to see where Galen had been mistaken. Nowhere, in any of these rich and wealthy cultures, did thinkers develop anything like the scientific method. No schools established laboratories and attracted teams of researchers, laying out hypotheses and training younger scientists to test them. No one set up faculties for the steady advancement of medicine by trial and error, or carefully tested the theories of the men who had gone before them. When seeds of scientific genius popped up in the ancient soil, they found it dry and rocky, with none of what science needed to nurture its steady, predictable growth.

Why was this true in so many cultures throughout world history, but not true in our own modern Western civilization? What was it that led to the growth of experimental science with such pioneers as St. Hildegard of Bingen, St. Albert the Great, and the monk Roger Bacon? What elements in our culture laid the groundwork for the theories of Newton, Kepler, Leibniz, and even Galileo? What set the Christian West apart?

A broad consensus of scholars of the history of science agree: it was the unique worldview of the Christians, inherited from the Jews, implanted in the rationalism of Greece and Rome, and guaranteed by faith. It is easy for

A Book You're Not Supposed to Read

The Genesis of Science: How the Christian Middle Ages Launched the Scientific Revolution by James Hannam (Washington, DC: Regnery, 2011).

us to miss the distinctive characteristics that set this distinctively Western, Christian mindset apart from its competitors, in the same way that we forget that we are breathing—until something goes wrong, and we choke on a noxious gas. Let us go through these characteristics one by one, using as a guide the work of Father Stanley Jaki, a distinguished scientist and historian of science. In *The Savior of Science* and other works, he notes the peculiar features of Jewish-Christian thinking that made it friendly to the scientific method, in contrast to other great worldviews, which weren't:

- We believe that God is rational, and that He created an orderly world that mirrors His rationality. So by testing the way the world responds to our activity—via experiments—we can gain reliable knowledge for the future

- We believe that we are images of God. Therefore the world's rational structure is transparent to the light of our own God-given reason, so that we can gradually come to know it better than our ancestors did

- We believe that the world did not always exist, and that it won't disappear and reappear in an endless cycle of meaningless cosmic cycles

- We believe that the world was created "good," is sharply distinct from God Himself, and has been entrusted to us as its "stewards." So it is legitimate and good for us to try to improve it

- We believe in progress and think that the world can and should become a more humane place, where suffering diminishes and justice prevails more widely[7]

These statements cannot be proven, disproven, or even tested. They are what Jacques Maritain called "pre-philosophy,"[8] and in thought about the physical world they serve the same role as axioms in mathematics. If you accept them, a whole world of new thought and understanding suddenly becomes possible. Reject one or more of them, and you will end in a hopeless cul-de-sac.

None of these principles was the fruit of intellectuals' brooding about the nature of the universe. Instead, they are the lessons the Jewish people took from God's revelation to them, spread out through their history and recorded in the Old Testament. Their message is so much more hopeful than anything offered by any pagan philosophy that by the time of Christ there were thousands of Gentile converts to Judaism all over the Roman world— and many more "Godfearers" who were deeply attracted to the Jewish revelation but unwilling to commit to circumcision and the other rigors of Jewish law. Some of these "Godfearers" were among the men and women to whom St. Paul opened the door when he championed the cause of Gentile converts to Christianity and convinced the other apostles to let them join the Church without first becoming Jews.

The importance of this "pre-philosophy" to the scientific inquiry that has resulted in such astonishing technological progress since the Middle Ages ought to be obvious, but Jaki also goes through the other great world civilizations and shows how their very different beliefs about the universe blunted and halted the development of science in those civilizations—often after initial explosions of intellectual progress. Jaki describes great civilizations with cultural premises that retarded the development of science. To summarize:

- **The ancient Egyptians, who developed the engineering prowess to build the pyramids and invented the world's first written language—but never went on to advance in abstract**

mathematics or even geometry. The universe, seen through Egyptian eyes, was not a place that the human mind could confidently master, but instead was a single pantheistic organism—whose ruling powers were symbolized by gloomy, inscrutable gods whose inhumanity Egyptians pictured vividly by giving them animal heads. A brief revolt in favor of monotheism by a single Pharaoh, Akhenaten, might have changed the course of that culture—but he was quickly overthrown by the hierarchy of pagan priests, who locked Egypt back into its timeless, static grandeur.

- **The Hindus of India, whose native genius produced the single most decisive discovery in the history of mathematics—the zero, and with it the decimal system of numbers, which we call "Arabic" because the West learned it from India's Arab conquerors.** Just try some time to do a simple multiplication or division problem using Roman numerals for an idea of how world-shaking an invention decimals are. Despite this unique advantage, for all the exquisite temple art and religious epics that India would produce, it never made notable progress in any empirical science or technology. Why not? The Hindus' extraordinary, poetic religious creed told Indians that such progress was not even possible, so they taught themselves to believe that it was not desirable. The Hindus believed that each man's fate was determined by the nature of the age (Yuga) into which he was reincarnated. Almost the whole of human history so far, they believed, was part of the debased "Kali Yuga," which could yield only poverty, ignorance, and disease. That age should have ended, as Jaki notes, around 300 BC. When the date passed and things did not improve, Hindu sages did not reject their cyclical view of existence; instead they rejiggered their math, and determined that the "Kali Yuga" would last for another four hundred thousand years—an unimaginably long period in which progress and happiness were simply cosmically impossible. One Hindu King, Brihadrata, expressed the hopelessness his religion taught: "In the cycle of existence, I am like a frog in a waterless well."

- **China, the oldest and perhaps the greatest world civilization, whose highly talented people came up with many individual inventions—but whose worldview, imposed by a rigid bureaucratic system of Confucian intellectuals, prevented those discoveries from yielding practical results of benefit to society.** The Chinese invented block printing, which allowed them to reproduce beautiful carvings, but never moveable type, which would have allowed for the printing press. The Chinese discovered gunpowder—and used it not for weapons or engineering projects, but fireworks displays. The Chinese sent out explorers who traveled as far afield as Columbus—then outlawed ocean-going journeys and forgot how to build the ships that had made those voyages possible. The same story can be repeated for every Chinese invention. What was it that blunted the intellectual curiosity of the Chinese? The loss of monotheism. Very ancient Chinese had believed that there was one God who served as lawgiver in a lawful universe. But this belief decayed into Taoism, a view of man,

Starvation Is So Spiritual

As late as the mid-twentieth century, Mohandas Gandhi would lecture the world that poverty-stricken, famine-prone India should be the model for other societies because of its freedom from materialist hubris. Happily, Indians would shrug off his advice and embrace the high-tech agriculture of the Green Revolution, ending millennia of cyclical food shortages and making India an exporter of grain.

nature, and the divinity as all inextricable and finally indistinguishable elements in a vast, smooshy whole (the Tao). The human mind could not stand separate from the Tao, and so could never hope to master nature. With this belief deeply engrained in the mind of China, no individual stroke of brilliance could be much more than a flash in the cosmic pan.

- **Ancient Babylon, home to a two-thousand-year tradition of succeeding Semitic civilizations, whose intellectual output can be read in the unique writing system that developed autonomously in the region (no mean feat in itself—inventing the alphabet!).** On the clay tablets found in Babylon can be found advanced feats of mathematics, accurate descriptions of the chemical properties of plants—and endless, mind-numbing superstitions, magical spells, and mystical attempts to predict the future. Babylonians saw no distinction, it seems, among these various activities, because their picture of the universe was finally quite irrational: a battle of forces personified as dangerous animals, ending in the bloody dismemberment of Tiamat, the Mother Goddess. From the pieces of her corpse are formed the world. Such a cosmos cannot be understood and brought under human stewardship. Instead, these primal forces must be kept at bay with violent sacrifices and orgiastic rituals.

- **Ancient Greece, which indeed pioneered the extraordinary philosophical and mathematical heritage from which—once it was married to the Biblical view of the cosmos—the West would someday create an apparatus for scientific progress.** But Greek philosophy at its most empirical, in the hands of Aristotle, could not escape from the rigid mechanistic determinism that he saw as driving all human and animal action, beginning with the (utterly impersonal) Prime Mover, and ending with every movement of every stone, and each human decision. The Greeks could see no real distinction between inhuman motion and human decisions, and so Aristotle theorized that objects move in the same way that human beings make choices—to reach a telos, or goal. The goal of a stone when it fell was to reach the center of the earth, or at least the ground (presumably as close as it could get). A stone that was twice as heavy would hence have twice the motion and fall twice as fast. As Jaki points out, it would have been easy for any Greek to test this crucial assertion of Aristotle's and see that it is not true. But the Greeks never developed a tradition of empirical experimentation, believing that we could understand even physics through introspection and logical deduction. This completely doomed Greek science to the status of a learned hobby.[9]

- **The Muslim world, which included thousands of subjugated Eastern Christians, who in many places saved ancient texts and served as librarians or physicians to sultans and caliphs.** As Pope Benedict XVI reflected in his famous address at Regensburg, the orthodox Muslim theology of Allah rejects the idea that the deity can be bound in any way—not by reason, not by His past decisions, not even by His promises.[10] This "voluntaristic" deity is a completely unpredictable, capricious being, whose will—not His reason or love—is the only ultimate principle in the universe. Robert Reilly, in *The Closing of the Muslim Mind*, shows the real-world effects of accepting such a theological principle: it crippled Islamic science, as puritanical Muslim "reformers" decreed that laying down rationally knowable laws of nature was an act of blasphemy, a pretense that we can "chain" the will of Allah to predictable causal patterns.[11]

★ ★ ★

Why Did the Roman Empire Fall?

Famed French historian Henri Pirenne offered a thesis about the collapse of ancient Western civilization that was provocative even when he published it in 1937: he suggested that the worst damage to European civilization after the fall of the Western Roman Empire came courtesy of Islam. When Muslim armies conquered, subjugated, and Islamized North Africa—especially Egypt—they also inflicted vast damage on the remaining Christian territories north of the Mediterranean. In his classic *Mohammed and Charlemagne* Pirenne explains that the Muslim rulers of North Africa imposed an absolute trade blockade on "infidel" lands such as France and Italy. Those who have read Roman history will remember that cities throughout Italy and Southern Gaul were heavily dependent on imported grain from Egypt to feed their burgeoning populations; in return, they would trade gold and manufactured items, such as cloth. With a Muslim blockade in place, these cities began to starve, and their populations plummeted—with cities such as Marseilles and Rome losing more than half their people. High culture dried up, roads were not maintained, and life retreated to the closed world of the feudal plantation—where at least there was enough food, most of the time. Using evidence such as the collapse of the money supply shortly after the Muslim boycott, Pirenne argues that this economic collapse was the real cause of the Dark Ages. For a recent work that vindicates Pirenne and refutes his Islamophile critics, see Emmet Scott's *Mohammed and Charlemagne Revisited: The History of a Controversy* (New English Review, 2012).

Such an attitude, pounded into a population over centuries by its religious authorities, dried up intellectual curiosity and stifled empirical research. Pervez Amirali Hoodbhoy quantified the outcome in *Physics Today*: The 57 countries of the Organization of the Islamic Conference (OIC) have 8.5 scientists, engineers and technicians per 1000 population, compared with a world average of 40.7, and 139.3 for countries of the OECD.... Forty-six Muslim countries contributed 1.17% of the world's science literature, whereas 1.66% came from India alone and 1.48% from Spain. Twenty Arab countries contributed 0.55%, compared with 0.89% by Israel alone. The U.S. National Science Foundation records that of the 28 lowest producers of scientific articles in 2003, half belong to the OIC.[12]

The Christian world inherited the crucial tenets of pre-philosophy from the Jews, and also certain elements of classical philosophy from ancient Greece. But the monks who retreated from the chaos of a Roman empire collapsing under the weight of immigration did not accept the mechanistic materialism that had hampered pagan Aristotle—many of whose works were lost in the West for centuries. Crucially, as we have seen, the Benedictine Order and its many offshoots also rejected another fallacy that had plagued the ancient world: the notion that practical work was somehow degrading, the proper domain of slaves, while free men must demonstrate their status by sticking exclusively to the "liberal" arts. No, the Benedictines learned from their founder, Benedict of Nursia (480–543), that honest, humble work is a form of prayer. Because they knew from the Jews that the world was created good, and made as an orderly cosmos in which man was free and history traveled in just a single direction—forward—these monks were neither too proud nor too despondent to engage in experiments to find out how God's world really worked. Instead of sitting back like Roman aristocrats to ponder the nature of man as slaves tilled their fields outside their windows, these monks worked the land themselves and set themselves to the task of understanding agriculture—to name just one discipline where they undertook sustained empirical scientific and technical experiments for the first time in Western history.

In a series of indispensable works of revisionist history, Baylor University scholar Rodney Stark has documented the enormous practical improvements in human life for ordinary people that the Christian worldview made possible, and that monks were the first to pioneer. In *The Victory of Reason* Stark shows

★ ★ ★
Saintly Experimenters

After Archimedes, an ancient pagan outlier in innovation, there is no record of sustained experimental science being practiced in the West—or anywhere else in the world—until Christian monastics embarked on practical experiments in the High Middle Ages. Saint Hildegard of Bingen (1098–1179), whom you may know better for her exquisite polyphonic musical compositions, was also an herbalist and proto-chemist who carefully explored the medical uses of local herbs. As Jacques Maritain notes, Saint Albert the Great (1200–80) "was remarkable as a botanist, chemist, geographer, geologist, mechanic, and anatomist."[13] Secular scientists have named some thirty-five craters on the moon after pioneering scientists in a single religious order, the Jesuits,[14] and to this day the Vatican maintains one of the leading space observatories in the world. For a daily dose of famous Catholic scientists—there really are that many, including biologist Louis Pasteur and physicist Georges Lemaître, the priest who first conceived of the Big Bang—follow @Catholiclab on Twitter.

how the focused efforts of monastic innovators helped develop the three-field system of agriculture, the improved plow, the systematic use of manure as a fertilizer, and extensive fish farming. In a world where more than 90 percent of the population lived directly off the land, these inventions made the difference between the constant threat of famine and a reliable food supply. More food meant that more people could survive the hazards of childhood, fewer farmers were needed on the land, and more people could move to cities—rebuilding the urban centers of Europe, which had become depopulated in the chaotic centuries after the collapse of the Roman Empire.

Stark documents an explosion of technical inventions that took place in the "Dark Ages" under the aegis of a Christian worldview—and that had never been dreamt of in the supposedly higher pagan culture of the Greco-Roman world. Here is just a representative sample:

- Eyeglasses
- Mechanical clocks
- Improvements in construction technology, such as cranes and hoists
- Advancements in mining, smelting, and metallurgy
- The wheelbarrow[15]

All that Jewish-Christian pre-philosophy in the hands of learned monks and hopeful laymen who believed in a good God and a rational world quite literally worked wonders, feeding hundreds of millions. Medieval universities—invented by the Church, mostly as outgrowths of school at local cathedrals—provided the first institutional site in Western history for the growth, transmission, and perfection of learning. Unlike ancient philosophical academies, which dealt only in speculative traditions and catered only to tiny elites, Church-founded universities at Paris, Oxford, Bologna, and Salamanca (among many other cities) accepted entrants from every social class, devoured new learning from whatever source (including pagan texts translated by Muslims), and established extensive formal faculties that would freely debate the truth or falsehood of intellectual hypotheses. The intellectual life as we know it in the West and around the world today is the fruit of Catholic institutions.

Stark also demonstrates how monastic thinkers and pious businessmen pioneered the practices in finance, investment, law, and banking that made possible the explosion of the market economy—first in northern Italy, then in the Low Countries—which provided the wealth that funded the Renaissance. For a really detailed account of that dynamic, including a history of how the Church reconciled itself to lending money at interest, see Samuel Gregg's *For God and For Profit* (Crossroad, 2016).

Galileo: Self-Aggrandizing Jackass

We have seen that Aristotelian philosophy had made its way back into Christendom during the Middle Ages, and in many ways it proved a positive influence—encouraging theologians to think much more precisely, and with greater attention to the God-given biological basis of human life. For instance, while the Neo-Platonist St. Augustine had believed that sexual intercourse was degrading and even in marriage always at least venially sinful—he thought that the way man reproduces was in part a punishment for the Fall—St. Thomas Aquinas saw through his (profoundly Christianized) Aristotelian lens that sexuality was too deeply rooted in our natures to be considered anything but part of God's original plan. Indeed, he suggested that absent the Fall, sexual pleasure would have been even greater. Aquinas's account of the Seven Deadly Sins was also deeply Aristotelian; he saw that the opposite of each deadly sin was not a virtue, but a mirror-image sin, and that the virtue that Christians are called to is the golden mean between the two.

But not everything in Aristotle was compatible with the truths of Christian faith—for instance, his firm belief that the material universe was uncreated, had always existed, and could never cease to exist. Some Christian philosophers became so enamored of Aristotle that they embraced such errors, and in doing so they very nearly goaded the authorities of the Church to ban Aristotle's works. Aquinas, instead, worked his way through Aristotle very carefully, keeping firmly in mind the fact that however brilliant he was, the man was a pagan—whose views on ultimate things were therefore to be read critically. In fact Aristotle's thinking, like that of other Greek pagans, was stunted, because it lacked the truths of pre-philosophy that Judaism and Christianity carry deep in their "DNA."

Some of the Greek thought that Muslims had translated from Greek manuscripts from libraries their ancestors had pillaged contradicted

A Book You're Not Supposed to Read

One of my previous books is devoted to understanding the moral life by the Christian-Aristotelian scheme that Thomas Aquinas worked out. *The Bad Catholic's Guide to the Seven Deadly Sins* (Crossroad, 2011) lays out those sins, the neurotic overreactions to them that can yield fresh sins in themselves, and the sane, Christian middle ground between them. Hence the opposite of sinful Wrath is cringing, cowardly servility—but courageous, Christian patience is the genuine virtue we seek. And so on, through each of the seven, with real-life role models (such as Mother Angelica and J. R. R. Tolkien) for every virtue and lurid human trainwrecks (like Ayn Rand and Stalin) for each deadly sin, plus helpful self-diagnostic quizzes at the end of every chapter.

the observable facts of reality. We've already seen, courtesy of Father Jaki, that Aristotle's theory of gravity was deeply confused and misleading. The Ptolemaic system for understanding the movement of the planets, which Christians had absorbed along with much else from the Greco-Roman world, was also fundamentally flawed—a fact that was only demonstrated by Nicholas Copernicus (1473–1543), a faithful Christian monk who drew on the previous, scrupulously empirical astronomical work of fellow clergymen Jean Buridan (1295–1363) and Nichole Oresme (1320–1382).

Galileo Galilei (1564–1642) followed up on the work of these devoted Catholic clerics and scientists. Whereas their scientific work had never been condemned by Church authorities, Galileo found himself in trouble with the Holy Inquisition, which ultimately tried him—and sentenced him to house arrest. What was different about Galileo that earned him prosecution for the same kind of innovative ideas that others had published? He was, to put it in modern terms, an egomaniac and a publicity whore with the nasty habit of sucking up to powerful people (such as the pope), then insulting them in public. As Protestant writer Joe Carter recounted in a classic *First Things* article:

> In 1610, Galileo used his telescope to make some surprising discoveries that disputed Aristotelian cosmology. Though his findings didn't exactly overthrow the reigning view of the day, they were warmly received by the Vatican and by Pope Paul V. Rather than continuing his scientific studies and building on his theories, though, Galileo began a campaign to discredit the Aristotelian view of astronomy. (His efforts would be akin to a modern biologist trying to dethrone Darwin.) Galileo knew he was right and wanted to ensure that everyone else knew that the Aristotelians were wrong.
>
> In his efforts to cram Copernicanism down the throats of his fellow scientists, Galileo managed only to squander the goodwill

he had established within the Church. He was attempting to force them to accept a theory that, at the time, was still unproven. The Church graciously offered to consider Copernicanism a reasonable hypothesis, albeit a superior one to the Ptolemaic system, until further proof could be gathered. Galileo, however, never came up with more evidence to support the theory. Instead, he continued to pick fights with his fellow scientists even though many of his conclusions were being proven wrong (i.e., that the planets orbit the sun in perfect circles).

Galileo's primary mistake was to move the fight out of the realm of science and into the field of biblical interpretation. In a fit of hubris, he wrote the *Letter to Castelli* in order to explain how his theory was not incompatible with proper biblical exegesis. With the Protestant Reformation still fresh on their minds, the Church authorities were in no mood to put up with another troublemaker trying to interpret Scripture on his own.[16]

Worst of all, as Carter points out, Galileo decided to mock the pope who had befriended him, Urban VIII, by publishing a book, *A Dialogue About the Two Chief World Systems,* in which he used the pope's own words to exemplify what ignorant and stupid people say about science. Galileo's attempt to establish worldwide fame by humiliating the pope—and smuggling out said book to Protestant publishers in bitterly anti-Catholic countries—was what landed him in jail, not his scientific theories.

No, we do not approve of intellectuals being imprisoned for mocking authorities. So we can criticize Pope Urban for not embracing before his time the American principle of the freedom of the press. But just by way of perspective: the same secular critics who like to paint the Church as the enemy of unfettered inquiry and science usually hold up England as the pioneer of liberties that the West enjoys today. And that is true as far as it goes. But during Galileo's lifetime, Protestant England was furiously persecuting Catholics and other dissenters from the Anglican Church that had been invented by Henry VIII. Converting to Catholicism, encouraging others to do so, and getting ordained as a Catholic priest were legally acts of treason— which could be (and often were) punished by "hanging, drawing, and quartering," which entailed being hung up while still alive, having your abdomen sliced open, your entrails drawn out before your eyes, and then dying at some point as your body was being hacked into four unequal pieces. Any of the hundreds of British Catholic martyrs would have gladly settled for the comfy house arrest (complete with books and visitors) that Galileo endured.[17]

Will the Vatican Start an Infallible Weather Channel?

While the condemnation of Galileo was not really caused by Church animus against science, it did deeply embarrass Catholics by giving the appearance that the Church had invested its highest authority in defending a particular scientific theory—something that completely eludes the competency of the popes and bishops to speak about. Father Jaki himself, a great defender of the Church's role in advancing science, admitted that "papal infallibility escaped only by a hair's breadth from the crucible of the Galileo case."[18]

Sadly, the statements of Pope Francis on climate change have created anew the impression that papal authority is being wagered on a particular, far-from-certain reading of the scientific facts. There was great fanfare when Pope Francis issued his "climate" encyclical, *Laudatio Si*, in 2015. Media venues that in previous years, with previous popes, had treated the Church with derision or alarm, now fawned on the pope's words as prophetic. And there were many passages in that document that reiterated classical Christian teachings about our duties to steward creation, to respect human as well as animal and vegetable nature, and to discipline our appetites here on earth in view of the life to come. As Christians and as ethical citizens, we know that it's wrong to dump the side-effects of our lifestyles on innocent third parties without compensating them for it. That's a core principle of tort law, by the way, and it's only the fact that some such harms can't be localized and litigated that makes environmental regulation necessary.

But the Vatican under Pope Francis went much, much further than that—with high-placed Vatican officials practically claiming that the pope can predict the weather a hundred years out.[19] This reflects an attitude that Catholic convert novelist Evelyn Waugh once mined for humor. In *Brideshead Revisited*, the character Rex Mottram is an insincere convert to Catholicism who tells the priest instructing him whatever he thinks he will want to hear. Hence the following priceless exchange, which starts with a question from the priest, on the extent of papal infallibility:

> "Suppose the pope says that it's going to rain tomorrow. Does that mean it will rain?"
>
> "Oh yes Father."
>
> "But supposing it doesn't rain, what then?"
>
> "Well...Uh...I guess it would be, ah, spiritually raining. Only...We were too sinful to see it!"[20]

So the earth must be spiritually warming, but thousands of scientists are "too sinful to see it." That was the message of Argentine Bishop Marcelo Sánchez Sorondo, a close advisor to Pope Francis, who said as much during a contentious public colloquium on December 3, 2015, in Rome. As we have already seen in chapter two, Bishop Sorondo claimed magisterial authority for the pope's predictions on global warming, refusing to back down even when reporter Riccardo Cascioli pointed out that Catholics are required to submit to papal pronouncements only on faith and morals, not scientific fact. Sorondo went so far as to call Francis's thoughts on the climate "equal" in authority to the teaching that "abortion is a grievous sin."[21] So pro-life candidates who reject the Paris Climate agreement are no better than those who want to fund Planned Parenthood's baby-parts business.

In fact, the pope has no authority to settle a question of speculative science, any more than the pope of Galileo's day had divine guidance in condemning Galileo. That pope was relying on the verdict of scientific experts whom he trusted. He did the best that he could, as no doubt Pope Francis is doing.

So I guess I'll have to scratch that start-up idea I had, of an infallible Vatican weather channel.

Christ never promised that His Church would always get science right— which is just as well, since it has plenty enough on its plate defending basic human institutions and realities, such as marriage, the existence of two (count 'em, just TWO) sexes, and the humanity of unborn children. Those are issues on which the culture is in deep scientific denial.

The "scientific consensus" on "climate change" isn't a real consensus, and even if it were, so what? In the 1930s, all respectable economists agreed that capitalism was dead, and that the future lay with "planned economies" and technocratic leadership of the kind thought to be working miracles in Fascist Italy, Nazi Germany and Soviet Russia.

Back in the 1960s and '70s, a similar consensus agreed that the earth faced a desperate crisis of overpopulation, which would drive us to mass famines, wars over water and copper, and a return to the Iron Age. To stop it, we would need to give massive powers to governments, even global agencies, to control people's child-bearing choices.

None of those prophecies came true, but governments did gain a lot of power, and in places like India and Brazil, the UN and American "charities" like Planned Parenthood helped to sterilize millions of people by force.[22] In China, the communist government, again with such agencies' help, imposed the "one-child" policy, forcing millions of women to abort their children and provoking the "gendercide" of millions of baby girls.

Now we learn that population is crashing around the world, and not enough workers will be paying taxes to support tomorrow's elderly. So the generation that accepted population control and abortion will pay for it in their dotage. They won't be cared for by grandchildren, but euthanized by robots.

Today we're told by the same cast of characters who touted the "population bomb" that the same long list of catastrophes they predicted last time really will happen after all unless we give them lots of power—only these same things will happen for a completely different reason: global warming. If the climate stabilized tomorrow, it wouldn't be long before the international crisis lobby would be predicting the very same catastrophes, for still another reason. Maybe an impending attack by Smaug the Dragon.

They're always panicking about a different problem, but their solution is always the same: to shift massive power from citizens to governments, and from democratically elected governments to unaccountable international agencies run by the same kind of people who mismanage the Olympics and the EU. That seems to be the constant of the "scientific consensus": whatever is going on, it's terrible and will kill us all quite soon, unless we hand over power to the nice men in the white coats and those troops in the blue helmets. Then we'll be safe.

There was concrete evidence supporting the population panic, too. The global population boom was real, but it was grossly misinterpreted and extrapolated by people with deeply engrained ideological agendas. Those—including popes Paul VI, St. John Paul II, and Benedict XVI—who noted this and challenged the "scientific consensus" that there would be massive overpopulation were dismissed as biased hacks or religious cranks.

The irony is that the religious cranks are on the other side. Elites have used their media influence to create a quasi-religious movement among affluent secularists that lets people find redemption by joining the new, sacred cause.

And indeed climate change activism has become a kind of cult, according to a detailed 260-page report by the National Association of Scholars documenting how college administrators are devoting (collectively) $3.4

billion per year to transforming curricula, facilities, and student activities at their schools in service of the fuzzy zealotry of "sustainability advocates," who present their "solutions" to climate change as urgently necessary to "save the planet"[23] (as college tuition has skyrocketed far beyond the rate of inflation, along with federal aid to colleges and student levels of debt). The doctrine of "sustainability," which damns market freedom and the Western lifestyle as poisoners of the earth and enemies of our grandchildren, is drummed into students' heads via courses in science, humanities, the arts, and even mathematics. As the NAS demonstrates, free speech is being restricted on college campuses, as those skeptical of the need for massive restrictions on the use of carbon-based fuels are prevented from speaking to students—sometimes by threats of physical violence from outraged activists. In past decades "socialism" and "zero population growth" were the beneficiaries of the same zealotry, with its disregard for facts and the need for free debate.

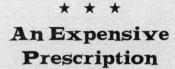

★ ★ ★

An Expensive Prescription

Imagine a doctor who, whatever your symptoms, always came back with a different, close-to-terminal diagnosis, and offered the same prescription. It's eight hundred dollars a pill, and he is the only supplier. You might start to get suspicious.

The Climate Changes—That's One of the Things It Does

Since we're quite as qualified as Pope Francis to form an opinion on global warming and the scientific "consensus" (or lack of one) surrounding it, let's review a few of the known facts. The planet is warming, evidence suggests—or at least it was until the fifteen-year "pause" in global warming that some scientists point out began around the year 2000.[24] But it has warmed (and cooled) many times before. The theory that mankind is causing most of that warming by using fossil fuels, and that we will soon push the climate past a point of no return that renders the earth uninhabitable, is absolutely unproven. The much ballyhooed "consensus" of scientists that this is happening and demands desperate urgent action is a soap bubble that pops when you try to examine it. As Mario Loyola observes in the centrist magazine *The American Interest*:

> It is true, and at least somewhat alarming, that the current atmospheric carbon dioxide level of 400 parts per million (ppm) is far higher than at any time in the past 800,000 years, almost entirely as a result of humans burning fossil fuels. What we hear less often, however, is that during the first 1.8 million years of the Pleistocene Ice Age, carbon dioxide levels were significantly higher than that. Major glaciation occurred a dozen or more times, without taking much notice at all of what should have been a much stronger greenhouse effect. And for 245 million years before that, carbon dioxide levels were vastly higher. So carbon dioxide levels are the highest they've been in 800,000 years, but they're also among the lowest they've been in 245 million years. Compared with that 245 million-year record, pre-industrial carbon dioxide concentrations of 280 ppm were perhaps perilously close to the level, around 150 ppm, below which plants cannot grow. It's always possible to have too much of a good thing, but it bears recalling that carbon dioxide has vital benefits. Plant photosynthesis, which sustains virtually all life on earth, requires an abundance of sunlight, water, and carbon dioxide....
>
> There is good scientific reason to believe that increasing concentrations of greenhouse gases almost certainly constitute a net contribution to global warming. But crucial questions remain about the relative importance of natural factors that influence climate. One of these is the sequestration of carbon dioxide by biomass on land and in the oceans. Another concerns

cloud cover, which reflects a large amount of solar radiation back into space, and which earlier models of climate change did not take into account (because it's very hard to get right). The simple climate models of ten or twenty years ago are now showing their age amid a flood of new data, and the far more complex, uncertain, and varied picture those data illustrate. The President [and, we might add, the pope] is therefore wrong in the sense that, for the most crucial scientific questions, the debate is just beginning.

The questions begin with the fact that while there is some correlation between temperature trends over the recent past and "anthropogenic" (or human-caused) carbon dioxide, the correlation is not very strong. The shape of the warming curve does not track the shape of the curve for increased carbon dioxide concentrations. For example, about 40 percent of the warming since 1900 happened in the first half of the 20th century, when "anthropogenic" carbon dioxide was insignificant. That warming could not have been caused by human behavior. Then, from 1945 to 1975, just as major amounts of carbon dioxide from burning fossil fuels start to appear in the atmosphere, there was a major "hiatus" during which global average surface temperatures held steady or actually dropped slightly—again, no correlation. From 1975 to 2000 there appears to have been very rapid warming. But then, as anthropogenic carbon dioxide levels continued to increase, another hiatus in temperatures appears to have set in with the strong El Niño year in 1998. While there are major discrepancies among different data sets, and new data are still being collected, the IPCC's latest report concedes that the rate of warming since 2000 has been substantially less than predicted by climate models in response to rising levels of carbon dioxide.[25]

The climate movement is not a conscious fraud, but then neither was socialism. Millions of people were willing to kill, torture, and die to create that earthly utopia. They weren't faking it. But the movement they supported was based on selective evidence and shaky theories, and it also promised them enormous power over their fellow man. So they were... *strongly motivated* to read the facts as pointing in just one direction. They should have been more skeptical, but that would have gotten them cast out of the movement, denounced by their former friends, and relegated to the "fever swamps" with all the "cranks"—who just happened, as things turned out, to be right.

Now there is a legitimate, complicated debate on the effect of carbon dioxide on climate. That's for scientists to settle. But nothing they've proven so far justifies the worldwide climate catastrophe movement. That requires a religious explanation—and the religion that's pushing it is not Catholicism.

It is possible that fossil fuels are adding to climate change, and that this will have destructive effects on nature and living systems. We should study this possibility and explore incentives for developing alternative sources of energy. But "erring on the side of caution"—exercising prudence, in other words—means taking account of *all* the grave risks involved, and looking for the least destructive means of exploring energy alternatives. It's Catholic laymen and women, in their roles as scientists and citizens, who are responsible for making those prudential decisions, not the pope.

Limiting Carbon Emissions: A Preferential Option for the Rich?

In his encyclical, Pope Francis said that the world must ensure that the transition to clean, sustainable energy doesn't harm the poor. But that's a lot easier said than done.

In an open letter to the pope, the Cornwall Alliance issued this warning:

Wind and solar energy, because of their higher costs and lower efficiency, account for only a few percent of total global energy use. Fossil fuels, because of their lower costs and higher efficiency, account for over 85%. Substituting low-density, intermittent energy sources like wind and solar for high-density, constant energy sources like fossil fuels would be catastrophic to the world's poor. It would simultaneously raise the cost and reduce the reliability and availability of energy, especially electricity. This, in turn, would raise the cost of all other goods and services, since all require energy to produce and transport. It would slow the rise of the poor out of poverty. It would threaten to return millions of others to poverty. And it would make electricity grids unstable, leading to more frequent and widespread, costly and often fatal, brownouts and blackouts— events mercifully rare in wealthy countries but all too familiar to billions of people living in countries without comprehensive, stable electric grids supplied by stable fossil or nuclear fuels....

The world's poor will suffer most from such policies. The poorest—the 1.3 billion in developing countries who depend on wood and dried dung as primary cooking and heating fuels, smoke from which kills 4 million and temporarily debilitates hundreds of millions every year—will be condemned to more generations of poverty and its deadly consequences. The marginal in the developed world, who on average spend two or more times as much of their incomes on energy as the middle class, will lose access to decent housing, education, health care, and more as their energy costs rise. Some will freeze to death because they will be unable to pay their electricity bills and still buy enough food. Tens of thousands died even in the United Kingdom in several recent winters due to Britain's rush to substitute wind and solar for coal to generate electricity.[26]

In any massive global transition, it is always the poor who suffer the most. The poor we will have always with us, and they will always bear the brunt, while the rich insulate themselves. Drive energy prices higher with burdensome taxes and constraints on fossil fuels, and you drive up the price of food and other essentials. There's no magic wand to prevent that. Those higher prices hit the poor the hardest, since they spend a higher percentage of their income on survival items, and have little margin of error. Will a single Hollywood star, college president, climate scientist, or UN bureaucrat suffer one night without heat or air conditioning as a result of the fight against climate change?

Much worse will happen to millions of people with names like Pedro, Lucia, Sandip, Maryam, and Chang. They will see their countries' economies stop growing, and that won't cut 25 percent from the value of their 401(k) accounts. It will mean that they can't go to college, or expand their farms, or maybe even get married and have a family. You might well see some famines—which the elites will blame, of course, on climate change, not their policies.

But maybe it doesn't matter to leading climate activists if millions of people suffer a relapse back into poverty. As Mario Loyola observed,

> Like proponents of bygone doomsday fads, most of today's climate alarmists share an unshakable conviction that humans are the problem and that nature in its "natural" state is pristine and perfect. That is the 19th century Romantic spirit at the heart of today's environmentalist movement, the hallmarks of which are a deification of nature and a revulsion for the works of human

beings, not to exclude innovations that lead to dramatic improvements in material well-being....

Man-made climate change...is the perfect vehicle for advancing that agenda. Dealing with it requires choking off fossil fuels, a top-down reorganization of economic activity, and income redistribution. If alarmists were really interested in protecting humans against climate change, they would be helping Bangladesh adapt to monsoon floods and thereby avoid thousands of deaths every few years, instead of insisting on green energy boondoggles that will never save a soul there or anywhere else.[28]

Not a Friend to the Human Race

Perhaps the most extreme of the climate panic activists is Hans Joachim Schellnhuber, the sole layman chosen by the Vatican to help present the climate encyclical. Schellnhuber has said publicly that the earth can only support fewer than one billion people, and that mankind needs to erect a global government to ensure that the other six billion...make their exit, one way or the other.[27] Why should we trust people with such manifestly evil ideas?

The international agencies that promise to protect the global poor are the same groups that led the population panic and gleefully took part in forced sterilizations and even forced abortions. Some of the people leading the charge, like Ban Ki Moon and Jeffrey Sachs, are still peddling population control to this day.[29]

The Real Threat to Science Is Not the Catholic Church, but a Competing Religion: Scientism

We see from the climate crisis that political ideologies driven by pseudo-religious impulses can distort the free play of discourse and research. But rankly political motives are distorting or muffling science in many other fields as well. Research into the causes and possible treatment of gender dysphoria (the psychological delusion that you aren't "really" the biological sex you were born) is hampered by "transgenderist" ideology—which asserts, contrary to all scientific evidence (not to mention the teachings of the Church) that biological sex is secondary to the "gender" with which a person identifies. There are at least fifty-one such genders, according to Facebook—each of which must be respected—now at the cost of legal penalties. According to Ryan Anderson of the Heritage Foundation, medical professionals will be forced by Obama administration HHS regulations to perform "sex change" operations and other treatments:

> [I]f a covered physician administers treatments or performs surgeries that can further gender transitions, that physician must provide them for gender transitions on the same terms, and insurance must cover it, regardless of the independent medical judgment of the physician.
>
> Furthermore, HHS allows no religious accommodation or exemption to its gender identity mandate or any other aspect of its new regulations.
>
> The regulations will force many physicians, hospitals, and other healthcare providers to participate in sex-reassignment surgeries and treatments, even if it violates their religious beliefs or their best medical judgment.[30]

Young children are especially endangered by transgenderist ideology, according to the American College of Pediatricians, which warned in 2016 that the attempt to "treat" gender dysphoria among children with hormones and surgery to make their bodies approximate their confused emotional self-perceptions can result in serious psychological and physical disorders—ranging from increased risk of suicide to high blood pressure, blood clots, and cancer. The College notes, "Rates of suicide are twenty times greater among adults who use cross-sex hormones and undergo sex reassignment surgery." And yet, as these physicians note, "According to the DSM-V, as many as 98% of gender confused boys and 88% of gender confused girls eventually accept their biological sex after naturally passing through puberty." In other words, the desperate rush to conform with transgender ideology by mutilating the bodies of confused adolescents threatens irreversible damage—all to "treat" what is overwhelmingly a passing emotional phase. Hence, these doctors conclude, "Conditioning children into believing that a lifetime of chemical and surgical impersonation of the opposite sex is normal and healthful is child abuse."[31]

Philosophers have coined a word for the unwarranted idea that empirical science can answer every question—and that those it cannot answer are meaningless or unimportant. The word is Scientism. A religion in competition with Christianity, Scientism is also the enemy of genuine scientific research, because it crowns the tentative results of today's research with the halo of objective truth, often closing off further research and forbidding ethical questions.

By truncating the search for truth and crassly dismissing the moral implications of any "conclusive" research, Scientism undermines the whole scientific quest—by attacking the crucial truths of the Jewish-Christian pre-philosophy which, as we have seen, made scientific and technological progress possible for the first time in one place: the Christian West. In his profound book *The Death of Humanity*, Richard Weikart documents how prominent spokesmen for Scientism such as "New Atheist" Richard Dawkins—and thousands who follow his lead—reject objective morality, free will, and the meaningfulness of life. Instead they blithely insist that everything—every single thing—in human nature can be traced to natural selection. Religious impulses, altruism, friendship, love, even scientific curiosity must all be explained away as the purely random side-effects of

A Book You're Not Supposed to Read

An entire book could be devoted to the ideological deformations of science and the abuse of scientific prestige to promote ideas and agendas that have no empirical basis. In fact, such a book already exists: *The Politically Incorrect Guide to Science*, by Tom Bethell (Washington, DC: Regnery, 2005). Appalling examples of ideological pseudo-science, all widely accepted at one time, that afflicted the twentieth century include:

• Eugenics, which led to the forced sterilization of thousands of Americans, and murder of hundreds of thousands in Nazi Germany and conquered countries

• Lysenkoist agriculture, which caused famines in Soviet Russia over decades

• Brutally reductionist psychology, which caused thousands of mental patients to receive crippling and useless lobotomies and electroshock treatments

• Population theories that convinced the Chinese government to impose millions of forced abortions through its One Child Policy

What made such atrocities possible is the brutal, ungrounded confidence that too many modern people have any questionable assertion that can be wrapped in the white lab coat of science.

positive mutations. Even human consciousness is a purely chemical, deterministic phenomenon entirely driven by the firing of neurons in the brain—which means that it is impossible to describe knowledge as objective, or any statement as really "true." The perception that each of us has that a proposition is provable, or an experiment is conclusive, is no guarantee of anything in external reality; instead it is the outcome of subatomic dominos falling in random patterns.

How can science continue if even scientists start to believe this about their minds? The answer is that it cannot. The death of humanity that Weikart describes will also be the death of science. A few more decades of such irrationalism will undermine completely the foundations of research and truth-seeking in the sciences, and the West will go into the same despairing stasis that haunted ancient Egypt, India, and China. Ironically, the only hope for science now is a rebirth of faith.

CHAPTER 11

Sex, Sanity, and the Catholic Church

I f a hostile alien race is monitoring us from space, learning about our institutions exclusively from the media, they must find this thing called the Catholic Church very puzzling indeed. A report on the subject filed by the Military Intelligence department of our future overlords would surely read something like this:

The largest global religion of the humans is organized around the principle of placating their invisible Deity and preparing them for future life with the same after their biological termination; yet this organization appears from all reports to be primarily concerned with their physical reproduction—generally in encouraging it, under longstanding social arrangements that for thousands of years have succeeded, allowing this species to increase its population tenfold in just a few centuries, while expanding lifespans and biological well-being. While for most of its existence this species was both predator and prey to other species, it has recently attained a biological dominance over its environment and stands atop the Earth's protein feeding chain.

Such reproductive arrangements entail one partner from each of the humans' two sexes pairing off with one from the other and cooperating in the care of biological offspring, who are born completely helpless and remain

Did you know?

★ Biologists, no less than popes, recognize that the primary purpose of sex is procreation

★ Legal abortion in America has killed more people than Hitler and Stalin put together

★ Giving out condoms in schools turns out to *increase* pregnancies and sexually transmitted disease

★ The Church is bound to the indissolubility of marriage by an infallible declaration of the Council of Trent

255

so for many years, learning skills and cultural codes from parents and nearby humans, typically in organized groupings, until they are prepared to pair off and reproduce in turn. Partners generally remain together even after termination of their fertility, exchanging affection and positive interaction, as well as sharing in the support of their offspring, who remain in extended contact with their birth-givers.

In recent decades, this organization ("the Church") has lost significant internal cohesion and prestige among the humans, for reasons that are not completely clear. This "Church" is frequently criticized for its adherence to the successful mammalian breeding customs by non-members and even by long-time members of the organization—who reject many of its recommendations and flout its taboos, yet insist on retaining their membership. We have been unable to understand their motives for doing so.

As best we can reconstruct the objections that are raised against the "Church" and its advocacy of traditional breeding patterns, they come from humans and organizations of humans that oppose the reproduction of the species—either wishing to drastically limit it out of (unfounded) fears that the humans are running out of food and other resources, or working to supplant reproduction among many of the humans with other forms of activity that mimic sexual reproduction, yet cannot produce offspring because they involve only members of one sex, which is insufficient, or employ technological devices that render reproductive activity ineffective.

Unsurprisingly, the regions of the earth where such new (and puzzling) strategies prevail are declining in population, while other regions that retain the traditional reproductive modalities supported by this "Church" are growing in numbers and power. The regions that are in self-imposed decline seem to be engaged in an energetic effort to spread their own (ineffective) reproductive practices to those which remain fertile, no doubt in order to maintain their comparative position of dominance. It is unclear whether they will succeed in doing so before they are simply overwhelmed.

Other elements in this puzzling scenario render it still more challenging to our analysts. The advocates of the new and ineffective reproductive strategies insist that their views are the result of research and scientific advancement—and that the "Church" retains its taboos based on information that it claims to have received from an invisible Deity, who (the "Church" claims) was responsible for the initial production of humans and has left them operating instructions for the species' ongoing benefit. Yet the modern, "scientific" strategies appear to be failing, by any empirical criterion one could imagine. Not only are populations stagnating or shrinking, with insufficient younger humans to provide care for the older when they become weak and feeble; fewer fertile humans appear to be pairing off at all, or they are doing so only for short periods of time, insufficient to provide human offspring with the care and training they require, or older humans with the companionship they seem to crave.

Still more incomprehensibly to us, the most advanced and technologically competent populations on earth now claim to have "discovered" the fact that their biological sexual difference is purely imaginary—that any member of the species can in fact be a member of either sex or both, or an amalgam of the two, and may switch between them at will, aided by crude chemical and surgical techniques that serve no purpose apparent to external observers, except to render the humans in question sterile.

It almost appears as if this highly intelligent species has fallen victim to the kind of experiments they sometimes perform on lesser earth mammals, such as "rats" and "mice," whereby they insert electrical devices into the "pleasure centers" of those animals' brains, allowing them to choose between intense surges of gratification and desperately needed nourishment. Such animals typically expend their scarce energy reserves attaining pleasure, and starve to death.

Most counter-intuitive of all these facts: the organization that favors the continued reproduction of the humans by the only effective means so far known to them is entirely dominated by members of one sex who do not themselves reproduce, but bend their efforts instead to providing a more welcoming environment for the reproduction of others. Yet those others appear to be increasingly hostile to the organization, its members, and leadership. It seems to our analysts that this species has chosen transitory pleasure in preference to survival, like the rodents upon which it experiments. Barring some intervention by the putative Deity that this "Church" claims to represent, the humans will forget how to reproduce.

RECOMMENDATION: Because of the crude but highly effective explosive weapons that the members of this species still retain, annexation should be postponed until depopulation and social decay are so advanced that resistance will be minimal. We estimate that three or four more human generations will suffice.

If you showed such an alien analysis of recent changes in human sexual behavior and the Church's response to a contemporary secularist, or an angry dissenting Catholic, he wouldn't be able to argue with you on the facts. But he wouldn't be persuaded either. Which is funny, because such an objective look is exactly what modern science would seem to demand.

Step back and look at sex "scientifically," pretending that you and I are merely the accidental by-products of random mutations and natural selection. That isn't true, but such a thought experiment will help us to bracket the hopes, dreams and aspirations that motivate most of our decisions on sexual questions, and view the matter objectively.

And objectively, the strategies that we have been trying since roughly 1960 have backfired. So maybe our society should try something else—perhaps something that worked well in the past, such as monogamous, fertile, lifelong marriage as the norm of human life, which our laws could support with incentives aimed first and foremost at protecting the best interests of children. Because, as the Whitney Houston song says, they're the future.

And that's exactly what the Catholic Church's teachings on sexuality say. Based on reason and empirical observation, we see that *the primary purpose of sex is reproduction*—not just the breeding but also the rearing of the next generation of our species. Any biologist would tell you the same thing about orangutans and squirrels. This is what the Church calls the "procreative" end of marriage.

The *secondary purpose*, which matters more to us than to lower animals, is social—creating bonds of affection and love that will outlast the initial spark between two young fertile creatures driven by instinct. This is what the Church calls the "unitive" end of marriage.

The third and *least essential purpose* of sexuality would have to be the short-lived excitement and pleasure that Nature attached to it so that we would be strongly motivated to go through all the trouble.

Any analysis of other bodily appetites would yield the same results: the primary purpose of eating is nutrition, then second to that the social benefits of sharing meals with others; dead last would come the exquisite gourmet delight we take in a fancy multi-course meal.

Any species would be in trouble if it got these priorities wrong and developed a preference for food that wasn't nourishing. No scientist would dispute that, championing the "right" of a population of koalas to feed on dirt instead of leaves. They would stand back and watch sadly while that mutant group disappeared, taking copious notes—which would read like a history of twentieth-century sex.

But as we see from the Catholic Church's efforts over recent decades to explain—then patiently re-explain using smaller, simpler words—its perennial teaching on human sexuality, few people are persuaded. Why is that?

If we were (as dogmatic Darwinists insist) just one of the higher primates, with no immortal souls and perhaps not even free will, why shouldn't we view ourselves the way biologists see other animal species, and act accordingly? Why is it that human beings, alone among all the species, do not seem

★ ★ ★

Satire Is Dead

In 1931 Aldous Huxley's *Brave New World*—portraying a time in which universal contraception had reduced sex to a meaningless but fun exercise involving no babies, no marriage, no love, and no emotional pain—struck its readers as an outrageous, implausible *reductio ad absurdum*. But some of those who read it seem to have taken it not as a warning but as a blueprint. We should hope that Huxley's example makes future satirists more cautious: there is no nightmare scenario, apparently, that somebody will not mistake for a utopia.

to respond in an uncomplicated way to the deep Darwinian drive to reproduce and pass along the "selfish genes" that New Atheists like to pretend are simply using us as tools for self-replication?

Instead we write poems, fall hopelessly in love with inappropriate people, elevate our emotional gratification over the well-being of our children, and pretend that the pleasure of sex—and that pleasure alone—somehow transcends every other biological drive, to the point where we feel almost virtuous in flouting its biological and social purpose. The Sexual Revolution, and the sullen feminist reaction that it provoked, could never have happened if we did not really, deep down, realize that human beings are special, unique, and free.

The Church agrees. Indeed, she has been saying that all along. But part of our uniqueness, the part that Genesis tells us emerged not long after we finished naming the animals, is that we sin. We choose our own immediate gratification, and the delusions of our own imaginings, over the needs and interests of others.

And that's the whole problem with sex, the reason that it has built into its very nature a far more complex set of ethical obligations than every other bodily instinct. (That's right—these obligations are part of the package, not arbitrary taboos imposed from outside by envious celibate clerics.) If every time we ate, or drank, or slept, our activity necessarily and profoundly involved another equal human being with complex emotions and an immortal soul, then eating, drinking, and sleeping would also carry profound moral implications, which the Church would have to recognize. What if any of those ordinary activities could also in fact create a whole new human being, with a body and soul all his own? Just imagine the detailed ethical rules that would have arisen around food, drink, and sleep!

When it comes to sex, we can't do without such rules. It once seemed as if we could; that's what Hugh Hefner, Margaret Sanger, and the Marquis de Sade all argued when they called for society to dismantle every obstacle to pleasure—denying the universal, pan-cultural human recognition that sex is somehow special—in favor of a sexual anarchism that's only really suited to the short-term cravings of a sixteen-year-old boy. Energetic libertine anthropologists like Margaret Mead went far afield hoping to find some "primitive" culture that didn't recognize that the sex act entails profound moral issues and instead treated it as a harmless innocent sport like water polo or volleyball. They didn't find one—though some, like Mead, were careless and biased enough to falsely report that they had. Scientists with hidden agendas such as Alfred Kinsey conducted skewed "research" on prostitutes and recently released prisoners, then reported those outliers' sexual activities as representative of all Americans'. (Kinsey also encouraged a pedophile molester of tiny infants, to gain his valuable insights on sexual performance in the crib.) Mead's reports and Kinsey's studies were cited by journalists and hyped by the media as evidence that all the fuss that religious people—and especially the benighted Catholic Church, with its repressed celibate clergy and their ideas from the Dark Ages—made about sexual morality came down to a needless, destructive taboo that targeted pleasure.

We know better now. The Sexual Revolution has triumphed, and its results are even bloodier than the French or Russian revolutions. Let's start with the most obvious and appalling outcomes, and work our way down to those that are merely depressing and soul-draining, shall we? Keep in mind that every one of these miserable fruits of sexual anarchism was something that the Catholic Church warned us about long beforehand, and still condemns today.

Two Books You're Not Supposed to Read

Sexual Sabotage: How One Mad Scientist Unleashed a Plague of Corruption and Contagion on America by Judith Reisman (Washington, DC: WND, 2010). Dr. Reisman exposed Kinsey's dishonest and criminal "research."

Margaret Mead and Samoa: The Making and Unmaking of an Anthropological Myth by Derek Freeman (Cambridge: Harvard University, 1983). Dr. Freeman followed up on Mead's reports that Samoa was a guiltless sexual playground and discovered that she had completely, perhaps even willfully, misunderstood what the natives told her.

Abortion: The American Gulag, Holocaust, and Ukrainian Famine All Rolled Up in One

Global abortion statistics are tricky, and they include the vast totals for communist countries such as China, so let's just look at America. Since 1973, there have been more than 58.5 million legal abortions in America, which has abortion laws much less protective than those in Western Europe—permitting abortions for any reason (including sex selection), and allowing them through all nine months of pregnancy in each of our fifty states (some state laws do attempt to ban late-term abortions, but the Supreme Court has declared that it is a Constitutional right to abort babies up to the point of birth for "the health of the mother," including her psychological health—which Paul Ryan, a Catholic and the Speaker of the House of Representatives, has called "a loophole wide enough to drive a *Mack*® Truck through)."[1] This death toll exceeds the Holocaust, Stalin's purges and artificial famines, and all the deaths of the Second World War. It comes close to scholars' estimates of the number of people who died at the hands of Mao Zedong in China.

When population controllers and feminists promoted legal abortion in the 1960s, they relied on "hard cases," such as victims of rape or women with medically dangerous pregnancies, to break down our long-standing natural and cultural aversion to the willful murder of the helpless and the innocent. (Before 1960 or so, the very word "abortion" was treated as a profanity, and not used in polite society.) Abortion advocates also counted on medical ignorance about fetal development, assuring people that all they sought was the right to remove a "clump of cells" that endangered a woman's happiness. The Catholic Church even then taught definitively that life begins at conception, and it has opposed abortion consistently since the earliest days of the Church, echoing the Jewish concern for the sanctity of life that saw Jews condemning the pagan exposure of infants, and early Christians working at the walls of the city of Rome, rescuing unwanted

★ ★ ★
If We Love Our Liberties

The regime of abortion on demand in the United States is by any reckoning one of the great crimes of history, and it casts a deep shadow on our love for this great country—especially when the Supreme Court affirms, as it did in *Casey v. Planned Parenthood*, that the right of abortion is implied in the very "liberty" we treasure as distinctively American. If we would preserve the real good of freedom, we must distinguish it clearly from such a barbarous abuse.

infants whom pagans had abandoned there to die.[2] The Church was one of the few institutions of any influence to speak out clearly against abortion under all circumstances—and it was Catholic laymen, with some backing by bishops, who created the pro-life movement even before *Roe v. Wade* in 1973, a decision that was applauded at the time by, of all things, the Southern Baptist Convention. (To its credit, the SBC under new leadership has apologized for that statement, and Evangelical Christians are now equally as visible as Catholics in the pro-life movement.)

We know now that abortion is not a desperate measure to which a tiny minority of women resort after a brutal rape or to avoid almost certain death. It is a back-up form of birth control, made necessary by the massive explosion in extramarital sexual activity since the early 1960s. Advocates of birth control such as Margaret Sanger had assured us that contraception would reduce the need for and number of (then-illegal) abortions. But that was a lie—as we learn from Ann Furedi, former director of British Pregnancy Advisory Service, Britain's largest abortion provider:

> Often, arguments for increased access to contraception and for new contraceptive technologies are built on the assumption that these developments will bring down the abortion rate. The anti-choice movement counter that this does not seem to be the case in practice. Arguably they are right. Access to effective contraception creates an expectation that women can control their fertility and plan their families. Given that expectation, women may be less willing to compromise their plans for the future. In the past, many women reluctantly accepted that an unplanned pregnancy would lead to maternity. Unwanted pregnancies were dutifully, if resentfully, carried to term. In days when sex was expected to carry the risk of pregnancy, an unwanted child was a chance a woman took. Today, we expect sex to be free from that risk and unplanned maternity is not a price we are prepared to pay.
>
> It is clear that women cannot manage their fertility by means of contraception alone.
>
> Contraception lets couples down. A recent survey of more than 2000 women requesting abortions at clinics run by BPAS, Britain's largest abortion provider, found that almost 60% claim to have been using contraception at the time they became pregnant. Nearly 20% said that they were on the pill. Such findings are comparable to several other smaller studies published during the last decade. ... It is clear that contraceptives let couples down...The simple truth is that the tens of thousands of women who seek abortion each year are not ignorant of contraception. Rather they have tried to use it, indeed they may have used it, and become pregnant regardless.[3]

This outcome should have been obvious: imagine if liquor distributors responded to deaths caused by drunk driving by assuring alcoholics and rowdy college students that they could drink and drive safely by installing airbags in their cars and wearing seatbelts. Would that reduce the death rate, or raise it? And it turns out that in this case, the liquor distributors have taken over Mothers Against Drunk Driving: The Playboy Foundation, whose cash derives from one of the earliest "mainstream" forms of pornography, was a major financial supporter of pro-abortion activists.[4] In December 1965, *Playboy* was the first national magazine to call for legal abortion.[5] To men who have imbibed Hefner's hedonism, a pregnant woman is a broken toy, and the abortionist is the toymaker who "fixes" her.

On top of the butcher's bill, there are the often devastating effects of abortion on women, the silent price many pay in guilt and regret for the "harmless" indulgence of casual sex. E. Joanne Angelo casts a little light on this dark place in our culture:

> When a woman finds herself pregnant in a crisis situation, she immediately calculates the date when her child would be born. She is aware of the tender feelings she has for her child who, if she takes no

★ ★ ★

If You Must Drive Drunk, Please Wear a Condom

Activists in the 1980s and '90s heaped scorn on St. John Paul II for rejecting condoms (in favor of marital fidelity or abstinence) as the solution to the AIDS crisis. Didn't the pope care that people were dying? How could he prefer medieval religious principle to people's lives? Secular authorities paid no attention to the pope's advice, and, as the liberal news site Vox reports, "In the early 1990s, with panic over the AIDS epidemic rising, hundreds of school districts began making condoms more accessible to students. The hope was to encourage students to practice safe sex and better protect themselves from sexually transmitted diseases." But now, a quarter century later, as Vox also reports, "A new research paper suggests that decision may have backfired. It finds that access to condoms in school led to a 10 percent increase in teen births.... Those schools also saw that gonorrhea rates for women rose following the condom programs.[6]

action to terminate the pregnancy, she will hold in her arms at that time. Simultaneously, however, she is often overwhelmed by dread, anxiety, external pressures, a sense of unworthiness to be a mother, and fear of loss of the relationship with the child's father. Strong ambivalent feelings cloud her ability to think clearly regarding the decision she is about to make. She is pressured to present herself for an abortion during the first three months of the pregnancy, because later abortions may not be available at the local abortion clinic due to their higher risk of complications, and also to safeguard her secret.

After the abortion she may feel numb, her grief over the death of her child being blunted by her strong ambivalent feelings—her tender feelings for her child, and the defensive denial of these feelings which enabled her to submit to the abortion procedure. She may continue in this emotional state for days, weeks, or even for many years. Societal expectations are that she feel relieved and grateful that "her problem is solved," and in fact this is the answer she typically gives to surveys and polls. In reality, however, her inner life is often plagued by guilt and shame, nightmares of babies being sucked down tubes or dying in horrific accidents or violent crimes. She may seek medical treatment for insomnia and anxiety or medicate herself with alcohol and illicit drugs to ease her pain. As time goes on she may experience intrusive thoughts, day and night, and flashbacks to the abortion experience may be triggered by such ordinary experiences as a gynecological exam or the sound of the suction in a dentist's office. She may become seriously depressed and even suicidal. Her affect is blunted, she feels numb. She may develop psychosomatic symptoms, an aversion to sexual intimacy, or, conversely, become promiscuous as a result of her terribly low self esteem.

When she is in this state she may enter a cycle of multiple pregnancies and repeated abortions.[7]

Replacing the Sexual Gold Standard with Monopoly Money

Even when contraception doesn't fail and abortion isn't "necessary," the costs of promiscuity are profound. Since sex is the most profound physical act of intimacy available to our kind, decoupling it from commitment has the same effect as printing vast amounts of currency: mass inflation and crass devaluation. Since the early 1960s we have transformed sex from a scarce, precious good to the equivalent of those almost worthless Reichsmarks that Weimar Germans had to pile high in wheelbarrows to purchase their daily groceries. The effects of this sex inflation have hit women harder than men, as Steven E. Rhoads reports:

> Collegiate men in the fifties would have been interested in sleeping with a variety of women on weekends just as they are today, but few attractive, educated women were available for those sorts of encounters. Now they are. The sexual culture has changed. The collegiate women are available because most of the women's movement has insisted that sexual liberation is an important part of women's liberation and because the Pill seemed to make sexual liberation costless.... The problem is...the enduring fact that, despite all the huffing and puffing of androgynous feminists, casual sex is not a good fit for women's natures....
>
> Edward S. Herold and Dawn-Marie Mewhinney found that females who hook up get less enjoyment and feel more guilt than men do. Denise Hallfors and colleagues found that female teens are many times more likely than male teens to become depressed

after sexual encounters with multiple partners. Catherine Grello, a clinical psychologist, and colleagues found that the college men who sleep around the most are the least likely to report symptoms of depression whereas female college students who engage in casual sex the most are the most likely to report depression.

In their book, *Premarital Sex in America,* [Mark] Regnerus and coauthor Jeremy Uecker report that having more sexual partners is associated with "poorer emotional states in women, but not in men." The more lifetime partners the women have, the more likely they are to be depressed, the more likely they are to cry almost every day and the more likely they are to report relatively low satisfaction with their life as a whole.[8]

Given the evident difference between male and female sexual impulses, and the grossly incomparable impact of promiscuity on women and men, traditional cultures have rested on a negotiated compromise: as the price of access to a regular sexual partner (to use an old-fashioned word, a "wife") men have been expected to grow up, get jobs, shed addictions, and show evidence of being suitable caregivers and providers for future children. In return, they would come to learn the deeper joys of commitment and lasting love, which their "natural" promiscuity if indulged might have denied them. In other words, as the price of sex, they had to grow up from boys to men. The Church observed this primal fact of mankind, accommodated in the structure of the sacraments, in which Matrimony is on an equal footing with Ordination to the priesthood as one of just seven central Christian mysteries.

When sexual radicals tried to overturn this arrangement, the Church looked to human nature much more than to divine Revelation to warn that they would fail. But they succeeded—in a sense. If your goal was to demolish human society into a whirling mass of self-seeking, mistrustful individuals living outside of families and hence dependent for many of their daily needs (from cradle to grave) on the federal government, then the Sexual Revolution was a triumph. The New Left, which abandoned Stalinist Puritanism and weaponized "sex, drugs, and rock and roll" for the purpose of destroying the bourgeois family—that perennial obstacle to socialism—has succeeded beyond its wildest dreams, making huge swathes of the American population effective wards of the state: welfare programs, social workers, and day care centers now strain to make up for the missing fathers of the huge proportion of American children who now live in single parent homes (that's public policy-speak for "desperate, overtaxed mother with children and no spousal support"). The numbers are profoundly depressing: as the Pew Research Center reports, "Fewer than half (46%) of U.S. kids younger than 18 years of age are living in a home with two married heterosexual parents in their first marriage. This is a marked change from 1960, when 73% of children fit this description, and 1980, when 61% did."[9]

A Book You're Not Supposed to Read

The Next Conservatism, by Paul Weyrich and William Lind (South Bend: St. Augustine's Press, 2009) offers a perceptive account of how "cultural Marxism" infused American elites via the pseudo-scientific work of the Frankfurt School, whose partisans strove to portray any resistance to progressive goals as symptomatic of mental illness of the sort that gave rise to fascism. That school's favorite buzzword was the "authoritarian personality."

The Least Binding Contract You'll Ever Sign— How Marriage Became Much Less Sacred (and Eternal) than Student Loans

Feminists and libertines fought hard in the 1960s to change divorce laws, removing in most states the requirement that one spouse had to have committed a grievous "fault," such as physical abuse, adultery, or abandonment. The happy suburban fable that "irreconcilable differences" were sufficient to void a lifelong covenant, which could end with an "amicable parting," became the conventional wisdom that justified an epidemic of divorces for frankly trivial reasons. A government that grimly enforces other contracts to the letter of the law—think of those student loans you're still paying off—blithely decided to walk away from this one, the central bond that is meant to hold society together and protect the interests of children. And children certainly suffered, as Focus on the Family documents:

> Psychologist Judith Wallerstein followed a group of children of divorce from the 1970s into the 1990s. Interviewing them at 18 months and then 5, 10, 15 and 25 years after the divorce, she expected to find that they had bounced back. But what she found was dismaying: Even 25 years after the divorce, these children continued to experience substantial expectations of failure, fear of loss, fear of change and fear of conflict. Twenty-five years!
>
> The children in Wallerstein's study were especially challenged when they began to form their own romantic relationships. As Wallerstein explains, "Contrary to what we have long thought, the major impact of divorce does not occur during childhood or adolescence. Rather, it rises in adulthood as serious romantic relationships move center stage...Anxiety leads many [adult children of divorce] into making bad choices in relationships, giving up hastily when problems arise, or avoiding relationships altogether."
>
> Other researchers confirm Wallerstein's findings. Specifically, compared to kids from intact homes, children who experienced their parents' divorce view premarital sex and cohabitation more favorably. (This is disturbing news given that cohabiting

couples have more breakups, greater risk of domestic violence and are more likely to experience divorce.)

Behind each of these statistics is a life—a child, now an adult, still coping with the emotions brought on by the divorce.

As Wallerstein put it, "The kids [in my study] had a hard time remembering the pre-divorce family…but what they remembered about the post-divorce years was their sense that they had indeed been abandoned by both parents, that their nightmare had come true."[10]

You will often hear the statistic thrown around that 50 percent of all marriages end in divorce. In fact that is not true across the board, as the *New York Times* points out:

As the overall divorce rates shot up from the early 1960's through the late 1970's…the divorce rate for women with college degrees and those without moved in lockstep. . . .

But since 1980, the two groups have taken diverging paths. Women without undergraduate degrees have remained at about the same rate, their risk of divorce or separation within the first 10 years of marriage hovering at around 35 percent. But for college graduates, the divorce rate in the first 10 years of marriage has plummeted to just over 16 percent of those married between 1990 and 1994 from 27 percent of those married between 1975 and 1979.

About 60 percent of all marriages that eventually end in divorce do so within the first 10 years, researchers say. If that continues to hold true, the divorce rate for college graduates who married between 1990 and 1994 would end up at only about 25 percent, compared to well over 50 percent for those without a four-year college degree.[11]

I suppose you could call this good news, if your sole concern were for the happiness of upper middle class people. But they can afford to go to therapy and take time off to deal with the emotional strains imposed on children by divorce. It's the poor and working class that need the stability, security, and cooperative economic effort of marriage the most, and are getting it the least. Again, from the *New York Times*:

> Jonathan Rauch, another fellow at the Brookings Institution and a leader of the Marriage Opportunity Council, a new multi-institution project, said, "Marriage is thriving among people with four-year college diplomas, but the further down you go on the educational and economic totem pole, the worse it's doing."
>
> "There's a growing danger that marriage, with all its advantages for stability, income and child well-being, will look like a gated community for the baccalaureate class, with ever-shrinking working-class participation," Mr. Rauch said. "We're not there yet, but that's the trajectory we're on."[12]

Not only is marriage now fragile, it is also shrinking: "After decades of declining marriage rates and changes in family structure, the share of American adults who have never been married is at an historic high. In 2012, one-in-five adults ages 25 and older (about 42 million people) had never been married, according to a new Pew Research Center analysis of census data. In 1960, only about one-in-ten adults (9%) in that age range had never been married."[13]

This social experiment in catering to the emotional whims of adults while reassuring ourselves that children are "resilient" has run its course, and we have the results: social collapse, massive unhappiness, and on top of it all a crime wave. The National Center for Fathering collected the relevant data in a single sobering report. In the words of the report:

- Children in father-absent homes are almost four times more likely to be poor. In 2011, 12 percent of children in married-couple families were living in poverty, compared to 44 percent of children in mother-only families[14]
- Children living in female headed families with no spouse present had a poverty rate of 47.6 percent, over 4 times the rate in married-couple families[15]
- The U.S. Department of Health and Human Services states, "Fatherless children are at a dramatically greater risk of drug and alcohol abuse"[16]
- There is significantly more drug use among children who do not live with their mother and father[17]
- A study of 1,977 children age 3 and older living with a residential father or father figure found that children living with married biological parents had significantly fewer externalizing and internalizing behavioral problems than children living with at least one non-biological parent[18]
- Children of single-parent homes are more than twice as likely to commit suicide[19]
- Children in grades 7–12 who have lived with at least one biological parent, youth that experienced divorce, separation, or nonunion birth reported lower grade point averages than those who have always lived with both biological parents[20]
- Children living with their married biological father tested at a significantly higher level than those living with a nonbiological father[21]
- Adolescents living in intact families are less likely to engage in delinquency than their peers living in non-intact families. Compared to peers in intact families, adolescents in single-parent families and stepfamilies were more likely to engage

in delinquency. This relationship appeared to be operating through differences in family processes—parental involvement, supervision, monitoring, and parent-child closeness—between intact and non-intact families[22]

The Catholic Church's Alternative to the Chaos: Same as It Ever Was

In the face of all these indisputable facts, you might think that progressives who profess to care for the weak and the vulnerable—and who better fits that description than the children of the poor?—would gain some respect for the Catholic Church for having warned against all these evils, and at great institutional cost clung to the doctrine of marriage it received from Jesus Christ: *marriage is a holy bond, open to children, between one man and one woman, that persists as long as both spouses are alive—and because of the very nature of sex itself, marriage is the only proper context for sexual relationships.* Even if liberals found such a stance a tad idealistic, you might think they'd at least doff their hats to it—as they do to the much more exotic beliefs of other world religions. But of course you would be wrong; it is only non-Western creeds that receive the courtesy of cosmopolitan deference, even when they are socially destructive (like Muslim misogyny). The Left rightly perceives that the Catholic Church stands guard at the (very faintly) beating heart of the civilization that frustrates and enrages them, the West. Combine that fact with the sexual libertinism that leftists still cling to, even as they oppose virtually every other kind of freedom, and you understand the storm that rages continually among the cultural cognoscenti against the teachings of the Church.

There's no reason to pretend that the Church's vision of marriage isn't challenging. One of the "hardest sayings" of Jesus in the Gospel remains His teaching on divorce, in which He revokes the license that Moses had given the Jews to dispose of wives (not husbands) at will (Matthew 19:3–12). Christ ends with the ringing line: "And I say to you, whoever divorces his wife, except for unchastity, and marries another commits adultery."

The apostles' reaction was telling: "If such is the case of a man with his wife, it is not expedient to marry" (Matthew 19:10). Our Lord answers their objection with what seems to be a shrug—and makes this a teaching moment where He introduces the idea of religious celibacy: "[T]here are eunuchs who have made themselves eunuchs for the sake of the kingdom of heaven. He who is able to receive this, let him receive it" (Matthew 19:12). Not very pastoral, if you ask me.

Christians over the centuries have struggled with this teaching, and over time most churches have succumbed, one way or the other, and reverted to Old Testament practice. The Eastern Orthodox churches, while affirming the lifelong character of marriage, for various reasons began to allow Christians whose first marriages had failed to marry again—albeit not in a festive manner, but via a ceremony whose dominant note is penitential. Those in second marriages are called to atone for the failure of their first, but are not expected to avoid marital intercourse.

Most Protestant churches, which venerate marriage as a covenant but not a sacrament, clung to the Biblical teaching at first. But many of these churches began to make exceptions, and by the mid–twentieth century divorce was becoming mainstream even for faithful Protestants. That left Catholics mostly alone, among world religions, in resisting the tide of marital dissolution.

And for some decades, Catholics' divorce rate lagged far behind that of other Christians, as even unhappy spouses resisted the prospect of leaving their Church marriages for either legally sanctioned adultery or a life of celibacy.

Then the Sexual Revolution hit, just after the Second Vatican Council had put in progress a series of jarring reforms to Church discipline and liturgy, changes that ordinary Catholics, encouraged by liberal clergy and nuns, misinterpreted as a sign that *all bets were off* (see chapters three and

★ ★ ★
A Binding Decision

The Catholic Church is bound to the indissolubility of marriage by a declaration of the Council of Trent—which is every bit as binding and infallible as the Council of Nicaea—which affirmed the divinity of Christ. If a pope or a council overturned that teaching, it would completely discredit the Church's teaching authority, and prove that the Eastern Orthodox theory of the Church was true, not the Catholic one.

four). If the Church could revolutionize something as central as its liturgy, they imagined, surely its dusty old marriage laws would be the next thing to go. Thus many Catholics acted accordingly, and began to divorce and remarry at rates not much lower than the rest of the population.

But the Catholic Church didn't change its teaching. Indeed, it can't, without committing institutional suicide.

Constrained by this attachment to lifelong marriage, but pressured by millions of Catholics whose marriages had failed, many bishops around the world have mostly surrendered in practice, while insisting on a fig leaf of respect for official Church teaching. To finesse this, they turned to the long-standing process of annulment. An annulment is a decree that a given marriage never really existed in the first place because one or more of the conditions required for making it valid was not present. There are real and valid reasons for granting an annulment: for instance, if one of the parties was kidnapped, coerced, insane, or under age. The Vatican has been dispensing annulments for centuries in cases like these. But liberal priests and bishops did not view annulments as what they rightly are—the recognition of a rare, exceptional injustice, such as forced marriage.

Instead, many bishops, especially in America, began to hand out annulments to almost anyone who asked, on spurious psychological grounds such as "emotional immaturity." In my own Catholic high school, the quarters that had once housed Christian Brothers (who all cleared out after Vatican II) were turned into an annulment tribunal with the highest "success" rate in the world. Some 99 percent of marriages examined in that tribunal turned out to have been invalid. Nor was my diocese an outlier. As veteran Vatican reporter John Allen has written, even today, "the United States accounts for at least half, and sometimes more, of all the annulments granted by the Catholic Church every year, even though it represents only 6 percent of the global Catholic population."[23] That means one of two things: (a) We Americans are very good at faking annulments of perfectly valid marriages, so that couples can contract second, adulterous marriages with a clear conscience; or (b) We are very bad at creating valid marriages. If the latter is the true explanation, then American Catholic marriages today are a lot less reliable than American cars built in the 1980s. Perhaps it is time for imports?

Popes St. John Paul II and Benedict XVI saw the American annulment rate as an international scandal, and tried to tighten the rules from Rome, making it harder for local bishops to accommodate the divorce culture, and giving some support to those spouses who didn't want their marriages (sometimes of twenty or thirty years, with multiple children) declared null and void in retrospect.

In 2015 Pope Francis reversed most of the reforms that the previous two popes imposed, and made annulments easier, quicker, and cheaper. That surely will mean that they will become more common.

What were his motives for doing that? John Allen suggested that Francis wanted to defuse the growing crisis between the Vatican and the German church—some of whose bishops were threatening to openly flout the pope's authority unless he allowed divorced and remarried Catholics whose marriages had not been declared null by the Church to receive Communion, which would imply that their second marriages didn't amount to living in adultery after all.

There aren't many practicing, faithful Catholics left in Germany, but that doesn't mean that a schism would be trivial; German Catholics send millions to the Vatican every year through that country's curious "church tax,"

A Book You're Not Supposed to Read

Shattered Faith: A Woman's Struggle to Stop the Catholic Church from Annulling Her Marriage by Sheila Rauch Kennedy (New York: Pantheon, 2013). An abandoned Kennedy wife famously fought her powerful husband's annulment petition—and when she lost had the bad manners to write a book exposing what a farce the procedure had become.

to which every registered Catholic contributes via payroll deduction—on pain of excommunication. If Germany cut off that money, Pope Francis would have to suspend most of the Vatican's spending on missions and aiding the poor. Such a schism might very well spread through other countries in Europe where the Catholic population is mostly well to the left of even their bishops.

So instead of changing church doctrine and driving faithful Catholics into the arms of an antipope or the Eastern Orthodox, or writing off the whole German church and all its money, it seems the pope has steered a middle ground: permitting the mass abuse of annulments to continue, and issuing a document on marriage, *Amoris Laetitiae*, whose chief effect has been to confuse people. In that apostolic exhortation, Pope Francis seems to present the Catholic vision of a lifelong, loving, and fruitful marriage not so much as the ordinary plan God has in mind for the vast majority of humans, but rather as a noble ideal toward which we can strive hopefully—something like the lofty Franciscan vision of absolute, Christlike poverty. And who could blame someone for failing at that?

The document is full of reaffirmations of Christian morality on marriage, but it leaves a theological gap the size of the Lincoln Tunnel that dissenters are sure to exploit. As Catholic historian Roberto de Mattei explained,

> Everyone was expecting the answer to one basic question: Can those who have remarried civilly after a first marriage, receive the Sacrament of the Eucharist? The Church *has always given a categorical no*[.] . . .

The answer of the post-synod Exhortation is, instead: along general lines—no, but *"in certain cases"—yes*. (no. 305, note 351)…

What is obvious is this: the prohibition to receive Communion for the divorced and remarried *is no longer absolute*. The Pope does not authorize, as a general rule, Communion to the divorced, but neither does he prohibit it.[24] [Emphasis added]

The decision on whether to give the Body of Christ to Catholics who are living in what the Church considers adultery will apparently be left to local pastors. How many will have the moral courage to hold firm in the face of anguished or angry parishioners?

Nor does the pope offer much encouragement to pastors placed in this position, as de Mattei explains: "The pastors wishing to refer to the Church's commandments, would risk acting…'as arbiters of grace rather than its facilitators' (310)….For this reason, a pastor cannot feel that it is enough simply to apply moral laws to those living in 'irregular' situations, as if they were stones to throw at people's lives. This would bespeak the closed heart of one used to hiding behind the Church's teachings, 'sitting on the chair of Moses and judging at times with superiority and superficiality difficult cases and wounded families (305).'"

How much of this same rhetoric will dissenting Catholics apply to people in same-sex relationships? I fear that the correct answer is *all of it*. If Catholics living in adultery are to be fully "included" in Church life, to be welcomed as godparents, religion teachers, and lectors, what exactly is the argument for rejecting those in homosexual relationships calling themselves "married"? Isn't that simply and blatantly homophobic? While Francis does not himself open the door to this conclusion, history tells us that the revolutionaries in the Catholic Church never wait for encouragement from the pope.

Many of the major liturgical changes that took place after Vatican II were rejected at first by Rome—which, a few years later, was faced with a *fait accompli*, since the liberals had ignored the Vatican's orders, and now millions of Catholics were accustomed to the new practices, and it would be "disruptive" and "unpastoral" to disturb their new "local traditions."

The same thing will happen now, as theological liberals claim that Francis's call to be "welcoming" to same-sex-attracted people implies that they deserve the exact same treatment now expected for those living in adultery—a policy liberal bishops pushed for, hard, at last year's Synod on the Family, only to be rebuked by the votes of conservative bishops from places like Poland.

How soon will it be before pastors in Germany, the Netherlands, Belgium, and other post-Christian wastelands are authorizing transvestites to hand out Holy Communion, same-sex couples to teach Pre-Cana classes, and activists promoting sodomy to serve as principals of Catholic schools and seminaries—citing the language Pope Francis used to encourage compassion toward Catholics who have abandoned their sacramental marriages?

Under previous popes, faithful Catholics at least had firm, unambiguous papal statements to cite against such destructive local abuses, and to use in court when they had to defend their religious freedom against intolerant secular activists: "I'm sorry, Your Honor, but my Church explicitly requires this." How long will it be until a well-informed judge, or a homosexual activist attorney, finds it useful to cite *Amoris Laetitia* against such beleaguered Catholics, and accuses them, in the pope's own words, of "sitting on the chair of Moses"?

Not just our faith's integrity, but our religious liberty is endangered by the pope's ill-chosen words—which just goes to prove once again that the pope only speaks infallibly when he explicitly invokes that divine protection, in an ex cathedra statement. Pretending otherwise is a sure recipe for losing one's faith, especially with a pope such as Francis.

Why has Pope Francis apparently given so much ground to secular and dissenting Catholic pressure on such a crucial issue as marriage? We can gain some insight from his own words on the subject. Quoting the bishop who preceded him in Buenos Aires, the pope told reporters, "Cardinal Quarracino, my predecessor, said that for him half of all marriages are null. That's what he said. Why? Because they are married without maturity, they get married without realizing that it's for an entire lifetime, or they are married because socially they must get married."[25]

What if the pope is right? A lifelong Christian marriage is quite a commitment—much less like forming a business partnership than it is like donating a kidney. It is perfectly plausible that a high percentage of the Clinton lovers who skip into American Catholic parishes seeking to use those Gothic buildings as backdrops for wedding photographers are not entirely sold on the whole "till death do us part" thing. If even one party in the marriage goes into it thinking that if things "don't work out" he can divorce and marry someone else, then the union really is void and invalid from day one. If the other partner was in fact sincere, she is the victim of an injustice—to be quite frank, of a fraud.

But wouldn't a pastor who lends out the sanctuary of his church for such a union be an unwitting party to that fraud? Surely it is his solemn duty to the souls whom he is called to evangelize to do all he can to prevent such sacrilegious marriages. Some priests and some bishops are taking such steps. Unfortunately, the pope has just made their job much harder. The fact that annulments are so easy to get undermines the seriousness with which Catholics treat marriage, and ensures that this year's crop of Catholic weddings, and next year's, will be equally flawed and eligible for annulments down the road.

Most Catholics outside of a few traditional societies have grown up in a divorce culture, where lifelong bonds are the exception, not the rule. Few of them have received decent education in their faith, either from parents or

★ ★ ★
Quality Control

Imagine if Toyota learned that half of its cars exploded when drivers exceeded 55 mph. And its CEO decided not to stop the assembly lines until such time as the error was rooted out and corrected. Instead, he told consumers that they could trade in their defective Toyotas, no questions asked—for new cars just as likely to have the same design flaw. You wouldn't think that executive was serious, either about safety or about the future of Toyota.

schools. The short, mostly pop psychology Pre-Cana classes that the Church requires rarely emphasize how obedience to Jesus requires that Catholic marriages are indissoluble. Even good pastors who do teach that lesson know that it is undermined by the Church's annulment policy. Whatever ringing scriptural words a holy priest uses to drive home the Church's teaching to a couple, they are multiplied by zero by the universal awareness that annulments are easier to get than debt forgiveness for student loans.

What if this or a future pope were to take solid pastoral steps to ensure that more Catholics marriages are valid? I have a simple, painful, five-point plan for Catholics, which if undertaken could make us prophetic witnesses to the reality of marriage, in the face of the pale pansexual temporary sex contract that our laws call by that name:

1. Each pastor could require of couples that wish to marry that they be trained in the methods and moral underpinnings of Natural Family Planning. This should be a non-negotiable part of Catholic marriage prep.

2. A boilerplate "covenant" prenuptial agreement could be drawn up by our bishops, and provided to pastors, that binds Catholic spouses to lifelong marriage, renounces divorce and remarriage, and awards all community property to the wronged party in any civil divorce. Our courts almost certainly wouldn't enforce any such agreements—but requiring people to sign them would weed out the unserious. And where, as in Louisiana,

Arizona, and Arkansas, the state does offer the option of a more binding "covenant" form of marriage whose terms the courts will enforce, Catholics who wanted to get married in church could be required to take that option. Anyone who objects is admitting in advance that he lacks sacramental intent. Give him directions to City Hall.

3. A civil divorce would no longer be a prerequisite for an annulment, but its legal aftermath. Catholics unsure of their marriage's validity would be required to await the Church's judgment before they seek the remedies of the state. Again, they could sign a document agreeing to this before the marriage takes place.

4. With marriages contracted after measures 1, 2, and 3 have been implemented, it would be much easier for Pope Francis or his successor to require annulment tribunals to be much stricter in their application of canon law. If either party going into a marriage secretly thinks that divorce and remarriage might be an option, that is enough to invalidate the bond, so that's the seed of the cancer which we must root out. It's not so much the annulments we approve that are scandalous farces, but the invalid weddings.

5. The party whose intent was found to be defective in any annulment would have to wait some length of time, say three to five years, before contracting a Catholic marriage, complete a rigorous marriage prep that fully explicates the conditions of the sacrament—and, of course, sign a "covenant" prenup so that this never happens again.

This would require some modifications of canon law, and perhaps it would have to be phased in over time. But a movement this radical and counter-cultural could be a beacon of bright light in the gathering global darkness, showing to all the world what Christian marriage really looks like. The question is whether the world really wants to see.

CHAPTER 12

Temptations and Opportunities for the Church

Either the Church is true, and the Holy Spirit will guard the Church's leaders from solemnly teaching error, or it isn't and He won't. Either way there is nothing to worry about on that score. So let's leave the job of protecting the Church from error between God and the pope, and look at the ways in which this-worldly politics, both on the micro and macro scale, could exert an important impact on the Church's religious witness—and yours and mine, in our day-to-day lives among our neighbors and fellow citizens. In this final chapter, I'd like to lay out some of the danger zones that we Catholics must steer clear of, and point to the hopeful opportunities that still exist in this place and time, the exact moment in history where God saw fit to plant each one of us to do our part.

If the Church's leaders, or large numbers of faithful Catholics, were to align themselves with destructive political and social movements, that would give scandal—and make other people less likely to join the Church. It might even drive Catholics out. That happened on a massive scale in Latin America, when that KGB invention, Liberation Theology, began to take over Catholic universities, seminaries, and parishes. Subjected to thinly veiled Marxist propaganda instead of solid preaching, millions of people whose

Did you know?

★ *Humanae Vitae* is no longer a sufficient litmus test for orthodox Catholic belief—as college-educated Catholics raising big families on welfare embrace socialism

★ The "New Homophiles" follow Church teaching on abstaining from sodomy, but see same-sex attraction as a gift from God

★ Catholics and Evangelical Christians cooperated in the pro-life movement and are now allies on religious liberty

families had been Catholic for five hundred years felt spiritually starved—and went elsewhere for nourishment, swelling the ranks of Evangelical and Pentecostal churches. After all, you will learn much more about Jesus at a holy roller church where the pastor and his wife speak in tongues than you will at a church where a German-trained Jesuit who can't tell the difference between "the People of God" and "the Proletariat" explains that the "new heaven and new earth" Christ promised us refers to the future collectivist society after the Revolution. (Think: Venezuela, the land without toilet paper.) Faithful Catholics have much more in common with Evangelical Protestants than we do with Marxists, even ones wearing Roman collars. I've gotten to know Evangelicals where it counts—on the front lines of the war for unborn life and religious liberty—and you won't meet better people anywhere. God bless and keep them!

Not every problematic Catholic you'll encounter will be quoting *Das Kapital*, or claiming that "the goddess" speaks to her on Jungian retreats where addled nuns "run with the wolves." Sure, there are plenty of open extremists out there who blatantly dissent from settled Church teaching on abortion, same-sex marriage, or the ordination of women. But the Devil is far from a fool. He knows that serious Catholics are already on to the con of Cafeteria Catholics, who pick the "social justice" teachings that appeal to them, while leaving aside all the nourishing guidance on personal morality. So when the Enemy wishes to assail and cripple the Church's mission today, he employs much subtler snares.

In the 1970s and 1980s, when most of the money, power, and institutions of the Church, at least in America, were in the hands of open dissenters, a safe litmus test of a Catholic's fidelity was his position on *Humanae Vitae*—an encyclical so widely scorned and rejected that there was no reason for anyone to accept it besides honest obedience to the Church (see chapter four). But since then, overtly dissenting religious orders and liberal seminaries have hemorrhaged vocations and lost much of their influence over anyone under age sixty-five. Two brilliant popes (St. John Paul II and Benedict XVI) inspired a renaissance of orthodox Catholic activism, which led to the founding of many new institutions to pass along the Faith—religious orders and colleges, organizations and media outlets, which are acquiring the money, visibility, hiring power, and influence that dying orders like the Jesuits and the IHM nuns once had. Why should we think that Beelzebub wouldn't try to infect these new institutions, too?

If you were a vaguely Catholic leftist with not much of a work ethic, looking for an undemanding job among trusting, forgiving people, why not try one of these new institutions? All you need to do to prove your bona fides is whisper the secret password: *Humanae Vitae.* Tell the nice folks who are hiring—who may have suffered bitterly for their fidelity to the pope in past decades—that you embrace that one encyclical, and they will assume that you are a faithful brother in arms! Then you can get busy mining Catholic documents for passages to wrestle out of context to serve your own agenda—which includes opposing pro-life Republicans who might cut the public assistance on which you rely to support yourself (and perhaps your spouse and children) while you spend all day on social media. You can justify those massive welfare programs by pointing to the danger that if poor people don't get large checks from the government they might use birth control or get abortions—and presto chango!—you have obliterated the Church's teaching on subsidiarity, and found a pretext for urging your fellow Catholics to vote for pro-choice Democrats. I have seen such arguments made over and over again by Catholic writers—people who work at orthodox, not dissenting venues, as this chapter will show. Sometimes it seems that Catholic media have been taken over by people with a great deal of time on their hands—since many of them don't have day jobs.

The go-to argument leftists use when they wish to borrow the mantle of Catholic orthodoxy is that tattered poncho from the early 1980s, the "seamless garment" (see chapter five), now rebranded as "the Whole Life" movement, a term that real pro-life conservative Jason Scott Jones argues credibly was simply lifted from his own writings in an astonishing act of intellectual theft.[1] (Why is it that discredited leftist ideas always have to be sold under a new label?)[2] In a series of columns during the 2016 election season, Robert Christian, Democrats for Life fellow and graduate student at Catholic University, promoted the seamless garment's distorted moral priorities. Christian claims that a "consistent" pro-life position must address "unjust social structures" (such as the free market) that allegedly cause "indirect threats to life, such as the absence of access to healthcare or food." In other words, conservatives who oppose both abortion and Obamacare are hypocrites, no better than pro-choicers who at least favor socialized medicine. Christian goes on to muddy the pro-life waters even further, denouncing pro-lifers' "simplistic focus on a single issue," and insisting that the movement be "purified" by adopting his own views on how to save the environment, "empower women and girls," and solve "global poverty."[3]

Mark Shea is a columnist at the EWTN-owned Catholic paper *The National Catholic Register*. He has endorsed not only the seamless garment ("which is to say," according to Shea, "the actual real normative teaching of the Church"—apparently now defined by the Archbishop of Chicago)[4] but also Hillary Clinton in the 2016 election, writing on May 13, 2016: "[I]f I lived in a swing state, I would not only feel free to vote for Hillary with a clear conscience in order to stop Trump, I would actually feel bound by my conscience to do so, precisely *because* of my Catholic—prolife—faith."[5] Shea characterizes Catholics who disagree with his leftist politics as "us[ing] the unborn as human shields for FOX News talking points," "battling the Church in the name of the unborn," and "hiding behind their Precious Feet pin."[6]

Rebecca Bratten Weiss, who teaches English at the revitalized and famously orthodox Franciscan University of Steubenville, seconded this endorsement of the seamless garment, complaining, "From a feminist perspective, let's just put this out there, too: that the [pro-life] movement has been infected with misogyny, not just on the cranky edges, but right down the middle.... [The pro-life movement] vilifies theologians and feminists who wish to address the larger issues surrounding abortion, issues of poverty and abuse and lack of health care."[7]

Weiss has also denounced Steubenville for failing to offer her a "living wage" and full family benefits for her work as a part-time adjunct.[8] Rather than seek more lucrative if less culturally prestigious employment, Weiss and her children have relied on food stamps.[9] Weiss has written that "the most likely outcome" of the election of radically pro-choice Socialist Senator Bernie Sanders as president "would be fewer abortions. The same can't be said of any of the Republican candidates, no matter what pieties they mouth."[10]

Simcha Fisher, a longtime columnist at EWTN's *National Catholic Register*, justified support of pro-abortion candidates such as Hillary Clinton to her enormous Facebook following on May 29, 2016: "You can't vote for someone who says he's pro-abortion *because* he says he's pro-abortion and because you hope he will keep abortion legal, but you can vote [for that candidate] if you think that, on balance, his actual policies are *in effect* pro-life."[11]

Fisher's other writings suggest that what she considers "pro-life" policies include massive government poverty and health care programs[12]—on which she herself has been dependent, by her account, since childhood, later giving birth to and raising ten children on public assistance.[13] Indeed, Fisher quipped about a column she wrote entitled "The Day I Bought Steak with My Food Stamps"[14] that "I especially liked that gravy we made out of the blood of hard-working Americans. That was delicious." She added, "We sleep on mattresses filled with the dollars confiscated from hard working people, and it gives us SUCH SWEET DREAMS."[15]

Fisher is the author of a book on (of all things) Natural Family Planning published by Our Sunday Visitor Press, and in 2015 spoke by invitation on

★ ★ ★

Having a Large Family at Other People's Expense Is Not Responsible Parenthood

Mrs. Fisher recounts in her manual on Natural Family Planning (!): "My husband and I have been married for fifteen years, we have nine children [ten as of this writing].... We always wanted a big family and we hope to have at least a few more kids..."[16] She answers critics of her family's long-term dependence on government poverty programs this way: "Why, yes, America *is* being ruined by irresponsible people like us who go on and have forty-seven children that we can't even afford to outfit in Brooks Brothers suits with a Rush Limbaugh logo embroidered on the lapel. We should pull ourselves up by our boot-straps, quit whining, and take the triple extra overtime shift in the coal mine so we will have something to leave to the Pat Buchanan Young Monsters Brigade in our will."[17] More than 620,000 people on Facebook shared Simcha Fisher's column defending buying steak on food stamps. One commenter said proudly, "Government programs help me have my Catholic babies!"[18]

the same panel as Catholic bishops at the Vatican-sponsored World Meeting of Families. In August 2016, she addressed Catholic CEOs at the Colorado Springs Chapter of Legatus—an organization devoted to prudent steward-ship and Catholic philanthropy.[19]

Teaching at a small orthodox Catholic college, I encountered numerous students who themselves were raised on public assistance by highly edu-cated Catholic parents, and who planned to marry their fellow graduates straight out of college (combining their undergraduate debt, which going by the national average could add up to more than $50,000).[20] They intended to immediately start large families on their neighbors' dime, then teach their own children that it would be virtuous for them to do the same. Unlike the desperate, poorly schooled, and economically marginal members of inner city families that are inter-generationally dependent on welfare, these leisured liberal arts graduates had attended a private Catholic college.[21] In consciously planning to spend their lives dependent on public assistance while pursuing low-pay culturally prestigious careers in academia, journalism, or apologetics, such Catholics are actually *stealing from the poor*— abusing emergency programs aimed at the truly needy. Strangely, Fisher doesn't seem to have much sympathy for the actual intended beneficiaries of federal welfare programs: impoverished single mothers, whom she wishes would "fornicate less."[22]

In fact, the Church calls for "responsible parenthood,"[23] which surely means providing your own family with food, shelter, education, and health care out of the wages of your own labor. According to Pope Paul VI, being a "responsible" parent requires acting "generously"—but also "prudently."[24] In any case, how genuinely "generous" is it to live at your neighbors' expense? If married college graduates expect society to pick up the tab for their progeny while they freelance as amateur theologians, then who exactly is supposed to produce the goods they're consuming? This is socialism, pure and simple—something that, like contraception, has been clearly condemned by the Church (see chapter seven). Catholics who refuse to use Natural Family Planning to limit their families to a size they can actually support—something that, as we have seen, popes since Pius XII have been advising—are not following Church teaching.

Other "orthodox" Catholics whose pet issue is not welfare programs but open borders have pointed to the fact that Americans and Europeans are contracepting as a reason that they *deserve to be replaced* in their native countries by fresh populations who are "open to life" (though many of them might also be intolerant Muslims). I heard that argument made publicly at the Acton University conference in 2015 by a conservative priest. Most of the (conservative) audience nodded uncertainly, aware in their guts that there was something perverse in Father's logic. You could almost see people thinking, "But he cited *Humanae Vitae*...."

★ ★ ★

No Work for Me—I'm Catholic!

Daniel Schwindt, a columnist for *The American Conservative*, wrote on February 1, 2016, at his Patheos Catholic blog the following revealing lines: "I have abhorred work for as long as I can remember. I don't mean that I'm against exerting myself. I do that all the time, but my exertions, it has always been made abundantly clear, do not qualify as 'work.' Work, as an American institution—work with capital 'W'—is something foreign to my nature. It isn't just that I find it unpleasant and unfulfilling. It is also that I've never been able to force myself to respect it, even way back when I still felt ashamed for that failure. Even when I felt that I was genuinely in the wrong, and that I was in some way sinning through my work-aversion, I couldn't bring myself to see work as a worthwhile endeavor, much less could I see a "career" as anything other than a veritable hell that awaited me....

"Work has been presented to me as a sacrament. It is the religion that surrounds me and that has drowned out all the others. But it isn't mine. I don't believe in it, and the more I see it worshiped, the more repulsive and blasphemous it becomes.

"It is the very opposite of my religion, which is the religion of creative activity. Through all the jobs I have had, and all the jobs I've not had but only seen, insofar as the work was 'work,' it was anti-human. It was the reverse of creative activity.

"God created because to create is divine. He didn't create because he needed employment or because work was good in itself. God does not have a job. The Divine Artist, like just about every artist, is unemployed, and in his unemployment he gives perpetual birth to the cosmos.

"But the world worships work, and America worships with unsurpassed devotion. So great and recognized is this devotion that America acts as the world-priest of the religion of work and productivity. Any refusal to worship at the altar of work is punished by death. But death is better. Starvation is better."[25]

I have encountered not dozens but hundreds of vocal "orthodox Catholics" who adopt stances like those I've just described, especially in the years since Pope Francis assumed the papacy—a development that seems to have emboldened them to come out of the closet. They throng social media and fill up the unpaid blogging spots at Catholic venues. They have found positions at orthodox Catholic publications and at recently founded Catholic liberal arts colleges. They take jobs with "conservative" bishops or worm their way into pro-life organizations—which they try to hijack in favor of "seamless garment" policies that equate poverty programs, gun control, and motorcycle helmet laws with measures to stop the intentional killing of a million babies each year.[26] And mostly, they get away with it.

Clearly, *Humanae Vitae* is no longer an adequate litmus test. The enemies of the Church's real social teaching have figured out that they can use that document to their advantage.

Putative Pro-Lifers and Verbal Pacifism

The Planned Parenthood videos released in 2015 have changed the abortion debate, forcing millions of Americans—those with the courage to watch them—to confront the full humanity of unborn children and the sheer barbarism of organizations like Planned Parenthood who sell their butchered body parts.[27] Repeated efforts by Congressional Republicans came achingly close to stripping that organization of its half billion dollars in annual taxpayer subsidies.[28]

What's the last thing you'd expect in response? That putative pro-lifers would condemn those who had exposed Planned Parenthood's baby parts business, claiming that the Center for Medical Progress *used evil means* to uncover the truth about Planned Parenthood—so evil that Christians should denounce the CMP, so sinister that these videos themselves will backfire and discredit the pro-life movement. Because, you see, the CMP's investigators *told Planned Parenthood employees things that weren't true.* And that is evil. By this logic, the Planned Parenthood videos are the fruit of a poisoned tree and should not even be made public or shared. Like Nazi doctor Josef Mengele's experimental results, or sins we overheard from someone else's confession, we should shun them and help Planned Parenthood keep its secrets hidden.

EWTN columnist Mark Shea is leading the charge against Planned Parenthood's critics. On July 21, 2015, Shea condemned the Center for Medical Progress in an online Catholic radio broadcast, in which he also said that families sheltering Jews during the Holocaust sinned by deceiving the Nazis who hunted those Jews. At 35:30 he quipped, "The issue is not and never has been figuring out how to lie well; the issue is figuring out how to hide your Jews well." Then he chortled heartily.[29]

Curiously, Shea has no track record of condemning the use of deception by police trapping pedophiles, CIA operatives fighting terrorism, or animal rights activists infiltrating factory farms.[30] But Shea has written countless words denouncing pro-life investigative reporters who infiltrated Planned Parenthood,[31] even alleging that these pro-lifers have compromised Catholic morality by "tempting" professional abortionists into sin.[32] You see, the pro-life investigators of Live Action, including Lila Rose, showed up at abortion clinics and made fake appointments, trying to see if the clinics were willing to violate the law. According to Shea, Rose was playing the evil temptress by doing that, urging someone to sin...because they *intended* to give her an abortion, so they sinned as gravely as a murderer who shoots but misses. She "tempted" them to do that, so she is just as guilty.[33] Really?

Clearly Shea doesn't understand the difference between entrapment and legitimate undercover work. If someone is already in the business of habitual acts of evil, presenting him an opportunity to express that fixed intention *in order to stop him* is not considered entrapment under law. Nor is it a sin. By Shea's logic, if a sniper were picking off pedestrians, police who shoved out a mannequin to draw away his fire would be "tempting" him to murder, since he *intended* to shoot a real person. To say that such policemen were guilty of "incitement to murder" would not just be false; it would be slander.

Such absurdities aside, let's examine the question that deserves our serious scrutiny: *to win the trust of the abortionists and obtain the video evidence of their human organ trafficking, the investigators from the Center for Medical Progress lied. And that's always evil.*[34] Or is it?

Not every killing is murder. Is every verbal deception a sinful "lie"? There isn't space here to review two thousand years of the still unsettled theological debate over whether the commandment forbidding you to "bear false witness *against* your neighbor"—which we find in both Divine Revelation and the natural moral law—extends to deceptions *for our neighbor' sake.* Saints and theologians have weighed in on both sides of that question, and so has the *Catechism of the Catholic Church.* In its initial edition, the *Catechism* said, "To lie is to speak or act against the truth in order to lead into error someone *who has the right to know the truth.*"[35] But when the official Latin version came out, that definition had been amended to say, "To lie is to speak or act against the truth in order to lead someone into error."[36] We can't resolve this question by an easy appeal to authority. We must each use our reason to consider it seriously and come to honest conclusions whose implications we're willing to live with. An argument that yields ludicrous conclusions has got a flaw in it somewhere, usually way back in its unexamined premises.

Any principled person will admit that the end does not justify the means. Not if the means is something intrinsically, *that is, under every imaginable circumstance and by its very nature,* evil. To clarify the point, let's choose an extreme example. If it would have beaten Hitler sooner and stopped the Holocaust, should the Allies have been willing to recruit French and Belgian children as suicide bombers? No, because using children as weapons of war is evil, the same kind of evil as the Nazis were committing. You can't use "a little bit" of real evil to fight for the good, a point which lay at the heart of *The Lord of the Rings.* The One Ring is an allegory for any truly evil means, which always corrupts the user.

But the end can reveal an error in the chosen means. Keeping your hands clean and your conscience perfectly shiny is no excuse for letting the real world go to hell, or allowing the vulnerable to suffer at the hands of the utterly ruthless. When Gandhi advised Europe's Jews (and also the Allies) to resist the Nazis by exclusively non-violent means, he played the role of a callous purist—as George Orwell pointed out.[37]

Pacifism is not merely quixotic and self-indulgent. It is actively sinful. It empowers the killers, thugs, and rapists of this fallen world by disarming the forces of justice. When only your own pride or even wellbeing is at stake, it can be right to turn the other cheek. But when the lives of others are involved, that amounts to reckless cowardice empowered by moralistic preening. So, I will argue, does refusing to fool the guilty in order to save the innocent—a stance I call "verbal pacifism."

Here are just a few of the implications of verbal pacifism. The following activities would be intrinsically evil, just like using child suicide bombers against the Nazis—and it would be better to die, and let millions of others be tortured, raped, or killed, rather than engage in them:

- Deceiving the Pharaoh who wished to kill all the newborn male Hebrews—as the midwives did in Exodus 1:15–21 (The Bible tells us that "God dealt well with the midwives.")
- Deceiving priest-hunters by using assumed names, as Jesuit missionaries did in Reformation England, and St. Miguel Pro did in Mexico in the 1920s[38]
- Deceiving the Nazis to rescue Jews from the gas chambers, as Oskar Schindler did[39]
- Distributing false baptismal certificates so that Jews could pass as Gentiles and escape extermination, as John XXIII did during World War II[40]

- Using false documents and false statements in a plot to assassinate Adolf Hitler, like the conspirators working with Dietrich Bonhoeffer, who were aided by Pope Pius XII (who passed their messages via Vatican couriers)[41]
- Deceiving the brutal dictators who hoped to hunt down and torture leftist priests, as Pope Francis did while serving as Archbishop of Buenos Aires[42]
- Posing as a child in online forums in order to catch child porn distributors and pedophiles, as police routinely do—having found it the only effective means of capturing such predators
- Pretending to be an Islamist in order to infiltrate terrorist organizations like al-Qaeda and ISIS, as CIA operatives do
- Misleading criminal suspects about the evidence you have, as police do to obtain truthful confessions without coercion
- Infiltrating an abortion business like Planned Parenthood to see if it is breaking laws about statutory rape and organ trafficking, as Live Action and the Center for Medical Progress did

Any moral philosophy that claims that all these activities are intrinsically evil has got some explaining to do. By insisting on premises that yield such repugnant conclusions, and claiming that the only alternative is a crass and unprincipled pragmatism, verbal pacifists are cutting off their nose to spite their face.

Verbal pacifists' profound confusion can be traced to one of the greatest writers and thinkers in history, St. Augustine, who wrote in *De Mendacio* that it would be wrong to deceive murderers at your door who asked about their hoped-for victim within.[43] (Augustine found falsehood especially repulsive because it had played such a major role in his previous life as a pagan, when he worked as a rhetorician, by his own admission flattering and lying for hire.) Augustine was not a physical pacifist, however, just a

★ ★ ★

A Catholic B.S. Detector

Given some of the things that appear in the "orthodox" Catholic press these days, you might think some people are using the Church and its social teaching as a screen for secular leftist views, for their own dependent lifestyle, or for both.

1. Those on the "orthodox" Catholic Left talk about "Catholic Social Teaching" *a lot*—and they suggest that it is infallible. But as we have already seen in chapter seven, in fact it's a set of wise *suggestions* offered over many centuries by holy men on how to apply the Church's infallible, magisterial teaching on morality to the complex, shifting realities of politics and economics. Leo XIII,[44] Pius XI,[45] and John Paul II[46] each explicitly denied that the Church offers a political or economic system—a "third way" between capitalism and socialism, for instance. It is our job as laymen to take these very broad principles and apply them—determining, for instance, whether a particular welfare program violates subsidiarity.

2. They disparage ordinary work at ordinary jobs, the virtue of thrift, and the need to plan for one's future—pretending that married parents are called to the same mindset as mendi-cant friars vowed to poverty, with no children to educate as faithful, productive citizens.[47]

3. They use their own idiosyncratic readings of Catholic social teaching to justify endorsing pro-choice Democrats.[48]

4. Their contempt for capitalism leads them to denigrate Christian-owned companies like Hobby Lobby threatened by secular big government.[49]

5. They encourage Catholics to act as members of a separate tribe or totalitarian political party, with duties only to the Church and its institutions, and not to our fellow citizens and neighbors.[50]

6. They talk about G. K. Chesterton, who would have starved to death if his wife hadn't run his finances, as an expert on economics and pretend that Chesterton's utopian scheme for wealth-redistribution by the state (distributism) has somehow been endorsed by the Church's Magisterium.[51] No economic system has—though the market economy with a basic social safety net comes closest to matching the principles that Leo XIII unfolded in *Rerum Novarum* and St. John Paul II explained in greater detail in *Centesimus Annus*.

7. They respond to defenders of the market economy with unhinged, explosive rage. On May 31, 2015, Sean Dailey, longtime editor-in-chief of *Gilbert!* magazine (published by the American Chesterton Society) attacked Catholic conservatives on Facebook: "All of you, with your smug contempt for the working poor: how does it feel to fellate the prince of darkness? Do you swallow too? Am I crude? Too bad, because your hatred for the working poor is simply diabolical."[52] I brought this profane public outburst—not Dailey's first—to the attention of his boss, Dale Ahlquist, host of a TV series at EWTN and president of the American Chesterton Society.[53] As of this writing, Dailey is still editor-in-chief of *Gilbert!*. Indeed, just a few months after this pornographic tirade, Dailey spoke in August 2015 to the thirty-fourth Annual Chesterton Conference on (of all things) "Chesterton as a Model of Lay Spirituality." In a public exchange on Facebook with Mr. Dailey, another contributor to *Gilbert!* responded to my own writings on economics by posting a lurid death threat against me and wishing for my eternal damnation[54] (To his credit, Sean Dailey did suggest that the commenter needed to go to Confession; months later he published the commenter's writings on G. K. Chesterton in *Gilbert!* magazine.)

verbal one. While he wouldn't allow you to lie to these would-be killers, if they tried to force their way in, you might be justified in *killing them*. Thomas Aquinas agreed; he likewise condemned all deception, but allowed for defensive wars, and even the use of torture on Christian "heretics."

How can we make sense of such a position, which sees physical violence as almost morally neutral—its merits dependent on the situation at hand—but verbal falsehood as evil beyond excusing? Seminary professor Janet Smith has done the heavy lifting here. In an article for *First Things* provoked by Mark Shea's relentless campaign against pro-life activists, she critiqued the fundamental premise of the Augustinian tradition: that human speech was created exclusively for speaking the truth, and we sinfully pervert it by using it deceptively, in however worthy a cause.

As Smith writes, that claim is correct as far as it goes. Just so, human hands were not made to kill or fight with other men, but to tend the Garden of Eden. However, given the Fall, God permits us and even commands us to use our bodies in new ways that would have been unnecessary and wrong in an unfallen world. Thus Christian soldiers and policemen can use deadly force when needed in defense of the innocent. Why should our words be held to such a radically different standard from our bodies?)[55]

At this point in the argument, someone is bound to start misquoting scripture, pointing to the fact that Christ is called "the Word," and suggesting that what we say is morally more significant than what we do, since it reflects our inner selves more purely or perfectly or something. That is Gnostic nonsense. Christ saved us not by what He said but by what He did. On the Cross. With His body.

In the early Church, non-Christians were invited to attend the liturgy long enough to hear the Gospel—but then ushered out before the sacrifice of Christ's sacred Body and Blood. Even today, we let the unbaptized read the Bible, but not partake in Communion. And so on. It is frankly bizarre to treat words, made by man, as more significant than bodies that took life from God.

Just so, the words of intrepid undercover reporters, spoken to professional killers who have no right to expect the truth, were nothing sacred. What was sacred were the lives of those tiny, helpless humans whom Planned Parenthood sells like scrap metal or chicken parts. We must choose our words very carefully in such innocent children's defense. We will each someday be called to answer for what we did or didn't do to help "the least" among us.

"Celibate" Gay Catholic Wedding Ceremonies in Church?

Identity politics are seemingly unstoppable in this age of social fragmentation. Disgruntled groups with political agendas have learned to ape the tactics and rhetoric of the upright and justified Civil Rights Movement, and apply them to much more dubious causes—from legalizing abortion to dismantling heterosexual marriage. Once a group of people claims that they are receiving unequal treatment, it's easy to get the compliant liberal media to make your new cause out to be the heir of Martin Luther King, Jr. and the Freedom Riders, and your opponents the newest crop of bigoted southern sheriffs. Soon your group will have the political upper hand, and its opponents will be smeared as bigots, outside the political mainstream and even polite society. That has happened with amazing speed to opponents of same-sex marriage in just the past few years, with bakers and florists facing prosecution and crippling fines for following their consciences—and churches facing threats from local governments for hiring policies that follow Catholic teaching.

Now, alas, that tactic is having its impact in orthodox Catholic circles, on people who seem to wish to remain within the Church but whose thinking seems to be sadly clouded by gay identity politics. If they prevail in their attempt to alter Catholics' thinking on homosexuality, they will spread confusion to millions of otherwise faithful Catholics and add their voices to the massive pressure that secular society and a hostile state are exerting on the Church to cave in and start performing same-sex marriages—as mainline Protestant churches have already begun to do.

In 2013, Catholic pro-life activists and social commentators Austin Ruse and Deacon Jim Russell identified a growing movement which Ruse dubbed "the New Homophiles." (Its partisans prefer the more anodyne title "Spiritual Friendship.") Ruse noted that this group consists of people who suffer from same-sex attraction and affirm the chastity that the Christian faith demands. But these writers and activists are "out and proud; they insist upon being known by their same-sex attractions."[56] Just like black or Asian people, these self-consciously "gay Catholics" seem to believe, with Lady Gaga, that they were "born that way," and they talk about their sexual attraction to members of their own sex as if it were a gift from God. They believe that their homosexuality gives them special insights, including, as one has argued, a "more intuitive understanding of certain forms of mysticism."[57]

At the site "Spiritual Friendship," Mike Allen has accused heterosexual Christians of something he calls "Straight Fragility" and argued that the Christian "church's exaltation of the nuclear family isn't biblical, but cultural."[58] Melinda Selmys is a columnist for EWTN's *National Catholic Register* and for *First Things* magazine. A married Catholic mother who nevertheless identifies as "Queer," she refers to her sacramental union with her heterosexual husband as a "mixed orientation marriage."[59] Perhaps the best known of these authors is Eve Tushnet, who in her book *Gay and Catholic* has called for the Church to encourage profound lifelong friendships between same-sex-attracted couples, which ought to be blessed in quasi-sacramental ceremonies at the altar.[60] But those relationships, of gay or lesbian couples in deep, lifelong friendships blessed in a church, will be celibate. Of *course* they will. No "near occasion of mortal sin" here, people. Move along! Of course, Pope Francis's dithering in the footnotes of *Amoris Laetitiae* over whether couples committing adultery—because one or both of them were previously married to someone else—need to stop having sex if they wish to receive Holy Communion isn't terribly helpful here.

Deacon Jim Russell, who has carefully studied the writings of the "New Homophiles" and engaged with them extensively, warns:

> As philosophers and theologians know, a mistake buried deep in your premises will have long-term, serious consequences. Put bluntly: How plausible is it to believe that God made you a certain way, with sexual attractions that you have accepted as unchangeable, while holding on to the judgment that acting on

these attractions would be sinful? To believe that God "made" you gay, with overwhelming feelings He will never allow you to act on? Today our culture screams at us from every medium—including our nation's highest court—that sexual "diversity" is a sacred good. Believers everywhere call the historic Christian teaching into question. When a person's commitment to chastity rests on such a shaky foundation, at some point, it's likely to bend and even break.[61]

Joseph Sciambra, a courageous Catholic who became an eloquent apostle for chastity after hellish years in the gay lifestyle—including appearances in gay porn films—warns against the "spiritual friendship" proposals as a "slippery slide into gay sex."[62]

As Robert Reilly has pointed out, if we encourage people to build their identity on the shifting sand of sexual impulses—granting that people *are* gay, rather than accurately describing them as fellow creatures of God afflicted with an abiding temptation—then the power of identity politics will pressure the Church to accommodate their lobbying group's demands. In fact, the 2 percent or so of human beings who experience same-sex attraction are much more like people inclined to alcoholism, or clinical depression. We should (and the Church does) offer pastoral outreach to help

A Book You're Not Supposed to Read

Catholic author Robert Reilly, former head of the Voice of America under George W. Bush, is one of the most consistently courageous and incisive writers alive. As we have already seen, he was willing to challenge the hostility of Islam to reason and science in *The Closing of the Muslim Mind*—a book every worried Westerner needs to read. But Reilly really earned a pundit's Bronze Star for Valor when he published *Making Gay Okay: How Rationalizing Homosexual Behavior Is Changing Everything*—which explains in sober philosophical detail why the Church simply cannot accept or in any way bless same-sex relationships. (Tellingly, Reilly had trouble finding conservatives willing to endorse or even review his book—they knew that the knives were out.)[63] Perhaps even more important, Reilly shows the danger in treating people's sexual temptations as constitutive of their identity.

them resist temptation, find consolation, and become saints. (From what I can see in his writing, Mr. Sciambra is well on the way—and will make it to Heaven long before a mediocrity like me.) But calls for the Church to accept and celebrate the gay "orientation" are profoundly dangerous. While the "New Homophiles" for the moment insist that they only want the Church to bless *celibate* same-sex couples, and while they currently treat homosexual desires as a call to chastity, that seems like the thin end of the wedge. For the Church to claim that God made someone gay is to open the door for that person to act on the desires that God apparently gave him. And the Church can never do that, without betraying the Gospel.

The "Benedict Option": Hiding Our Light under a Bushel in the Vain Hope the World Will Leave Us Alone

In *Obergefell v. Hodges*, the 2015 decision legalizing same-sex marriage in fifty states, the Supreme Court redefined both liberty and marriage, and opened the door to punitive taxes, crippling lawsuits, and criminal prosecutions against Christian churches, schools, and hospitals. The Court knew exactly what it was doing. During the oral arguments in the case, Justice Samuel Alito had asked Solicitor General Donald Verrilli whether acceptance of same-sex marriage would subject Christian churches to the treatment once accorded Bob Jones University, which lost its tax-exempt status because its ban on interracial dating contradicted federal policy. Verrilli seemed a little taken aback, then answered yes, "it's certainly going to be an issue."

Imagine if your house of worship needed to turn a hefty profit, so it could pay the same taxes on its property and income as a casino or a strip joint.

By rejecting natural marriage, the U.S. Supreme Court freed up the feds to target the Catholic Church and the Southern Baptist Convention, among other religious organizations that cling to the classical definition of marriage. (In theory, the government might also take aim at every mosque in America, but something tells me that the mosques are likely to get a pass.) Remember that the Obama administration had already tried to force faithful Christians—including the Little Sisters of the Poor—to provide abortifacients to their employees. Attacking churches' tax-exempt status over Biblical sexual ethics is peanuts compared to that.

This is not the script for a paranoid, low-budget Christian film. Stripping churches of non-profit status is exactly what many progres-

> ★ ★ ★
> ## Second Class Citizens
> If the federal government yanks the Catholic Church's tax exemption, it will be effectively establishing a two-tiered religious system akin to that in communist China, with the churches that are still preaching the unadulterated gospel banished to the fringes of society along with the white supremacists. And the media will present it as progress: *love has won, now it's time to shoot the prisoners.*

sives plan. Pundits are already calling for the end of tax exemptions for churches—not on fringe websites, but in *Time* magazine.[64]

And sadly, that same publication has featured a call by The *American Conservative* blogger and former Catholic Rod Dreher for conservatives to abandon our alliance with Republican politicians who promise to protect us from persecution. As Dreher wrote, "Voting Republican and other failed culture war strategies are not going to save us now." Instead, he argued, faithful Christians should withdraw into scattered apolitical enclaves of like-minded fellow believers—in the hope that the gay totalitarians and their fellow travelers will decide to let our kids alone.[65]

Is it time to give up, hide, and hope for the best? Should we throw down the civic weapons we still have, which God provided us? Shall we surrender America to the sex radicals, and leave our children without the liberty that we inherited from our parents? Is it moral to abandon our fellow citizens and neighbors to the ever-escalating demands of the secular culture of death? Is it time to dissolve the activist divisions of the pro-life movement, which has made so many strides, and accept that abortion on demand, up until the minute of birth, will be legal in America forever?

All of these outcomes would flow from the misnamed "Benedict Option" favored by Dreher, who for years has advocated a sort of irresponsible Christian separatism. Actually, the notion of laymen refusing the duties of citizenship and withdrawing into enclaves has nothing whatsoever to do with the historical St. Benedict. As I wrote at the Intercollegiate Review,

> That mystical ex-hermit never tried to organize laymen, but monks—men who could live and work together only because they took vows of celibacy, poverty, and obedience. Benedict drafted his famous Rule to teach monks how better to obey these particular, difficult vows. Married people make very different promises. They don't obey an abbot but are subject to each other. They're called to be fertile, not celibate; thrifty and prudent, not poor. The proper bourgeois virtues of responsible Christian parents are almost the diametrical opposite of monastic communalism. Most historical attempts to found such communities among married couples have ended in farce or disaster....
>
> The worst thing Benedict and his followers had to fear were bandits—and renegade monks.
>
> Today Christians face something that behaves much more like Islam. It is a rising empire of aggressive secularism, with a deep historical grudge against our faith. Gay activists, New Atheists, radical feminists, population controllers, multiculturalists, and other powerful interest groups see orthodox Christianity as their enemy. We once wielded power throughout the culture as they lived on the margins, and now they are looking for payback. They will know where to find us. . . .

We must fight for our freedom from an increasingly arbitrary and all-encompassing government. We must defend our property rights, our religious rights, our right to defend ourselves and raise our children with our beliefs. All those fights are political, and to say otherwise is simply slothful and escapist.

At the same time, we must fight for internal freedom from the deep addiction to sin. Otherwise, all the civic freedom in the world won't save our souls.[66]

I understand battle fatigue. I started exercising Christian citizenship in 1975 when I rang doorbells collecting signatures for New York's Right to Life Party at age eleven. I have been active in one way or another ever since—earning ostracism at Yale for defying gay rights groupthink; facing down most of my grad school professors across the picket line at an abortion clinic while one of them recorded our faces with a video camera; leading a successful fight (with a budget of one hundred dollars) against a state-wide multiculturalist pro-gay brainwashing mandate for the entire LSU system; and so on, ever since. I am sure that many readers have similar stories to tell.

A Book You're Not Supposed to Read

One of the greatest saints of the twentieth century is Josemaría Escrivá, founder of Opus Dei. (No, I'm not a member.) He pioneered a theology of work that resonated with St. Benedict's embrace of humble, faithful labor and St. John Paul II's endorsement of the sanctifying power of work in *Laborem Exercens*. In his collection of lucid, uplifting homilies called *Christ Is Passing By* (Scepter, 1985) St. Josemaría challenges Catholics to shed their pretense of changing the world via grandiose or separatist schemes and instead to fill the state in life that God has given them with faithfulness and charity—inspiring and attracting nonbelievers in the same way early Christians did, by the power of good example.

A Book You're Not Supposed to Read

Philip Jenkins's brilliant *The Lost History of Christianity* makes for a wrenching read. It chronicles the vast and vibrant Christian churches that once extended from Antioch to China, whose well-schooled believers almost equaled the number of recently baptized Western barbarians as late as 1000 AD. All that is gone now, with the last few brave, abandoned believers cowering on mountaintops hiding from ISIS while the West concentrates on creating "safe spaces" free from "transphobia." What happened to the great churches of the East? As Jenkins reports, one church after another *lost the protection of the government*. At first persecution was mild, and tolerant Muslim or Confucian rulers would sometimes leave breathing space for local Christians. But finally, over centuries, the slow drip of humiliation, punitive taxes, and periodic massacres, ground down all the Christians, till no one was left. Once-mighty monasteries are now dusty masjids, or abandoned ruins. Cathedrals are now mosques or museums. Once-Christian cities from Constantinople to Mosul are now almost wholly purged of Christians.[67] Churches can withstand a lot—including even the sixty-plus years of communist oppression in China. And Christ has promised us that the Church universal will prevail to the end. But we know from history that Christianity can be purged from entire regions. Should we invite such an appalling outcome, by retreating to holy enclaves?

And like you, I am bone tired. Worn down, frustrated, and tempted to curl up in apathy and just binge-watch *Daredevil* on Netflix. But as that show reminds us, "The world is on fire." I won't just hunker down and watch Rome burn. I am not fireproof and neither are you. Nor are your kids. You may decide that you've had enough, that you're tired of worrying about other people's unborn children, and their marriages, and their intergenerational dependency on welfare programs, and the wretched public schools, and the low-skill immigration that drives down their wages. You're sick of it all. You just want to hang around with your fellow Christians and live your life in peace. You'd like to crawl into a cell where you can hide.

But there is nowhere to hide, no ghetto so obscure that the gay totalitarians will leave you alone. Think of all the money that Germany spent persecuting a single homeschooling family, the Romeikes—whose daughter they seized and placed in a psychiatric facility because her parents had violated Germany's Hitler-era law forbidding homeschooling.[68] In 2016, the Norwegian government seized a Christian family's children, accusing the parents of "indoctrinating" them—and only returned them after an international firestorm that involved appeals to the European parliament.[69] Persecution like this is coming here soon, if we don't fight tooth and nail. Remember the thousands of bureaucrats who dutifully audited Tea Party groups for the IRS? Soon thousands more will be scrutinizing your church, its school, and every Christian organization in the country. The anti-religious Left has tasted blood, and intends to feed. Even if you piously decide to turn the other cheek and congratulate yourself on being persecuted for Christ, you have no right to make that decision for your children or your neighbor.

It is delusional to expect most Christian families to pass along the Faith in wartime conditions for generation upon generation. It almost certainly will not happen. God can grant a miracle, but as Our Lord made clear in the desert, we should not test Him by jumping off the Temple Mount.

Here let me anticipate and knock down the straw man that Rod Dreher trots out every time he is contradicted. *Of course it is not enough to simply vote for pro-Christian conservatives.*[70] No one has ever claimed that it is. We must witness our faith in dozens of non-political ways, by building strong Christian families and institutions, caring for the poor, sick, and dying— through exactly the kinds of institutions that progressives intend to co-opt or close, using same-sex marriage or "transgender rights" as the steamroller in a war on civil society. If we let them get away with that—by abandoning our solemn responsibilities as Christian citizens to defend human rights and the common good—then we act like hirelings and abandon the lambs to the wolves. We will answer for it to the Good Shepherd who laid down His life to save them.

When Christians Give Up on Freedom

Here's a quick smell test that I use when someone presents me with what he considers a brave and "radical" interpretation of the Gospel: are this theory's implications so appalling—not just for me, but for the whole human race—that they would make me hope from the depths of my very soul *that Christianity isn't true?* Does this reading of the Christian message:

- So outrage our natural instincts that it makes God seem like a sadistic monster or a bumbling incompetent Who made men fundamentally wrong—and now expects us to torture ourselves to correct His initial mistake?
- Suggest that the Fall obliterated from the human heart any inkling of the Good, effectively re-creating the race of man according to Satan's specifications?
- Cut Christianity off completely from Judaism by making nonsense of the Old Testament—suggesting that the Pharisees and Sadducees were right to reject Jesus?

Such theories stink of brimstone. Gnostic attempts to remake Christianity as a hatred of life on earth are not so much real intellectual options as temptations from the Devil aimed at the virtue of Faith. And countless saints have warned us to "flee the occasion of sin." *Any version of Christianity that would send a reasonable person on a quest for the nearest synagogue is false.* Catholicism is, in the words of G. K. Chesterton an "outline of sanity," not a pinched creed hostile to human nature.

Employing the Brimstone Test has saved me going down countless blind alleys over the years. It helped me to shrug off the fringe arguments of those who claim that all non-Catholics are doomed to hell, and that for this grim reason we Catholics should seek to reinstate the Inquisition—using totalitarian means to save as many souls as possible from plummeting into the Fire.

The Brimstone Test helped me quickly reject the idea—which bedeviled some in the early Church—that really every Christian ought to live as a monk or nun, leaving marriage as a quasi-pagan halfway house that the truly devout should reject. The same test helps me know right off the bat what to think of Christians who call for pacifism or open borders (see chapters eight and nine).

I used the Brimstone Test again when I read a famous essay, "Catholicism and the Bourgeois Mind" (1935), by Catholic historian Christopher Dawson, whom we have briefly met in chapter seven. In that essay Dawson (who was born into money and later handed an endowed chair at Harvard) argued that any *kind of financial planning*, any effort to turn a profit or provide for your children's future, *is profoundly unchristian.*[71] All Christians, even fathers of families, should live as St. Francis did, existing from day to day on whatever tithes come over the transom. Hence *business, the free market, banking, insurance, savings, inheritance, and children's college funds are all fundamentally evil.* Soldiers, noblemen, artists, clergy, kings, and even conquistadors make better Christians than businessmen, said Dawson.

Dawson's argument is false but it isn't dead. In fact, his ideas have found new apostles. Students at the small, orthodox Catholic college where I used to teach used his argument to justify making reckless decisions about their lives.[72] And Dawson is serving as inspiration to a broad and influential movement of Catholics who reject business and the free market—and indeed freedom itself—as forbidden fruit that fell from the Enlightenment's poison tree. In such Christian circles you will hear sneering references to "liberalism," by which the authors don't mean the ideology of the Democrats. Instead, what they're rejecting is the worldwide movement for freedom—religious, political, and economic—that might be better called "classical liberalism."

It's a movement America's founders imported from England, and its roots reach back beyond the Reformation to the Catholic England that gave us the

Magna Carta. This liberalism is the heritage of the Anglosphere, and its benevolent effects can be seen from India to Australia, from Texas to the Falkland Islands. Pope St. John Paul II, who had endured in communist Poland the only viable modern alternative to classical liberalism—ideological tyranny—wrote in *Memory and Identity* that such liberalism reflects in politics the Christian vision of the person, as a free, responsible being answerable finally only to God.[73] Yes, it is possible to take such liberalism too far—as some libertarians do when they follow Murray Rothbard, embracing abortion rights or rejecting all welfare programs. But a firm grasp of classical natural law is sufficient to avoid stumbling into such extremes. Indeed, a free society based on a firm grasp of natural law seems to be the closest system imaginable to what Catholic social teaching actually calls for. See the writings of the Reverend John Courtney Murray, the work of the Acton Institute for Religion and Liberty, and the political platforms of pro-life statesmen who champion Constitutional freedom, such as Senators Ted Cruz and Mike Lee.

This broad-based movement of liberalism was the force behind demands for religious, economic, and political freedom first in England, then in America, and then around the world. This freedom movement was what caught fire in Poland and brought down the Soviet empire. Such freedom is what persecuted Christians seek in the Middle East, and dissidents call for in China. Our Constitution's guarantees of this freedom serve in America as the last, fragile bulwark against government repression of Christianity, such as the kind we saw with the Obama administration's attempt against Hobby Lobby and the Little Sisters of the Poor.

And now there are Catholics who reject such freedom as incompatible with the Gospel. They crave a return of the old paternalistic order, which saw priests collude with governments to maintain a religious monopoly, suppressing non-Catholic speech, outlawing Protestant churches, and censoring the press. The Church renounced this power, all too belatedly, in the mid-1960s at Vatican II—but there are Catholics out there who reject the

Council's teaching, or try to get around it by looking for loopholes in the text. Nor are such arguments confined to mimeographed tracts distributed at coffee hours after Latin Masses; ironically they appear in *First Things* magazine, which was founded as an ecumenical journal by a Catholic priest to further the alliance of faithful Christians and classical liberal.[74]

And more common by far are Christians—we are seeing them in various denominations now—who, skipping lightly over the question of whether the state should impose their religious ideas by force, turn their attention almost obsessively to the economy. Classical liberalism entails a basically free economy, where citizens strive to maximize their wellbeing by adapting what they produce to what others wish to consume—allowing the billions of choices of individuals, measured and implemented by the price system, to coordinate the vast and incomprehensibly complex neural net of human cooperation, instead of handing that power to bureaucrats and "scientific" managers, as the Soviets tried to do.

Most Christians favor a safety net (as I do) designed to protect those who cannot take care of themselves, one constructed with respect for subsidiarity—the principle protecting the free institutions of civil society, favoring voluntary over coerced charity, and keeping power as decentralized as possible. But there are other Christians out there who seem to oppose freedom in principle.[75]

Eastern Orthodox theologian David Bentley Hart has used the pages of *First Things* to preach what we might call "Illiberal Christianity."[76] It's an ideology that would seem to flow from resentment of the dynamism, unpredictability, and spontaneity of an economy driven by the free choices of billions of people, without the guidance of wiser souls with advanced humanities or theology degrees. But Illiberal Christians are running out of cudgels with which to beat the free economy.

In past decades, it was perhaps plausible to blame the market economy for failing to serve the interests of the global poor. Cold hard statistics now show

★ ★ ★

Marx and Marcion

The entirety of the Old Testament is predicated upon God promising blessedness, prosperity, happiness, and freedom on earth to the Jewish people if they obey Him. Christianity teaches us that there is another and higher happiness to be found in the next life. But God could never have promised worldly blessings to His people in the first place if wealth were an "intrinsic evil," as David Bentley Hart pretends. Hart's rejection of life's good things—such as better prospects for one's children—which Jews craved from Abraham onward strikes me as frankly Marcionite, partaking of the early Christian heresy that starkly opposed the "wicked" and "unspiritual" Old Testament to the New. Theologian Hans Urs von Balthasar was the first to note the deeply Marcionite, and sometimes frankly anti-Semitic, biases of certain modern radicals who reject the market economy as evil.[78]

that in the past twenty years, economic globalization has lifted more than a billion human beings from the grinding misery of absolute poverty. India, China, South Korea, and parts of Africa have moved or are quickly moving out of the perennial cycle of subsistence agriculture and periodic famines.[77]

Of course, it was only the market economy that, between the early nineteenth and mid–twentieth centuries, lifted the populations of Western Europe and America from the perennial want and anxiety that characterized most of human existence.

Illiberal Christians know by now that the economic effect of classical liberalism and the free economy on the poor is overwhelmingly beneficial. Apparently, they just don't care. Since they cannot blame freedom for global poverty, they now damn it for creating global wealth, which engenders "consumerism." The market feeds people's bodies, and thereby endangers their souls. As Hart writes in *First Things*, the market system cannot "coexist indefinitely with a culture informed by genuine Christian conviction. Even the fact of the system's necessary reliance on immense private wealth makes it a moral problem from the vantage of the Gospel, for the simple reason that the New Testament treats such wealth not merely as a spiritual danger, and not merely as a blessing that should not be misused, but as an intrinsic evil."

Hart goes on to say, "In the Sermon on the Plain's list of beatitudes and woes, [Jesus] not only tells the poor that the kingdom belongs to them, but explicitly tells the rich that, having had their pleasures in this world, they shall have none in the world to come. He condemns those who buy up properties and create large estates for themselves. You cannot serve both God and mammon."

But the Church has never regarded wealth as evil in itself.[79] We learn from the Gospels and the Church's traditions that we must imitate Christ, Who healed the sick and sought to alleviate worldly suffering. Indeed, the extraordinary and Christ-like work of Christian doctors and nurses, teachers, and abolitionists, is all devoted to alleviating suffering. If suffering is in fact spiritually preferable to decent comfort and freedom, then Christians have no business trying our best to stamp it out, *we ought to be spreading it.* Imagining the highly "spiritual" austerity which Hart prefers to modern prosperity, I cannot help thinking of the program favored by Ingsoc in Orwell's *1984*, which was organized around suppressing pleasure of any kind. If that really were Christianity, then (as Catholic novelist Flannery O'Connor said of another heresy), "To hell with it."

The free market's success in uplifting the poor did not cure the resentment of the Illiberal Christians. One begins to wonder whether their real motivation might be a visceral, aesthetic, pseudo-spiritual disgust at the outcome of freedom, resulting in ordinary people making choices of which intellectuals disapprove—picking country music over string quartets, suburbs over historic neighborhoods, and *Guideposts* magazine over Carmelite mysticism.

Respect for the dignity and autonomy of others, and the realization that God is at work in their consciences every bit as powerfully as in their own, should teach elitists to reject the use of force to train other human beings "for their own good" like recalcitrant pets. As early as 1850, the great

Catholic classical liberal Frédéric Bastiat diagnosed the satanic pride involved in presuming to engineer human souls. As Bastiat wrote of social- ists, so we must now say of Illiberal Christians, they:

> ...look upon people as raw material to be formed into social combinations. This is so true that, if by chance, the socialists have any doubts about the success of these combinations, they will demand that a small portion of mankind be set aside to experiment upon....
>
> In the same manner, an inventor makes a model before he constructs the full-sized machine; the chemist wastes some chemicals—the farmer wastes some seeds and land—to try out an idea.
>
> But what a difference there is between the gardener and his trees, between the inventor and his machine, between the chemist and his elements, between the farmer and his seeds! And in all sincerity, the socialist thinks that there is the same difference between him and mankind!...To these intellectuals and writers, the relationship between persons and the legislator appears to be the same as the relationship between the clay and the potter.[80]

The Stench of Corruption: Child Abuse

A well-funded organization with a carefully groomed philanthropic public image and hundreds of millions of dollars (some of it in U.S. federal fund- ing or contracts) turns out to be allowing the systematic sexual abuse of children on its watch—in fact to be bending its efforts not toward stopping such abuse, but to covering it up from peering eyes and saving the culprits from prosecution. Intrepid journalists get wind of this abuse, and through dogged efforts expose the enablers of it. But no one goes to jail. Still, the organization is gravely discredited in the minds of those willing to face the facts.

What did I just describe—the Catholic Church in America, or Planned Parenthood? The answer, sadly, is both.

In February 2016, I had a searing experience that every Catholic should share: I went to see the powerfully written, beautifully acted movie *Spotlight*, starring Michael Keaton, Rachel McAdams, Mark Ruffalo, and Stanley Tucci. The film was highly praised and won the Academy Award for Best Picture—deservedly so. There wasn't an exploitative or manipulative moment in it. Instead, it showed with sober storytelling how honest, old-fashioned journalism at its best can be the servant of truth, the common good, and the innocence of children. The "Spotlight" reporter team at the *Boston Globe* won a Pulitzer Prize for the more than two hundred stories they published exposing hundreds of predator priests and thousands of conspiratorial acts by the Boston Archdiocese to cover their crimes. I think they deserved a papal medal, too, for their service to the Church.

The film depicts the appalling impact of child sexual abuse by criminals in the priesthood—and the even more disturbing reaction of senior clergy, not just in Boston, but all across the country. As the *Dallas Morning News*

The Gospel of the Grand Inquisitor

One of the greatest works of nineteenth-century literature, Dostoevsky's *The Brothers Karamazov*, adumbrates the eventual merging of socialist and religious Illiberals into a single movement that would suppress the unruly desires of the vulgar, grasping masses and herd them into orderly ghettos, walled in by coercion. Dostoevsky's dystopia is the "heavenly city" that would result if the Illiberals had their way. The Gospel they are preaching belongs not to Jesus Christ, but to the Grand Inquisitor: "Man is tormented by no greater anxiety than to find someone quickly to whom he can hand over that great gift of freedom with which the ill-fated creature is born."

I was so fascinated by the figure of the Grand Inquisitor that I wrote a whole book about it—a graphic novel imagining what it would be like if the Vatican itself adopted his philosophy, deciding to soften the Gospel and obscure Church moral teachings in order to spare people's feelings: *The Grand Inquisitor* (Crossroad, 2008). Thank goodness we don't have to worry about that now, do we?

documented in 2002, *two bishops out of three* in the United States covered up such abuse.[81] They shuffled predator priests from parish to parish, sent them for useless New Age "counseling," used legal threats and bribes to silence victims, and pulled political strings to discourage cops and prosecutors from sending these perverts to prison. What motivated all this? Partly bad, liberal theology, which first gave the priestly pederasts (like everyone else) in the Vatican II generation permission to explore their sexuality without reference to the guidance of Church teaching, and then refused to consider justice out of a misguided notion of mercy. But mostly, plain and simple corruption—the institutional willingness to put the interests of fellow insiders (in this case, priests) ahead of the safety and innocence of children.

Churchmen who cover up for sexual criminals enjoy long and comfortable careers amid circles of well-meaning pious folk who want to believe the best of them. It's good that outsiders stepped up to do some of the necessary policing, providing a crucial watchdog service for America's children.

Would that the media provided a similar watchdog service for the statutory rape victims Planned Parenthood is victimizing a second time by helping their rapists cover up the crime with secret abortions. As Catholic pro-life activist Lila Rose and the other undercover investigators at Live Action were able to document in undercover videotapes, numerous Planned Parenthood staffers demonstrated their willingness to help adult abusers—including pimps with stables full of trafficked teen prostitutes—get them birth control and abortions without reporting the crimes to the police.[82]

In the light of the *Boston Globe*'s reporting, in 2002 the U.S. bishops imposed a policy of "one strike and you're out" on the priests who serve under them: a single credible accusation *should* now get priests removed from service—and reported to police. (In practice, not all bishops are complying.)[83] Tellingly, the bishops didn't create a policy for punishing their own. It was only in June 2016 that Pope Francis trumpeted a new mechanism for removing bishops who behave like Boston's Bernard Law or Los Angeles's Roger Mahony—leaders who acted with callous disregard for the safety of innocent children, but doting concern for church insurance premiums and their own political influence.[84] It remains to be seen whether this mechanism will ever in fact be employed. As *the Guardian* reports, in the meantime:

> The Catholic church in Pennsylvania has been accused of employing "mafia-like" tactics in a campaign to put pressure on individual Catholic lawmakers who support state legislation that would give victims of sexual abuse more time to sue their abusers.
>
> The lobbying campaign against the legislation is being led by Philadelphia archbishop Charles Chaput, a staunch conservative who recently created a stir after inadvertently sending an email to a state representative Jamie Santora, in which he accused the lawmaker of "betraying" the church and said Santora would suffer "consequences" for his support of the legislation. The email was also sent to a senior staff member in Chaput's office, who was apparently the only intended recipient.
>
> The email has infuriated some Catholic lawmakers, who say they voted their conscience in support of the legislation on behalf of sexual abuse victims. One Republican legislator, Mike Vereb, accused the archbishop of using mafia-style tactics.[85]

What I'm waiting for next is the *Guardian* coverage and a high-budget, A-list Hollywood film depicting Planned Parenthood's systematic abuse of children, including not only underage girls, but the more than three hundred thousand babies it aborts every year; its illegal profiteering in the stolen body parts of butchered babies; the shoddy and inadequate health care it uses as a fig leaf for its abortion business; the half-billion dollars it gets from the U.S. taxpayer each year despite the pro-life Hyde Amendment; its vast network of political donations to abortion boosters like Hillary Clinton; and, for good measure, Planned Parenthood's origin as a white racist eugenics organization aimed at (in the words of an editorial that appeared in Margaret Sanger's *Birth Control Review*) arranging for "more children from the fit, less from the unfit."[86]

That's a movie I'd go to see. Because I have seen the raw reporting on which it would be based: Lila Rose's videotapes, plus the dozen undercover videos created by David Daleiden and the other heroic journalists at the Center for Medical Progress—videos which Democratic legislators and staffers (including "pro-choice" "Catholics" like Nancy Pelosi) refused to watch when they were shown on Capitol Hill, which biased judges have tried to ban, and which might land their makers not a Pulitzer Prize, but a twenty-year term in prison.[87]

If it ever got made, the Planned Parenthood version of *Spotlight* would be a Catholic movie too. Daleiden and his partner Sandra Merritt, who face the threat of imprisonment, are devout Catholics. In the decades when Planned Parenthood was worming its way into respectability by frightening mainline Protestants about the threat of "excessive" fertility among American blacks, Jews, and Catholic immigrants, our bishops took the lead in combating its propaganda. They fought against the laws that Planned Parenthood successfully imposed in thirteen states, mandating the sterilization or castration of people who failed that era's primitive, culturally biased IQ tests. American Catholics including Monsignor John Ryan argued that the best way to help the poor was to grow the economy and offer them jobs, instead of culling them like cattle.[88]

We have already seen how, when eugenics somehow lost its luster in the wake of the Holocaust, Planned Parenthood switched its story and discovered that instead of a flood of "human weeds" and "waste," to quote Margaret Sanger,[89] what threatened social progress was a "population explosion" that would devastate the planet—resulting in massive famines and resource wars, as doomsters such as Paul Ehrlich warned America about on Johnny Carson's top-rated *Tonight* show. Again, Planned Parenthood's story sold, and again the Catholic Church stood almost alone in rejecting Planned Parenthood's solution: massive contraception, and now abortion—in some places like China, coerced abortion, a policy that the local Planned Parenthood energetically helped to implement.[90]

Today the pro-life, pro-family movement is happily ecumenical. While the worst Catholic bishops are as bad as any mainline Protestant leader, the best Protestant laymen are praying alongside priests and nuns outside of abortion clinics across the country. We are joining hands to support pro-life, pro-family candidates and marching together to defend our First Amendment freedoms. Surely Our Lord is pleased at such progress toward "that they all may be one"(John 17:21).

Signs of Hope and Opportunity for Catholics

This is the single most hopeful development for the Church in the past fifty years—the coming together of faithful Christians across once-bitter denominational lines around the issues of "the culture war." Leftists (and political pacifists like "Benedict Option" promoter Rod Dreher) believe that with the Supreme Court's approval of same-sex marriage, those wars are finally over. The Church and its allies have been comprehensively crushed, and all that remains is to mop up the wounded. As leftist Harvard Law professor Mark Tushnet (an anti-Christian intellectual and the father of Catholic "New Homophile" organizer Eve Tushnet) wrote, religious conservatives ought to be treated like the defeated Nazi Germans or Japanese:

> The culture wars are over; they lost, we won. Remember, they
> were the ones who characterized constitutional disputes as

culture wars (see Justice Scalia in *Romer v. Evans*, and the Wikipedia entry for culture wars, which describes conservative activists, not liberals, using the term.) And they had opportunities to reach a cease fire, but rejected them in favor of a scorched earth policy. The earth that was scorched, though, was their own. (No conservatives demonstrated any interest in trading off recognition of LGBT rights for "religious liberty" protections. Only now that they've lost the battle over LGBT rights, have they made those protections central—seeing them, I suppose, as a new front in the culture wars. But, again, they've already lost the war.) For liberals, the question now is how to deal with the losers in the culture wars. That's mostly a question of tactics. My own judgment is that taking a hard line ("You lost, live with it") is better than trying to accommodate the losers, who—remember—defended, and are defending, positions that liberals regard as having no normative pull at all. Trying to be nice to the losers didn't work well after the Civil War, nor after *Brown*. (And taking a hard line seemed to work reasonably well in Germany and Japan after 1945.) I should note that LGBT activists in particular seem to have settled on the hard-line approach, while some liberal academics defend more accommodating approaches. When specific battles in the culture wars were being fought, it might have made sense to try to be accommodating after a local victory, because other related fights were going on, and a hard line might have stiffened the opposition in those fights. But the war's over, and we won.[91]

That's the same message given, with a different emotional spin, by advocates of the "Benedict Option," who add to it only a mewling hope that our triumphant opponents will be magnanimous in victory. They won't. It's not in their nature. The armies of tolerance are not going to tolerate us, any more than radicalized Muslims watching their numbers and influence grow in Europe are going to soak in Western liberalism and turn into peaceful Swedes. Indeed, there are many resemblances between the treatment that faithful Christians face under aggressive secularism and their condition in traditional Muslim societies such as Pakistan. If the anti-Christian Left succeeds, our freedom to evangelize will be legally circumscribed. Our right to educate our children as we see fit will be subject to laws that are biased against our religious beliefs. We will pay punitive taxes—not unlike the jizya under Islamic sharia law—imposed by an IRS that decertifies our churches because they will not cater to the homosexual agenda. We will even face legal prosecution for blasphemy—against the pieties of the Sexual Revolution. New York City has already criminalized "Failing to Use an Individual's Preferred Name or Pronoun," including the made-up transsexual pronouns "ze" and "hir," a "human rights" violation. If you exhibit a "willful, wanton" refusal to enable the mental illness of "transgender" persons (men who believe or pretend that they're women, or vice versa), you can be fined $250,000.[92]

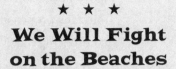

We Will Fight on the Beaches

There can be no truce, no respite, no surrender. As the price of calling ourselves Christians, we must make our case for natural law, religious and economic liberty, the sanctity of life, and the truth about sex year in and year out, regardless of the vagaries of particular candidates and party platforms. Pragmatically, we have no other option, but that is just as well: all those truths are either integral parts or inevitable implications of the gospel of Jesus Christ, which He ordered us to preach even in the face of literal, bloody persecution, offering us this promise: "Blessed are those who are persecuted for righteousness' sake, for theirs is the kingdom of heaven. Blessed are you when men revile you and persecute you and utter all kinds of evil against you falsely on my account. Rejoice and be glad, for your reward is great in heaven, for so men persecuted the prophets who were before you" (Matthew 5:10–12).

Millions of Evangelical Christians have seen the need to keep fighting as clearly as many Catholics have. In fact, Evangelical leaders and theologians have come a long way toward accepting the necessity of classically Catholic natural law reasoning, instead of relying on Biblical proof-texts, cultural inertia, and natural repugnance in fighting back against the latest outrages proposed by sexual revolutionaries. This is enormous progress, considering that Martin Luther once called reason "a whore."

We must meet our fellow citizens on the neutral ground of reason, and speak to them from our common store of faith. When we talk about economics or politics, we should never—literally, never, not even once—argue from authority, citing Vatican documents as if they settle a question. Those documents themselves do not pretend to do that. Instead, they wisely and richly explore the implications of today's problems in the light of reason, a reason illumined by the fundamental truth that God is real, that He made man, and did so in His image. We should no more try to resolve a debate with our non-Catholic fellow citizens about politics or economics by quoting a Vatican press release (or even an encyclical) than we would by citing Our Lady's words at Fatima to a Baptist preacher. It's not just ineffective; it's intellectually unsound.

As the ecumenical effort to fight back against the Obama administration's HHS mandate showed, Christians can prevail when we act together—when the Protestant owners of Hobby Lobby cooperate with the Little Sisters of the Poor. There are many organizations that serve the cause of protecting religious liberty and unborn life across denominational lines, and we should energetically support them:

- The Acton Institute for Religion and Liberty
- The Becket Fund
- The American Center for Law and Justice
- Eagle Forum
- The Family Research Council
- The Susan B. Anthony List
- Students for Life of America
- IamWholelife.com
- Movie to Movement

- The National Organization for Marriage
- The Homeschool Legal Defense Association
- The National Association of Scholars
- Alliance Defending Freedom
- The Center for Medical Progress

We should also work energetically with other organizations fighting to preserve the basic liberties of Americans, even if they are not religiously motivated, to protect our own rights to economic initiative, self-defense, private property, and free speech. We should embrace the vision of ordered liberty that America's founders inherited from the Catholics who fought for the Magna Carta and the teaching of Vatican II setting aside the idea of an intolerant Catholic state. Liberty is all the Church ever needs, and all it asks for today. It is profoundly under threat by a massive, expanding, inveterately hostile, and intrinsically secular modern state, which threatens the rights of many non-Catholics and even non-Christians. We cannot—as too many bishops seem still to dream—grab Leviathan and baptize it, infusing the modern leftist nanny state with a true Catholic vision of social justice. The vision of man that underlies modern progressivism is incoherent, rooted in pseudo-science and adolescent sexual rebellion, at once demonically proud and degraded by animalistic indulgence of brute instinct. We must look back to the dignified, free, responsible vision of man upon which our great Republic was founded, a profoundly Christian vision, which is also Catholic because it is true.

Core Principles We Can Cling To

One of the best efforts I have seen at presenting the rationally provable truths about human nature that animate real Catholic social teaching is the "Whole Life" program that Jason Scott Jones has developed. His presentation of these principles is so winning that he has become a highly sought-after speaker, addressing audiences at the March for Life in Washington, D.C., and in Canada; scholars at Notre Dame University; and pro-life students at Yale. I was so taken with Jones's distillation of these ideas that I collaborated with him on a book that spelled them out.[93] In it we unpack the five "Ideologies of Evil" that made the span from 1914 to 2014 the bloodiest century in human history:

- Racism and nationalism (which, as we have seen, is a very different thing from patriotism)
- Total war against civilian populations
- Utopian collectivism
- Radical individualism
- Utilitarian hedonism

The book refutes these ideologies and their false answers with the Catholic Church's balanced wisdom, spelled out in fundamental principles that must animate any decent politics:

- The sanctity of each human being as an image of God
- The reality of a transcendent moral order that is above all man-made laws
- The need for a free society that protects fundamental rights
- The virtues of a humane economy that allows humans to flourish
- The duty of solidarity among every member of the human family

Such a program can heal the sickness and divisions of our fractious body politic and unite citizens of good will in the quest to provide a more decent, truly human world for our descendants.

✝

Acknowledgments

First of all I would like to thank Faye Ballard for her exhaustive assistance researching this book, and her boundless encouragement and support. Thanks also to Jay Richards for suggesting this project to me, and to him and Jonathan Witt for their editorial understanding at *The Stream* as I was completing it. I am grateful to Jason Jones for his friendship and support; no colleague has ever been more valuable to me. My thanks to James Robison and Clare Brewster for their many kindnesses. Thanks to Harry Crocker and Elizabeth Kantor for top-notch editorial work, and to the various editors who kindly gave permission for me to repurpose pieces that they originally commissioned at various online publications. Finally, credit is due to Anthony Ottaviano, and Franz Josef and Susie Zmirak, without whom none of this would have been possible.

Notes

Chapter 1: The Church: What It Says about Itself, the World, and What Will Happen to You When You Die

1. *Catechism of the Catholic Church*, 892.
2. If you live in the Archdiocese of Chicago. See Blase Cupich, "Blase Cupich Op-Ed: Planned Parenthood and the Muted Humanity of the Unborn Child," *Chicago Tribune*, August 3, 2015, http://www. chicagotribune.com/news/opinion/commentary/ct-blase-cupich-abortion-planned-parenthood-perspec-0804-20150803-story.html.
3. The Church has never answered this question definitively. As a guide to responsible speculation, see Aquinas's *Summa Theologiae,* 1.97.1–1.102.2.
4. Walker Percy, *The Message in the Bottle: How Queer Man Is, How Queer Language Is, and What One Has to Do with the Other* (New York: Farrar, Straus, and Giroux, 1975), 6.
5. Walker Percy, *The Thanatos Syndrome* (New York: Farrar, Straus, and Giroux, 1987).
6. Massimo Introvigne, "The Catholic Church and the Blood Libel Myth: A Complicated Story," *Covenant: Global Jewish Magazine* 1: 2 (April 2007), http://www.covenant.idc.ac.il/en/vol1/issue2/introvigne.html.
7. See Edward Pentin, "The Framing of Piux XII: From Skepticism to Belief," *National Catholic Register*, August 17, 2012, http://www. ncregister.com/blog/edward-pentin/the-framing-of-pius-xii-from-skepticism-to-belief. See also Rabbi David Dalin, *The Myth of Hitler's*

Pope: Pope Pius XII and His Secret War Against Nazi Germany
(Washington, DC: Regnery History, 2005).

8. Hans Hermann Henrix, "The Covenant Has Never Been Revoked: Basis of the Christian-Jewish Relationship," Christian-Jewish Relations: Insights and Issues in the Ongoing Jewish-Christian Dialogue, http://www. jcrelations.net/The_covenant_has_never_been_revoked.2250.0.html.

9. "July 6: Clement IV and the Black Plague," *Jewish Currents: Activist Politics & Art*, July 5, 2012, http://jewishcurrents.org/july-6-clement-vi-and-the-black-plague-10952.

A Conversation You're Not Supposed to Have

1. Leskez Kolakowski, *Religion If There Is No God: On God, the Devil, Sin and Other Worries of the So-Called Philosophy of Religion* (South Bend: St. Augustine's Press, 2001).

2. John XXII, *Gloriosam Ecclesiam*, 1318.

Chapter 2: The Pope, the Other Bishops, and When and Why Catholics Have to Believe What They Say

1. "The Arabic Infancy Gospel of the Savior," in *Ante-Nicene Fathers*, Alexander Roberts, David Donaldson, and Arthur Cleveland Cox, eds., vol. 8 (Buffalo: Christian Literature Company, 1886), http://www.gnosis.org/library/infarab.htm.

2. Just go to the "Graduation Requirements" page of most ostensibly Catholic colleges (such as Georgetown, Marquette, or Holy Cross) to see that I'm right. What's worse, courses fulfilling these requirements often focus on "social justice," racial or cultural issues, or even (at Holy Cross a few years back) "Sacred Gardening" or (at Georgetown) "Dogs and Theology."

3. Second Vatican Council, *Dei Verbum* [Dogmatic Constitution on Divine Revelation], Vatican website, November 18, 1965, http://www.vatican. va/archive/hist_councils/ii_vatican_council/documents/vat-ii_const_19651118_dei-verbum_en.html.

4. Ibid.

5. J. Budziszewski, *What We Can't Not Know: A Guide* (San Francisco: Ignatius Press, 2011).

6. Vatican I's First Dogmatic Constitution on the Church, 4:9.

7. *Catechism of the Catholic Church*, 892.

8. Pascal-Emmanuel Gobry, "Let's Listen to Pope Francis on Economics," *First Things*, November 27, 2013, http://www.firstthings.com/web-exclusives/2013/11/lets-listen-to-pope-francis-on-economics.

9. One well-meaning attempt to do this is found in Stephen Krason, "The Secret Riches of Heinrich Pesch and Solidarism," *Aleteia*, January 23, 2014, http://aleteia.org/2014/01/23/the-secret-riches-of-heinrich-pesch-and-solidarism/.

10. Quoted in Catherine Heidt Zuchert, "Machiavelli's Revolution in Thought," in *Machiavelli's Legacy: The Prince after 500 Years*, ed. Timothy Fuller (Philadelphia: University of Pennsylvania Press, 2015), 63–64.

11. John Zmirak, *The Bad Catholic's Guide to the Seven Deadly Sins* (New York: The Crossroad Publishing Company, 2010), 50–51.

12. John-Henry Westen, "Vatican Bishop: Pope's View on Global Warming Is As Authoritative As the Condemnation of Abortion," LifeSite News, December 18, 2015, https://www.lifesitenews.com/news/vatican-bishop-popes-view-on-global-warming-is-as-authoritative-as-the-cond

13. Ibid.

14. "On many concrete questions, the Church has no reason to offer a definitive opinion; she knows that honest debate must be encouraged among experts, while respecting divergent views." Pope Francis, *Laudatio Si*, encyclical letter on Care for Our Common Home, Vatican website, May 14, 2015, https://w2.vatican.va/content/dam/francesco/pdf/encyclicals/documents/papa-francesco_20150524_enciclica-laudato-si_en.pdf.

15. Joseph Cardinal Ratzinger, *Principles of Catholic Theology* (San Francisco: Ignatius Press, 1982).

16. Joseph Cardinal Ratzinger, "Worthiness to Receive Holy Communion: General Principles," memorandum sent to Cardinal McCarrick, July 2004, https://www.ewtn.com/library/CURIA/cdfworthycom.HTM.

A Conversation You're Not Supposed to Have

1. Francis A. Sullivan, *Creative Fidelity: Weighing and Interpreting Documents of the Magisterium* (Eugene: Wipf and Stock, 2003).

Chapter 3: One, Holy, Catholic, and Thoroughly Splintered Church

1. See Michael Burleigh, *Earthly Powers* (New York: HarperCollins, 2005), as cited in Peter J. Leithart, "Secular Saviors," *Touchstone* (March 2007), http://www.touchstonemag.com/archives/article.php?id=20-02-041-b.

2. Margarita Marchione, *Pius XII: Architect for Peace* (Mahwah: Paulist, 2000).

3. "Introduction to the Inquisition," Catholic Bridge, http://catholicbridge.com/catholic/inquisition.php. Even Protestant pastor Nathan Busenitz, citing the research of Joseph Pérez, R. J. Rummel, and other "contemporary experts," puts the number of Protestants killed throughout the entirety of the Spanish Inquisition at "between 3,000 and 10,000." See"How Many People Died in the Inquisition? The Cripplegate, February 28, 2015, http://thecripplegate.com/how-many-people-died-in-the-inquisition/.

4. "Introduction to the Inquisition"; Thomas Madden, "The Real Inquisition: Investigating the Popular Myth," *National Review*, June 18, 2004, http://www.nationalreview.com/article/211193/real-inquisition-thomas-f-madden.

5. R.J. Rummel, "How Many Did Communist Regimes Murder? Powerkills, November 1993, https://www.hawaii.edu/powerkills/COM.ART.HTM.

6. Michael Davies, "Annibale Bugnini: The Main Author of the Novus Ordo," Catholic Apologetics Information, http://www.catholicapologetics.info/modernproblems/newmass/bugnini.html.

7. John Zuhlsdorf, "A Pentecost Monday Lesson: And Paul VI Wept," *Fr. Z's Blog*, June 9, 2014, http://wdtprs.com/blog/2014/06/a-pentecost-monday-lesson-and-paul-vi-wept-2/.

8. Josef Cardinal Ratzinger, "Address to the Bishops of Chile," July 13, 1988, http://unavoce.org/resources/cardinal-ratzingers-address-to-bishops-of-chile/.

9. Matthew Becker, "Holy Scripture in the Thought of Martin Luther," *The Daystar Journal*, November 10, 2013, http://thedaystarjournal.com/holy-scripture-in-the-thought-of-martin-luther/.

10. Rodney Stark, *The Rise of Christianity: How the Obscure, Marginal Jesus Movement Became the Dominant Religious Force in the Western World in a Few Centuries* (San Francisco: HarperSanFrancisco, 1997), 82–84, 124–25.

11. Richard A. Fletcher, *The Barbarian Conversion: From Paganism to Christianity* (Oakland: University of California Press, 1999), 268–71.

12. "The American Epoch in the Catholic Church," *The Chesterton Review* 35 (2009): 317–33.

13. Carlyle Murphy, "Half of U.S. Adults Raised Catholic Have Left the Church at Some Point," Pew Research, September 15, 2015, http://www.

pewresearch.org/fact-tank/2015/09/15/half-of-u-s-adults-raised-catholic-have-left-the-church-at-some-point/.

14. John Allen, Jr., *The Future Church* (New York: Image, 2012).

Chapter 4: How Birth Control Tore the Church Apart

1.   James Swan, "Luther, Contraception, and Onan's Sin," Beggars All: Reformation and Apologetics, November 16, 2013, http://beggarsallreformation.blogspot.com/2013/11/luther-contraception-and-onans-sin.html.

2.   Contraskeptic, "Calvin: Contraception 'Kills the Son,'" Contraception and Christianity, January 22, 2007, http://contraskeptic.blogspot.com/2007/01/calvin-contraception-kills-son.html.

3.   AP, "Farm Population Lowest Since 1850's," *New York Times*, July 20, 1988, http://www.nytimes.com/1988/07/20/us/farm-population-lowest-since-1850-s.html; "Fast Facts About Agriculture," American Farm Bureau Federation, http://www.fb.org/newsroom/fastfacts/.

4.   "Origins of Eugenics: From Sir Francis Galton to Virginia's Racial Integrity Act of 1924," Historical Collections at the Claude Moore Health Sciences Library, University of Virginia, 2004, http://exhibits.hsl.virginia.edu/eugenics/2-origins./.

5.   "Margaret Sanger Quotes, History, and Biography," Live Action, http://liveaction.org/research/margaret-sanger-quotes-history-and-biography.

6.   "Harry Laughlin and Eugenics," in the *Harry H. Laughlin Papers*, Truman State University, http://historyofeugenics.truman.edu/exchanging-ideas/international-discourse/nazi-connection/.

7.   Margaret Sanger, "America Needs a Code for Babies," *American Weekly*, March 27, 1934, https://www.nyu.edu/projects/sanger/webedition/app/documents/show.php?sangerDoc=101807.xml.

8.   Letter from Margaret Sanger to Dr. C. J. Gamble, December 10, 1939, http://genius.com/Margaret-sanger-letter-from-margaret-sanger-to-dr-cj-gamble-annotated.

9.   "Margaret Sanger Quotes, History, and Biography."

10. Ibid.

11. Paul Mankowski, "Flannery O'Connor: A Life," *First Things* (March 2003), http://www.firstthings.com/article/2003/03/flannery-oconnora-life.

12. Human Population: Population Growth," http://www.prg.org/Publications/Lesson-Plans/HumanPopulation/PopulationGrowth.aspx.

13. G. K. Chesterton, *The Defendant* (New York: Dover, 2012), 79.

14. Brian Clowes, "Exposing the Global Population Control Agenda," Human Life International, http://www.hli.org/resources/exposing-the-global-population-control/.

15. Penny Star, "400 Million Lives 'Prevented' Through One-Child Policy, Chinese Official Says," CNS News, October 10, 2014, http://cnsnews.com/news/article/penny-starr/400-million-lives-prevented-through-one-child-policy-chinese-official-says.

16. Jonathan P. Henderson, "Planned Parenthood: Eugenics & Organ Harvesting Under China's 'One Child Policy,'" Politichicks, July 22, 2015, http://politichicks.com/2015/07/planned-parenthood-eugenics-organ-harvesting-under-chinas-one-child-policy/.

17. Steven Ertelt, "China Reportedly Abolishes Pro-Abortion One-Child Policy, Will Allow Families to Have Two Children," Lifenews.com, October 29, 2015, http://www.lifenews.com/2015/10/29/china-reportedly-abolishes-pro-abortion-one-child-policy-will-allow-families-to-have-two-children/.

18. See Rev. Ryan Erlenbusch, "NFP: The Myth of the 'Contraceptive Mentality,' *Crisis*, November 3, 2011, http://www.crisismagazine.com/2011/nfp-the-myth-of-the-%E2%80%9Ccontraceptive-mentality%E2%80%9D; Angela D. Bonilla, "*Humanae Vitae*: Grave Motives to Use a Good Translation," *Homiletic and Pastoral Review*, March 25, 2008, http://www.hprweb.com/2008/03/humanae-vitae-grave-motives-to-use-a-good-translation/.

19. *Catechism of the Catholic Church*, 2221–25.

20. Janet Smith, "Moral Use of Natural Family Planning," Life Issues, http://www.lifeissues.net/writers/smith/smith_24moralusenfp.html.

21. Crista B. Warniment and Kirsten Hansen, "Is Natural Family Planning a Highly Effective Method of Birth Control? Yes: Natural Family Planning Is Highly Effective and Fulfilling," *American Family Physician* (November 2012), http://www.aafp.org/afp/2012/1115/od1.html.

22. Frank Newport, "Americans, Including Catholics, Say Birth Control is Morally OK," Gallup, May 22, 2012, http://www.gallup.com/

poll/154799/americans-including-catholics-say-birth-control-morally. aspx.

Chapter 5: Progressive Catholics and Their Permanent Revolution

1. Kenneth D. Whitehead, "How Dissent Became Institutionalized in the Church in America," *Homiletic & Pastoral Review* (July 1999), https://www.catholicculture.org/culture/library/view.cfm?recnum=1209.

2. "Frequently Requested Church Statistics," Center for Applied Research in the Apostolate, http://cara.georgetown.edu/frequently-requested-church-statistics/.

3. Elizabeth Mehren, "Priest Tried to Blackmail Cardinal, Files Show," *Los Angeles Times,* April 27, 2002, http://articles.latimes.com/2002/apr/27/news/mn-40342.

4. William A. Donohue, "A Crisis of Faith," *Catalyst* (June 2002), http://www.catholicleague.org/a-crisis-of-faith/; Associated Press, "Catholic Priest Attended First Man-Boy Love Meeting, Documents Show," Fox News, April 8, 2002, http://www.foxnews.com/story/2002/04/08/catholic-priest-attended-first-man-boy-love-meeting-documents-show.html.

5. William Donohue, *Secular Sabotage: How Liberals Are Destroying Religion and Culture in America* (Nashville: FaithWords, 2009).

6. William Marra and William Coulson, "We Overcame Their Traditions, We Overcame Their Faith," *The Latin Mass* 3, no. 1 (January–February 1994), https://www.ewtn.com/library/PRIESTS/COULSON.TXT.

7. Ibid.

8. The best number for homosexuals in the general public is 2.3 percent, according to a 2014 survey by the Centers for Disease Control and Prevention. The percentage of priests who identify as gay is obviously in dispute. The John Jay Report commissioned by U.S. bishops on sexual abuse reported that "homosexual men entered the seminaries in noticeable numbers from the late 1970s through the 1980s," and cited a range of estimates of homosexually-inclined priests from 15 to 58 percent. Karen J. Terry et al., *The Causes and Context of Sexual Abuse of Minors by Catholic Priests in the United States, 1950–2010: A Report Presented to the United States Conference of Catholic Bishops by the John Jay College Research Team*, May 2011, http://www.usccb.org/

issues-and-action/child-and-youth-protection/upload/The-Causes-and-
Context-of-Sexual-Abuse-of-Minors-by-Catholic-Priests-in-the-United-
States-1950-2010.pdf.

9. Pat Buchanan, "An Index of Catholicism's Decline," Townhall,
December 11, 2002, http://townhall.com/columnists/
patbuchanan/2002/12/11/an_index_of_catholicisms_decline.

10. Ibid; Peter Steinfels, "May 29–June 4; Catholics Question Article of
Faith," *New York Times*, June 5, 1994, http://www.nytimes.
com/1994/06/05/weekinreview/may-29-june-4-catholics-question-
article-of-faith.html.

11. Steven Ertelt, "58,586,256 Abortions in America Since Roe v. Wade in
1973," Lifenews, January 14, 2016, http://www.lifenews.
com/2016/01/14/58586256-abortions-in-america-since-roe-v-
wade-in-1973/.

12. Samuel Gregg, "The Consistent—and Not So Seamless—Ethic of Life,"
Catholic World Report, August 13, 2015, http://www.
catholicworldreport.com/Item/4098/the_consistentand_not_so_
seamlessethic_of_life.aspx.

13. Blase Cupich, "Planned Parenthood and the Muted Humanity of the
Unborn Child," *Chicago Tribune*, August 3, 2015, http://www.
chicagotribune.com/news/opinion/commentary/ct-blase-cupich-
abortion-planned-parenthood-perspec-0804-20150803-story.html.

14. George Neumayr and Phyllis Schlafly, *No Higher Power: Obama's War
on Religious Freedom* (Washington, DC: Regnery Publishing, 2012),
79–80.

15. Alana Goodman, "The Hillary Letters: Hillary Clinton, Saul Alinsky
Correspondence Revealed," *Washington Free Beacon*, September 21,
2014, http://freebeacon.com/politics/the-hillary-letters/.

16. "Newsviews: Archbishop Cupich," ABC 7 Eyewitness News, July 10,
2016, http://abc7chicago.com/religion/newsviews-archbishop-
cupich/1420373/. Transcript courtesy of Oakes Spalding, "It's Not That
Hard for Archbishop Cupich to Give Catholics the Wrong Advices,"
Mahound's Paradise, July 14, 2016, http://mahoundsparadise.blogspot.
com/2016/07/its-not-that-hard-for-archbishop-cupich.html?spref=tw.

17. Jason Scott Jones, "Archbishop Cupich's Seamless Bulletproof Vest for
Pro-Choice Politicians: An Open Letter to the Archbishop of Chicago
on Planned Parenthood and Poverty," The Stream, August 14, 2015,

https://stream.org/archbishop-cupichs-seamless-bulletproof-vest-pro-choice-politicians/.

18.   This is the thesis that runs throughout Gary Wills's *Papal Sin: Structures of Deceit* (New York: Image, 2001), and that pops up explicitly or implicitly in countless progressive Catholic polemics.

19.   Dietrich von Hildebrand, *The Trojan Horse in the City of God* (Bedford: Sophia Press Institute, 1967).

Chapter 6: They Kept the Faith

1.   Reprinted from "Free the Cognitive Dissidents," Takimag, July 17, 2008. http://takimag.com/article/free_the_cognitive_dissidents/print#axzz 44yQVQkBk.

2.   Raymond Arroyo, *Mother Angelica: The Remarkable Story of a Nun, Her Nerve, and a Network of Miracles* (New York: Image, 2007), 211.

3.   Stephanie Block, "The Underground Call to Action," CatholicCulture. org, http://www.catholicculture.org/culture/library/view.cfm?id=1318 &CFID=29203369&CFTOKEN=44056458.

4.   Malachi Martin, The Jesuits (New York: Simon & Schuster, 1988).

5.   Michael Davies, *Pope Paul's New Mass* (Kansas City: Angelus Press, 2009). Lefebvre's critique is the guiding principle of the whole book, which examines the "reforms" to the liturgy chapter by chapter.

6.   Josef Ratzinger, *Faith and the Future* (San Francisco: Ignatius, 2009), excerpted by Catholic Education Resource Center, http://www. catholiceducation.org/en/religion-and-philosophy/spiritual-life/the-church-will-become-small.html.

7.   Pope Francis, *Evangelii Gaudium* [Apostolic Exhortation of the Holy Father Francis to the Bishops, Clergy, Consecrated Persons and the Lay Faithful on the Proclamation of the Gospel in Today's World], Catholic Culture, November 24, 2013, http://www.catholicculture.org/culture/library/view.cfm?id=1318&CFID=29203369&CFTOKEN=44056458.

Chapter 7: The Church and the Free Market

1.   Leo XIII, *Rerum Novarum* [Encyclical of Pope Leo XIII on Capital and Labor], Vatican website, May 15, 1891, http://w2.vatican.va/content/leo-xiii/en/encyclicals/documents/hf_l-xiii_enc_15051891_rerum-novarum. html.

2.   Ibid.

3. Joe Hargrave, "How John Locke Influenced Catholic Social Teaching," Insidecatholic.com, November 5, 2010, http://www.catholicity.com/commentary/hargrave/08646.html.

4. Leo XIII, *Quod Apostolici Muneris* [Encylical of Pope Leo XIII on Socialism], Vatican website, December 28, 1878, http://w2.vatican.va/content/leo-xiii/en/encyclicals/documents/hf_l-xiii_enc_28121878_quod-apostolici-muneris.html.

5. Leo XIII, *Rerum Novarum*.

6. John Paul II, *Laborem Excercens* [On Human Work], Vatican Website, September 14, 1981, http://w2.vatican.va/content/john-paul-ii/en/encyclicals/documents/hf_jp-ii_enc_14091981_laborem-exercens.html.

7. Pius XII, "Allocution to Directors and Employees of the Bank of Italy," April 25, 1950; Pius XII, "In the Holy Gospels, the Divine Master Does Not Condemn Justly Acquired Riches," cited by Rupert J. Ederer in *Pope Pius XII on the Economic Order* (Lanham: Scarecrow Press, 2011), 224.

8. Franciscans even served as fundraisers, collecting money to fund the Crusades. See Christoph T. Maier, *Preaching the Crusades* (Cambridge: Cambridge University Press, 1994), 68.

9. St. Thomas Aquinas, *Summa Theologica*, Supplement, 49; John Paul II, *Familiaris Consortio* [On the Role of the Christian Family in the Modern World], Vatican website, November 22, 1981, http://w2.vatican.va/content/john-paul-ii/en/apost_exhortations/documents/hf_jp-ii_exh_19811122_familiaris-consortio.html.

10. Ines St. Martin, "Sights and sounds from the Iowa caucuses of the Catholic Church," *Crux*, http://www.cruxnow.com/church/2015/02/16/sights-and-sounds-from-the-iowa-caucuses-of-the-catholic-church/.

11. Jorge Velarde Rosso, "Pope Francis Meets Comrade Mr. President," Acton Institute, July 15, 2015, http://www.acton.org/pub/commentary/2015/07/15/pope-francis-meets-comrade-mr-president.

12. Al Kresta, *Dangers to the Faith* (Huntington: Our Sunday Visitor, 2013), 219.

13. Christopher Dawson, "Catholicism and the Bourgeois Mind," CatholicCulture.org, https://www.catholicculture.org/culture/library/view.cfm?recnum=2580. See also my January 11, 2012, critique, "Dawson's Usura Canto," in which I compare Dawson's economics with those of fascist poet and ideologue Ezra Pound: http://www.crisismagazine.com/2012/the-usura-canto.

14. Rodney Stark, *The Victory of Reason* (New York: Random House, 2005).

15. Leo XIII, *Quod Apostolici Muneris* [On Socialism], Vatican website, December 28, 1878, http://w2.vatican.va/content/leo-xiii/en/encyclicals/documents/hf_l-xiii_enc_28121878_quod-apostolici-muneris.html.

16. Aquinas, *Summa Theologica*, 2.77.4 quoted in Samuel Gregg, *For God and for Profit* (New York: Crossroad, 2016), 54.

17. David Gordon, "Three New Deals: Why the Nazis and Fascists Loved FDR," Mises Daily, September 22, 2006, https://mises.org/library/three-new-deals-why-nazis-and-fascists-loved-fdr.

18. Leo XIII, *Quadragesimo Anno*.

19. Jason Scott Jones and John Zmirak, *The Race to Save Our Century* (New York: Crossroad, 2014).

20. "Former Soviet spy: We created Liberation Theology," Catholic News Agency, May 1, 2015, http://www.catholicnewsagency.com/news/former-soviet-spy-we-created-liberation-theology-83634/.

21. "Is the Pope a Socialist?" CNA, July 22, 2015, http://www.catholicnewsagency.com/news/is-the-pope-a-socialist-95558/.

22. David Deavel, "What's Wrong with Distributism?" *Intercollegiate Review* (Summer 2013), https://home.isi.org/whats-wrong-distributism.

23. John Paul II, *Sollicitudo Rei Socialis* [For the Twentieth Anniversary of Populorum Progressio], Vatican website, December 30, 1987, http://w2.vatican.va/content/john-paul-ii/en/encyclicals/documents/hf_jp-ii_enc_30121987_sollicitudo-rei-socialis.html.

24. Dorothy Day, "Our Country Passes from Undeclared War to Declared War; We Continue Our Christian Pacifist Stand," *The Catholic Worker*, January 1942.

25. Michael Harrington, "Michael Harrington on the Uniquely Orthodox Radicalism of Dorothy Day," *In These Times*, September 25, 2015, http://inthesetimes.com/article/18451/pope-francis-dorothy-day-michael-harrington#_blank.

26. Dorothy Day, "About Cuba," *The Catholic Worker*, July/August 1961.

27. Dorothy Day, "Ho Chi Minh and Theophane Venard, the Hero and the Saint," *The Catholic Worker*, January 1970.

Chapter 8: Amnesty Equals Abortion

1. Jie Zong and Jeanne Batalova, "Frequently Requested Statistics on Immigrants and Immigration in the United States," Migration Policy Institute, April 14, 2016, http://www.migrationpolicy.org/article/frequently-requested-statistics-immigrants-and-immigration-united-states.

2. George Weigel, "The End of the Bernardin Era," *First Things* (February 2011), http://www.firstthings.com/article/2011/02/the-end-of-the-bernardin-era.

3. Daniel Halper, "Jeb Bush Says Pope's Meddling Helped Trump Win Primaries," *New York Post*, July 12, 2016, http://nypost.com/2016/07/12/still-bitter-jeb-bush-says-pope-brought-on-trumps-nomination/.

4. Jack Smith, "Archbishop Gomez—'Immigration Is the Great Civil Rights Test of Our Generation,'" The Catholic KeyBlog, April 8, 2010, http://catholickey.blogspot.com/2010/04/archbishop-gomez-immigration-is-great.html.

5. Joel Mathis, "Chaput Slams Trump on Immigration," *Philadelphia Magazine*, September 2, 2015, http://www.phillymag.com/news/2015/09/02/chaput-trump-immigration/.

6. "President Obama Quotes Pope Francis In Speech About Income Inequality," December 4, 2013, http://www.huffingtonpost.com/entry/obama-quotes-pope-francis_n_4386622.

7. "Islam in Belgium," Euro-Islam.info, http://www.euro-islam.info/country-profiles/belgium/.

8. Pope Francis, "Visit to Lampedusa: Homily of Holy Father Francis," July 8, 2013, http://w2.vatican.va/content/francesco/en/homilies/2013/documents/papa-francesco_20130708_omelia-lampedusa.html.

9. Patrick Donahue, "Germany Saw 1.1 Million Migrants in 2015 as Debate Intensifies," Bloomberg, January 6, 2016, http://www.bloomberg.com/news/articles/2016-01-06/germany-says-about-1-1-million-asylum-seekers-arrived-in-2015.

10. "PEGIDA Rally in Cologne Derailed by Violent Protesters," Breitbart London, January 9, 2016, http://www.breitbart.com/london/2016/01/09/exclusive-pictures-pegida-rally-in-cologne-derailed-by-violent-protesters/.

11. Oliver Lane and Chris Tomlinson, "German Students Should Take Compulsory Arabic Lessons Says Leading Professor," Breitbart, February 4, 2016, http://www.breitbart.com/london/2016/02/04/german-students-should-take-compulsory-arabic-lessons-says-leading-professor/.

12. Ruth Sherlock and Colin Freeman, "Islamic State 'Planning to Use Libya As gateway to Europe,'" February 17, 2015, http://www.telegraph.

co.uk/news/worldnews/islamic-state/11418966/Islamic-State-planning-to-use-Libya-as-gateway-to-Europe.html.

13. Isabel Hunter, "Let Down By the Pope on Lesbos," *Daily Mail*, April 22, 2016, http://www.dailymail.co.uk/news/article-3550138/Betrayed-Pope-Lesbos-Christian-brother-sister-desperately-disappointed-told-rescued-Holy-Father-left-red-tape.html#ixzz46laQMRzU.

14. Paul VI, *Dei Verbum* [Dogmatic Constitution on Divine Revelation], Vatican website, November 18, 1965, http://www.vatican.va/archive/hist_councils/ii_vatican_council/documents/vat-ii_const_19651118_dei-verbum_en.html.

15. *Catechism of the Catholic Church*, 2241.

16. "Some 57% of Hispanic Registered Voters Now Call Themselves Democrats or Say They Lean to the Democratic Party, While Just 23% Align with the Republican Party—Meaning There Is Now a 34 Percentage Point Gap in Partisan Affiliation among Registered Latinos," Pew Research Center, Hispanic Trends, December 6, 2007, http://www.pewhispanic.org/2007/12/06/hispanics-and-the-2008-election-a-swing-vote/.

17. Drew Desilver, "For Most Workers, Real Wages Have Barely Budged for Decades," Pew Research, October 9, 2014, http://www.pewresearch.org/fact-tank/2014/10/09/for-most-workers-real-wages-have-barely-budged-for-decades/.

18. Adam Shaw, "About Half of Immigrant Households on Welfare, Report Says," Fox News, September 2, 2015, http://www.foxnews.com/politics/2015/09/02/half-immigrant-households-on-welfare-report-says.html.

19. Mark Krikorian, "Mass *Legal* Immigration Will Finish Conservatism," *National Review*, August 31, 2015, http://www.nationalreview.com/article/423288/mass-legal-immigration-will-finish-conservatism-mark-krikorian.

20. Leo XIII, *Rerum Novarum*.

21. Joel B. Pollak, "Anti-Donald Trump Rally Waves Mexican Flags in L.A.," Breitbart, March 14, 2016, http://www.breitbart.com/big-government/2016/03/14/california-markets-roiled-by-water-pressure-fluctuations/.

22.	Michelle Malkin, "Police State: How Mexico Treats Illegal Aliens," Michelle Malkin, April 28, 2010, http://michellemalkin. com/2010/04/28/police-state-how-mexico-treats-illegal-aliens/.

23.	Jens Manuel Krogstad and Jeffrey S. Passel, "5 Facts about Illegal Immigration in the U.S.," Pew Research, November 19, 2015, http:// www.pewresearch.org/fact-tank/2015/11/19/5-facts-about-illegal-immigration-in-the-u-s.

24.	Jason Scott Jones and John Zmirak, "Immigration Crisis: Playing Chicken with Children's Lives," July 8, 2014, http://www.foxnews.com/ opinion/2014/07/08/immigration-crisis-playing-chicken-with-childrens-lives.html.

25.	Henri Pirenne, *Mohammed and Charlemagne* (North Chelmsford: Courier, 2012), 17–75.

26.	"Leading Sunni Sheikh Yousef Al-Qaradhawi and Other Sheikhs Herald the Coming Conquest of Rome" (quoting Al-Jazeera Television in Qatar), Middle East Media Research Institute, January 24, 1999, http:// www.memri.org/report/en/0/0/0/0/0/0/774.htm#_edn3; Al Jazeera (Qatar), http://www.aljazeera.net/programs/shareea/ articles/2001/7/7-6-2.htm.

27.	Ann Corcoran, "Refugee Resettlement and the Hijra to America," March 30, 2015, http://www.centerforsecuritypolicy.org/2015/04/20/ refugee-resettlement-and-the-hijra-to-america/.

28.	José Angel Gutiérrez (interview), "In Search of Aztlan," August 8, 1999, http://www.insearchofaztlan.com/gutierrez.html.

29.	In 2002, Maradiaga dismissed the clerical sex abuse crisis as an invention of Jews in the media outraged at the Church's support for Palestinian rights. See Alan Dershowitz, "Catholic Church Accused of Covering Up Pedophilia: Blame the Jews," *Jewish Journal*, April 6, 2010, http://www.jewishjournal.com/opinion/article/catholic_church_ accused_of_covering_up_pedophilia_blame_the_jews_20100406/.

30.	Rocco Palmo, "The Council's 'Unfinished Business,' the Church's Return to Jesus…and Dreams of 'the Next Pope'—a Southern Weekend with Francis' Discovery Channel," Whispers in the Loggia, October 28, 2013, http://whispersintheloggia.blogspot.com/2013/10/the-councils-unfinished-business.html.

31.	John Paul II, *Memory and Identity* (London: Weidenfeld & Nicolson: 2005), 65–89.

32. "America's Changing Religious Landscape," Pew Research Center, May 12, 2015, http://www.pewforum.org/2015/05/12/americas-changing-religious-landscape/.

33. Michael Lipka, "A Closer Look at Catholic America," Pew Research Center, September 14, 2015, http://www.pewresearch.org/fact-tank/2015/09/14/a-closer-look-at-catholic-america/.

34. Anna Sutherland, "Why Latinos Are Leaving the Catholic Church," *First Things*, May 12, 2014, http://www.firstthings.com/web-exclusives/2014/05/why-latinos-are-leaving-the-catholic-church.

35. Kelly Riddell, "Catholic Church collects $1.6 billion in U.S. contracts, grants since 2012," *Washington Times*, September 24, 2015, http://www.washingtontimes.com/news/2015/sep/24/catholic-church-collects-16-billion-in-us-contract/?page=all.

36. Ann Corcoran, "In 2014, Your Tax Dollars Paid 97% of the US Conference of Catholic Bishops Migration Fund Budget," Anne Corcoran, Refugee Resettlement Watch, July 25, 2015, https://refugeeresettlementwatch.wordpress.com/2015/07/25/in-2014-your-tax-dollars-paid-97-of-the-us-conference-of-catholic-bishops-migration-fund-budget/.

Chapter 9: Is the Catholic Church a Global Gun-Free Zone?

1. For detailed documentation of all these facts see Robert Spencer, *The Politically Incorrect Guide to Islam and the Crusades* (Washington, DC: Regnery, 2005).

2. Gregory Nazianzen, "Funeral Oration on the Great St. Basil, Bishop of Caesarea in Caapadocia," Oration 43, New Advent, http://www.newadvent.org/fathers/310243.htm.

3. Thomas Aquinas, quoted in *Catechism of the Catholic Church*, 2263–64.

4. Ibid., 2265.

5. Carol Glatz, "Gun Control: Church Firmly, Quietly Opposes Firearms for Civilians," Catholic News Service, January 14, 2011, http://www.catholicnews.com/services/englishnews/2011/gun-control-church-firmly-quietly-opposes-firearms-for-civilians.cfm.

6. John Paul II, *Apostolos Suos* [On the Theological and Juridical Nature of Episcopal Conferences], IV:1, Vatican website, May 21, 1998, http://

w2.vatican.va/content/john-paul-ii/en/motu_proprio/documents/hf_
jp-ii_motu-proprio_22071998_apostolos-suos.html.

7. Thomas Aquinas, *Summa Theologica*, 2.64.7.

8. "History," Saint Gabriel Possenti Society, http://www.gunsaint.com/
history.asp.

9. Jason Scott Jones, "Gun Rights: Human Rights Guaranteed by Natural
Law," *Legatus Magazine*, April 1, 2016, http://legatus.org/gun-rights-
human-rights-guaranteed-natural-law/.

10. Rudy Rummel, "Democide vs. Other Causes of Death," Democratic
Peace Blog, February 1, 2005, https://democraticpeace.wordpress.
com/2009/07/01/democide-vs-other-causes-of-death/.

11. Stephen Halbrook, "What Made the Nazi Holocaust possible? Gun
control," *Washington Times*, November 7, 2013, http://www.
washingtontimes.com/news/2013/nov/7/halbrook-the-key-to-this-
german-pogrom-is-confisca/.

12. George Rutler, "Hanging Concentrates the Mind," *Crisis*, February 8,
2013, http://www.crisismagazine.com/2013/hanging-concentrates-the-
mind.

13. Jason Scott Jones, "Give Us Barabbas!" The Stream, May 4, 2015, https://
stream.org/give-us-barabbas/.

14. Avery Cardinal Dulles, "Catholicism and Capital Punishment," *First
Things* (April 2001), http://www.firstthings.com/article/2001/04/
catholicism-amp-capital-punishment.

15. *The Catechism of the Council of Trent*, Catholic Publication Society,
http://www.ecatholic2000.com/trentcat/untitled-34.shtml.

16. *Catechism of the Catholic Church*, 2267.

17. Dulles, "Catholicism and Capital Punishment."

18. Christopher A. Ferrara, "Can the Church Ban Capital Punishment?"
Crisis, December 2, 2011, http://www.crisismagazine.com/2011/can-
the-church-ban-capital-punishment.

19. Rutler, "Hanging Concentrates the Mind."

20. *Catechism of the Catholic Church*, 2309.

21. Mark Tooley, "The Peacenik Campaign to Kill Just War," *Detroit News*,
April 18, 2016, http://www.detroitnews.com/story/opinion/2016/04/18/
peacenik-campaign-kill-just-war/83218164/.

22. Ryan Hammill, "Could Pope Francis Be Ready to Throw Out Just War
Theory," *Sojourners*, April 26, 2016, https://sojo.net/articles/could-
pope-francis-be-ready-throw-out-just-war-theory.

23. Philip Pullella, "Pope Says Weapons Manufacturers Can't Call Themselves Christians," Yahoo! News, June 21, 2015; Rafael Medoff, "Pope Francis: Why Didn't US Bomb Auschwitz and Why Don't We Take More Action Today?" *Algemeiner*, June 24, 2015, https://www.algemeiner.com/2015/06/24/pope-francis-why-didnt-us-bomb-auschwitz-and-why-dont-we-take-more-action-today/.

24. See Christopher Jones, "Christians in the Roman Army: Countering the Pacifist Narrative," Gates of Nineveh, April 20, 2012, https://gatesofnineveh.wordpress.com/2012/04/20/christians-in-the-roman-army-countering-the-pacifist-narrative/.

25. See Anscombe's classic essay "War and Murder," in Joram Graf Haber, ed., *Absolutism and Its Consequentialist Critics* (Lanham: Rowman & Littlefield, 1994).

26. In "Was There an Islamic 'Genocide' of Hindus?" Belgian scholar Koenraad Elst notes, "There is no official estimate of the total death toll of Hindus at the hands of Islam. A first glance at important testimonies by Muslim chroniclers suggests that, over 13 centuries and a territory as vast as the Subcontinent, Muslim Holy Warriors easily killed more Hindus than the 6 million of the Holocaust." The Koenraad Elst Site, http://koenraadelst.bharatvani.org/articles/irin/genocide.html.

27. Richard McCaffery Robinson, "Fourth Crusade," *Military History* (August 1993), http://www.historynet.com/fourth-crusade.htm.

28. Ibn Warraq, *Sir Walter Scott's Crusades and Other Fantasies* (London: New English Review, 2013).

A Conversation You're Not Supposed to Have

1. *Catechism of the Catholic Church*, 2309.

Chapter 10: Is the Church Anti-Science?

1. Historians rely on the account of Nicolaus of Damascus, which he admitted was at best second-hand. See "The Assassination of Julius Caesar, 44 BC," EyeWitness to History.com, 2004, http://www.eyewitnesstohistory.com/caesar2.htm.

2. Pius XII, *Humani Generis* [Concerning Some False Opinions Threatening to Undermine the Foundations of Catholic Doctrine], Vatican website, August 12, 1950, http://w2.vatican.va/content/pius-xii/

en/encyclicals/documents/hf_p-xii_enc_12081950_humani-generis.
html.

3. Augustine of Hippo, *The City of God* (New York: Penguin Classics, 2004), 11:6.

4. Augustine of Hippo, *The Literal Interpretation of Genesis* (Washington, DC: The Catholic University of America Press, 2001), 1:19-20.

5. Ibid., 2:9.

6. Richard C. Lewontin, "Billions and Billions of Demons," *New York Review of Books*, January 9, 1997, http://www.nybooks.com/ articles/1997/01/09/billions-and-billions-of-demons/.

7. Stanley L. Jaki, *The Savior of Science* (Grand Rapids: William B. Eerdman's, 2000).

8. Jacques Maritain, *An Introduction to Philosophy* (New York: Sheed and Ward, 2005).

9. Jaki, *The Savior of Science*.

10. Benedict XVI, "Papal Address at University of Regensburg," September 12, 2006, https://zenit.org/articles/papal-address-at-university-of-regensburg/.

11. Robert Reilly, *The Closing of the Muslim Mind* (Wilmington: ISI, 2011).

12. Jaki, *The Savior of Science*; Pervez Amirali Hoodbhoy, "Science and the Islamic World," Andy Ross, August 2007, http://www.andyross.net/ hoodbhoy.htm.

13. Jacques Maritain, "The Experimental Sciences—Albertus Magnus—Roger Bacon," University of Notre Dame, http://www3.nd.edu/ Departments/Maritain/etext/staamp3.htm.

14. Joseph MacDonnell, "The 35 Lunar Craters Named to Honor Jesuits," Fairfield University, http://www.faculty.fairfield.edu/jmac/sj/ scientists/lunacrat.htm.

15. Rodney Stark, *The Victory of Reason* (New York: Random House, 2006).

16. Joe Carter, "The Myth of Galileo," *First Things*, September 8, 2011, http://www.firstthings.com/blogs/firstthoughts/2011/09/the-myth-of-galileo-a-story-with-a-mostly-valuable-lesson-for-today.

17. Patrick Barry, "The Penal Laws," EWTN (from *L'Osservatore Romano*, November 30, 1987), https://www.ewtn.com/library/CHISTORY/ PENALAWS.HTM.

18. Jaki, *The Savior of Science*, Chapter 3.

19. John-Henry Westen, "Vatican Bishop: Pope's View on Global Warming Is As Authoritative As the Condemnation of Abortion," Lifesitnews,

December 18, 2015, https://www.lifesitenews.com/news/vatican-bishop-popes-view-on-global-warming-is-as-authoritative-as-the-cond?.

20. Evelyn Waugh, *Brideshead Revisited* (New York: Penguin, 2012), 185.

21. Westen, "Vatican Bishop: Pope's View on Global Warming Is As Authoritative As the Condemnation of Abortion."

22. Mike Gallager, "Population Control: Is It a Tool of the Rich?" BBC Magazine, October 28, 2011, http://www.bbc.com/news/magazine-15449959

23. *Sustainability: Higher Education's New Fundamentalism*, National Association of Scholars, March 2015, https://www.nas.org/projects/sustainability_report.

24. Anthony Watts, "New Paper Shows Global Warming Hiatus Real after All," Watts Up with That? February 24, 2016, https://wattsupwiththat.com/2016/02/24/new-paper-shows-global-warming-hiatus-real-after-all/.

25. Mario Loyola, "Twilight of the Climate Change Movement," *The American Interest*, March 31, 2016, http://www.the-american-interest.com/2016/03/31/twilight-of-the-climate-change-movement/.

26. "An Open Letter to Pope Francis on Climate Change," Cornwall Alliance for the Stewardship of Creation, April 27, 2015, http://cornwallalliance.org/anopenlettertopopefrancisonclimatechange/.

27. William M. Briggs, "The Scientific Pantheist Who Advises Pope Francis," *The Stream*, June 22, 2015, https://stream.org/scientific-pantheist-who-advises-pope-francis/.

28. Loyola, "Twighlight of the Climate Change Movement."

29. "Vatican Hosts Two Leading Pro-Abortion, Population Control Activists at Climate Conference," LifeSite News, April 28, 2015, https://www.lifesitenews.com/opinion/vatican-hosts-two-leading-pro-abortion-population-control-activists-at-clim.

30. Ryan Anderson, "New Obamacare Transgender Regulations Threaten Freedom of Physicians," *The Stream*, May 15, 2016, https://stream.org/new-obamacare-transgender-regulations-threaten-freedom-physicians/.

31. "Gender Ideology Harms Children," American College of Pediatricians, April 6, 2016, http://www.acpeds.org/the-college-speaks/position-statements/gender-ideology-harms-children.

Chapter 11: Sex, Sanity, and the Catholic Church

1.   Steve Ertelt, "58,586,256 Abortions in America Since Roe v. Wade in 1973," Lifenews, January 14, 2016, http://www.lifenews.com/2016/01/14/58586256-abortions-in-america-since-roe-v-wade-in-1973/; "Paul Ryan Calls the Health of the Mother Exception a 'Loophole' You Could 'Drive a Truck Through,'" YoutTube video, posted by Huffington Post Politics, August 22, 2012, https://www.youtube.com/watch?v=Tck6nnze1Sk.

2.   Diane Severance, "Jesus Loved Children," Christianity.com, http://www.christianity.com/church/church-history/timeline/1-300/jesus-loved-children-11629553.html.

3.   Abby Johnson, "Sorry Folks. Contraception Access Increases Abortions. And Here's the Proof," Lifesitenews, March 11, 2015, https://www.lifesitenews.com/blogs/tell-me-that-good-one-again-about-how-contraception-decreases-abortions.

4.   Staff, "Hugh Hefner: Activist for Women's Rights," Celebrity Café, August 2, 2010, http://thecelebritycafe.com/2010/08/hugh-hefner-activist-womens-rights/.

5.   Victor T. Cheney, *The Sex Offenses and their Treatments* (Bloomington: AuthorHouse, 2004), 9.

6.   Sarah Kliff, "Schools That Give Away Condoms See More Teen Births, Not Fewer," Vox, June 15, 2016, http://www.vox.com/2016/6/15/11925792/school-condoms-teen-births.

7.   E. Joanne Angelo, "Portraits of Grief in the Aftermath of Abortion," Hope after Abortion, August 8, 2011, http://hopeafterabortion.com/?page_id=843.

8.   Steven E. Rhoads, "Hookup Culture: The High Costs of a Low 'Price' for Sex," Springer Business Media, October 18, 2012, http://link.springer.com/article/10.1007/s12115-012-9595-z.

9.   Gretchen Livingston, "Fewer than Half of U.S. Kids Today Live in a 'Traditional' Family," Pew Research Center, December 22, 2014, http://www.pewresearch.org/fact-tank/2014/12/22/less-than-half-of-u-s-kids-today-live-in-a-traditional-family/.

10.   Amy Desai, "How Could Divorce Affect My Kids?," Focus on the Family, http://www.focusonthefamily.com/marriage/divorce-and-infidelity/should-i-get-a-divorce/how-could-divorce-affect-my-kids.

11. Dan Hurley, "Divorce Rate: It's Not as High as You Think," *New York Times*, April 19, 2005, http://www.nytimes.com/2005/04/19/health/divorce-rate-its-not-as-high-as-you-think.html.

12. Andrew L. Yarrow, "Falling Marriage Rates Reveal Economic Fault Lines," *New York Times*, February 6, 2015, http://www.nytimes.com/2015/02/08/fashion/weddings/falling-marriage-rates-reveal-economic-fault-lines.html.

13. Wendy Wang and Kim Parker, "Record Share of Americans Have Never Married," Pew Social Trends, September 24, 2014, http://www.pewsocialtrends.org/2014/09/24/record-share-of-americans-have-never-married/.

14. *U.S. Census Bureau, Children's Living Arrangements and Characteristics: March 2011, Table C8.*

15. *U.S. Department of Health and Human Services, Information on Poverty and Income Statistics.* September 12, 2012, http://aspe.hhs.gov/hsp/12/PovertyAndIncomeEst/ib.shtml.

16. *U.S. Department of Health and Human Services, National Center for Health Statistics, Survey on Child Health,* Washington, DC, 1993.

17. John P. Hoffmann, "The Community Context of Family Structure and Adolescent Drug Use," Journal of Marriage and Family 64 (May 2002): 314–330.

18. S. L. Hofferth, "Residential father family type and child well-being: investment versus selection," Demography 43 (2006): 53–78.

19. Gunilla Ringbäck Weitoft et al., "Mortality, severe morbidity, and injury in children living with single parents in Sweden: a population-based study," *The Lancet 361,* no. 9354 (January 25, 2003), http://www.thelancet.com/journals/lancet/article/PIIS0140-6736(03)12324-0/abstract; Sid Kerchheimer, "Absent Parent Doubles Child Suicide Risk: Experts Offer Tips on How You Can Reduce the Risk in Your Kids," WebMD, January 2003, http://www.webmd.com/baby/news/20030123/absent-parent-doubles-child-suicide-risk.

20. K. H. Tillman, "Family structure pathways and academic disadvantage among adolescents in stepfamilies," Journal of Marriage and Family (2007).

21. Ibid.

22. Stephen Demuth and Susan L. Brown, "Family Structure, Family Processes, and Adolescent Delinquency: The Significance of Parental

Absence Versus Parental Gender," Journal of Research in Crime and Delinquency 41, no. 1 (February 2004): 58–81, http://familyfacts.org/briefs/26/marriage-and-family-as-deterrents-from-delinquency-violence-and-crime.

23. John Allen, "Pope's Annulment Reform Will Recalibrate the Synod of Bishops, and More," Crux, September 18, 2015, http://www.cruxnow.com/church/2015/09/08/popes-annulment-reform-will-recalibrate-the-synod-of-bishops-and-more/.

24. Roberto de Mattei, "The Post-Synod Exhortation, Amoris Laetitia: First Reflections on a Catastrophic Document," Rorate Coeli, April 10, 2016, http://rorate-caeli.blogspot.com/2016/04/de-mattei-post-synod-exhortation-amoris.html#_blank.

25. "Full Transcript of Pope's In-Flight Press Remarks Released," Catholic News Agency, August 5, 2013, http://www.catholicnewsagency.com/news/full-transcript-of-popes-in-flight-press-remarks-released/.

Chapter 12: Temptations and Opportunities for the Church

1. Jason Jones,"Pro-Lifers, Don't Fall for This Sleazy Political Trick," The Stream, May 18, 2016, https://stream.org/pro-lifers-dont-fall-sleazy-polit-ical-trick/.

2. Note how socialist ideas often go by a name that makes them sound like the free market. Whether it's the European Union's government by bureaucrats getting its foot in the door as "the Common Market" or the Obamacare "marketplaces," socialism and top-down government control in defiance of the Catholic principle of subsidiarity regularly masquerade as economic freedom.

3. Robert Christian, "What Is the Whole Life Movement?" Millennial, February 3, 2016, https://millennialjournal.com/2016/02/03/what-is-the-whole-life-movement/.

4. Mark Shea, "An Honest and Heartfelt Exchange with a Friend Who Feels That I've Changed," Patheos, July 13, 2016, http://www.patheos.com/blogs/markshea/2016/07/an-honest-and-heartfelt-exchange-with-a-friend-who-feels-that-ive-changed.html.

5. Mark Shea, "Voting to Support a Lesser Evil vs. Voting to Lessen Evil," Patheos, May 13, 2016, http://www.patheos.com/blogs/markshea/2016/05/voting-to-support-a-lesser-evil-vs-voting-to-lessen-evil.html.

6.   Shea, "An Honest and Heartfelt Exchange."

7.   Rebecca Bratten Weiss, "Now Is the Time to Be Whole Life," Patheos, May 12, 2016, http://www.patheos.com/blogs/ suspendedinherjar/2016/05/now-is-the-time-to-be-whole-life/.

8.   Rebecca Bratten Weiss, Facebook posts, April 18, May 3, September 21, 2012, and May 30, 2015. Screenshots available upon request.

9.   Rebecca Bratten Weiss, Facebook posts.

10. Rebecca Bratten Weiss, Facebook post August 2, 2015; "Abortion, Collective Responsibility, and the S-Word," Patheos, February 22, 2016, http://www.patheos.com/blogs/suspendedinherjar/2016/02/abortion-collective-responsibility-and-the-s-word. Screenshot available upon request.

11. Simcha Fisher, Facebook post May 29, 2016. Screenshot available upon request.

12. Simcha Fisher, "Gov't Shutdown Means Food Pantries Need Help--UPDATED," Patheos, October 2, 2013, http://www.patheos.com/blogs/ simchafisher/2013/10/02/govt-shutdown-means-food-pantries-need-help/; "Behold the Fabled Welfare Leech," Aleteia, June 29, 2016, http:// aleteia.org/blogs/simchafisher/behold-the-fabled-welfare-leech/.

13. Simcha Fisher, "But What Will Poor People Do If Planned Parenthood Is Defunded?" Patheos, August 5, 2015, http://www.patheos.com/blogs/ simchafisher/2015/08/05/but-what-will-poor-people-do-if-planned-parenthood-is-defunded/.

14. Simcha Fisher, "The Day I Bought Steak with My Food Stamps," reprinted on Aleteia, February 21, 2016, http://aleteia.org/blogs/ simchafisher/the-day-i-bought-steak-with-my-food-stamps-2/.

15. Simcha Fisher, Facebook post, November 4, 2014. Screenshot available upon request.

16. Simcha Fisher, The Sinner's Guide to Natural Family Planning (Huntington: Our Sunday Visitor, 2014), 12.

17. Simcha Fisher, "Tax Return Tithing," National Catholic Register, March 1, 2011, http://www.ncregister.com/blog/simcha-fisher/tax-return-tithingPat.

18. Allison Sherlock Howell, Commenting on Simcha Fisher Facebook post, October 5, 2013. Screenshot of article's Facebook shares available upon request.

19.   Adult Congress Sessions: Thursday and Friday," World Meeting of Families 2015, Philadelphia, http://www.worldmeeting2015.org/about-the-event/adult-congress-sessions-thursday-friday/; Simcha Fisher, "What's for Supper? Vol. 44: AmeriCaCado 2016!," Aleteia, July 22, 2016, http://aleteia.org/blogs/simchafisher/whats-for-supper-vol-44-americacado-2016/; Simcha Fisher Facebook posts, August 2016 (screenshots available upon request).

20.   Jeffrey Sparshott, "Congratulations, Class of 2015. You're the Most Indebted Ever (For Now)," *Wall Street Journal*, May 8, 2015, http://blogs.wsj.com/economics/2015/05/08/congratulations-class- of-2015- youre-the-most-indebted- ever-for- now/.

21.   For a taste of the unapologetic welfare dependence shared by a subculture of graduates of Catholic liberal arts colleges, see Rosie Herreid, "7 Quick Takes: Ethical Dilemmas of a Welfare Queen," Check Out That Sunset! February 21, 2015, https://checkoutthatsunset.wordpress.com/2015/02/21/7-quick-takes-ethical-dilemmas-of-a-welfare-queen.

22.   Simcha Fisher, Facebook post, October 31, 2014. Screenshot available upon request.

23.   Paul VI, Humanae Vitae, 10.

24.   Ibid.

25.   Daniel Schwindt, "Journal Entry of a Working Man," Patheos, February 1, 2016, http://www.patheos.com/blogs/thedorothyoption/journal-entry-of-a-working-man/.

26.   For copious examples, see Jason Jones and John Zmirak, "Leftists Are Hijacking 'Pro-Life' to Ban Guns and Carbon Dioxide and to Open the Borders," The Stream, May 27, 2015, https://stream.org/leftists-are-hijacking-pro-life/.

27.   Luke Faulkner, "5 Things We Learned about Planned Parenthood from the 'Baby Parts' Videos," Lifesitenews, August 3, 2016, https://www.lifesitenews.com/pulse/5-things- we-learned-about- planned-parenthood- from-the- baby-parts- videos.

28.   Laura Bassett, "Congress Votes Yet Again to Defund Planned Parenthood," Huffington Post, January 6, 2016, http://www.huffingtonpost.com/entry/congress-votes- defund-planned-parenthood_us_568d5a67e4b0cad15e62fda6.

29. Connecting the Dots with Mark Shea and Tom McDonald—Chickens, Lying, and More," Breadbox Media, July 21, 2015, http://breadboxmedia.podbean.com/e/connecting-the-dots-with-mark-shea-and-tom-mcdonald-chickens-lying-and-more-072115/.

30. In fact, in tthat July 21, 2015 online radio broadcast, Shea admitted that he was "not confident" in saying that deception would be wrong if practiced by government agencies. Ibid. Though he claims that the ban on lying is part of the natural law and hence universal, Shea curiously seems to apply it only to pro-life Catholics. See Christopher Ferrara, "You Don't Shea!" *Remnant*, August 13, 2015, http://remnantnewspaper.com/web/index.php/fetzen-fliegen/item/1930-you-don-t-shea-why-planned-parenthood-digs-neo-catholic-schoolmarmery.

31. E.g. "Mark Shea, "Lying for Jesus: A Faustian Bargain," Patheos, June 5, 2012, http://www.patheos.com/blogs/markshea/2012/06/lying-for-jesus-a-faustian-bargain.html.

32. Mark Shea, "Why I Believe Live Action's Tactics Are Wrong," Patheos, May 3, 2013, http://www.patheos.com/blogs/markshea/2013/05/why-live-actions-tactics-are-wrong.html.

33. Ibid.

34. Christopher O. Tollefsen, "Truth, Love, and Live Action," *The Public Discourse*, February 9, 2011, http://www.thepublicdiscourse.com/2011/02/2529/.

35. *Catechism of the Catholic Church*, 2483, 1994 edition.

36. *Catechism of the Catholic Church*, 2483, 1997 edition.

37. George Orwell, "Reflections on Gandhi," *Partisan Review*, (January 1949), George Orwell's Library,3 http://www.orwell.ru/library/reviews/gandhi/english/e_gandhi.

38. "Votive Mass of Saint Edmund Campion, Priest and Martyr," Archdiocese of Baltimore, October 3, 2013, https://www.archbalt.org/about-us/the- archbishop/homilies/votive-mass-saint- edmund-campion.cfm; "Blessed Miguel Pro," Catholic Online, (undated), http://www.catholic.org/saints/saint.php?saint_id=86.

39. Knight-Ridder Newspapers, "'A Witness to the Truth' Tells Brave Story of Schindler, Who Tricked Nazis," *Baltimore Sun*, December 30, 1993, http://articles.baltimoresun.com/1993-12- 30/news/1993364198_1_oskar-schindler-leopold-page- holocaust.

40. Thomas Macdonald, "John XXIII and the Jews," Catholic World Report, April 3, 2014, http://www.catholicworldreport.com/Item/3048/john_xxiii_and_the_jews.aspx.

41. Thomas Williams, "New Book Reveals Vatican Plot to Assassinate Hitler," Breitbart, October 19, 2015, http://www.breitbart.com/national-security/2015/10/19/new-book-reveals-vatican-plot-assassinate-hitler/.

42. Bob Fredericks, "Pope Francis Saved Many from Argentina's Death Squads," *New York Post*, March 13, 2014, http://nypost.com/2014/03/13/pope-francis-saved-many-from-argentinas-death-squads/.

43. Jeffrey Mirus, "Is Lying Ever Right?" Catholic Answers, 19:7, http://www.catholic.com/magazine/articles/is-lying-ever-right.

44. Leo XIII, Rerum Novarum, 171.

45. Pius XI, *Quadragesimo Anno*, 41.

46. John Paul II, *Sollicitudo Rei Socialis* [For the twentieth anniversary of Populorum Progressio], Vatican website, December 30, 1987, http://w2.vatican.va/content/john-paul-ii/en/encyclicals/documents/hf_jp-ii_enc_30121987_sollicitudo-rei-socialis.html : "The Church's social doctrine is not a 'third way' between liberal capitalism and Marxist collectivism, nor even a possible alternative to other solutions less radically opposed to one another: rather, it constitutes a category of its own."

47. Schwindt, "Journal Entry of a Working Man."

48. John Medaille, of the University of Dallas, who calls himself a "distributist" and "monarchist," endorsed Barack Obama for president using such arguments. See John Medaille, "The RINO Party," *The Distributist Review* (October 2008), http://distributism.blogspot.com/2008/10/rino-party.html.

49. Patrick Deneen, "Even If Hobby Lobby Wins, We Lose," *The American Conservative,* March 25, 2014, http://www.theamericanconservative.com/2014/03/25/hobbylobby/.

50. See Sean Kenney, former executive director of the Republican Party of Virginia, "Fighting for the Catholic Restoration," Ethika Politika, July 15, 2010, https://ethikapolitika.org/2010/07/15/fighting-for-the-catholic-restoration/.

51. Thomas Storck, "Catholics, Distributism, and Occupy Wall Street," *The Distributist Review*, January 12, 2012, http://distributistreview.com/catholics-distributism-and-occupy-wall-street/.

52. Sean Dailey, Facebook post, May 31, 2015. Screenshot available upon request.

53. Correspondence available upon request.

54. Facebook post, September 23, 2015 (screenshot available upon request).

55. Janet Smith, "Fig Leaves and Falsehoods," First Things (June 2011), http://www.firstthings.com/article/2011/06/fig-leaves-and-falsehoods.

56. Austin Ruse, "An Intellectual Challenge to the Spiritual Friends," Crisis, September 4, 2015, http://www.crisismagazine.com/2015/an-intellectual-challenge-to-the-spiritual-friends.

57. Austin Ruse, "The New Homophiles," Crisis, December 20, 2103, http://www.crisismagazine.com/2013/the-new-homophiles.

58. Mike Allen, "On Straight Fragility," Spiritual Friendship, June 29, 2016, https://spiritualfriendship.org/2016/06/29/on-straight-fragility/.

59. Melinda Selmys, "Orientation Change vs. Mixed Orientation Marriage," Sexual Authenticity, December 22, 2012, http://sexualauthenticity.blogspot.com/2012/12/orientation-change-vs-mixed-orientation.html.

60. Elizabeth Stoker Bruenig, "Is There a Christian Way to Be Gay?" The American Conservative, February 5, 2015, http://www.theamericanconservative.com/articles/is-there-a-christian-way-to-be-gay/.

61. Jim Russell, " 'Gay but Chaste' Is Not Enough for a Faithful Christian Witness," The Stream, September 8, 2015, https://stream.org/gay-but-chaste-is-not-enough-for-faithful-witness/.

62. Joseph Sciambra, " 'Spiritual Friendship:' Chaste Love or Slippery Slide into Gay Sex?" JosephSciambra.com, http://josephsciambra.com/spiritual-friendship-chaste-love-or-slippery-slide-into-gay-sex/.

63. Austin Ruse, "Conservative Media Refuse to Cover New Book on Gay Movement," Breitbart, June 8, 2014, http://www.breitbart.com/big-journalism/2014/06/08/conservative-media-refuse-to-cover-new-book-on-gay-movement/.

64. Mark Oppenheimer, "Now's the Time To End Tax Exemptions for Religious Institutions," Time, June 28, 2015, http://time.com/3939143/nows-the-time-to-end-tax-exemptions-for-religious-institutions/.

65. Rod Dreher, "Orthodox Christians Must Now Learn to Live as Exiles in Our Own Country," Time, June 26, 2015, http://time.com/3938050/orthodox-christians-must-now-learn-to-live-as-exiles-in-our-own-country/.

66. John Zmirak, "The Benedict Option Isn't One," *Intercollegiate Review* (Summer 201), https://home.isi.org/benedict-option-isnt-one#sthash. XoTWHc3L.dpuf.

67. Philip Jenkins, The Lost History of Christianity (New York: HarperOne, 2008).

68. J. Michael Smith, "Romeike Family Can Stay in U.S.," Homeschool Legal Defense Association, March 2, 2015, http://www.hslda.org/legal/cases/romeike.asp.

69. Carly Hoilman, "Norway to Return Seized Children to Christian Parents Accused of 'Indoctrination,'" The Blaze, June 6, 2016, http://www.theblaze.com/stories/2016/06/06/norway-to-return-seized-children-to-christian-parents-accused-of-indoctrination/.

70. Dreher, "Orthodox Christians Must Now Learn To Live as Exiles in Our Own Country."

71. Dawson, "Catholicism and the Bourgeois Mind."

72. John Zmirak, "Dawson's Usura Canto," Crisis, January 11, 2012, http://www.crisismagazine.com/2012/the-usura-canto.

73. John Paul II, Memory and Identity (New York: Rizzoli, 2005).

74. Thomas Pink, "Conscience and Coercion," *First Things* (August 2012), http://www.firstthings.com/article/2012/08/conscience-and-coercion.

75. John Zmirak, "Illiberal Catholicism," Aleteia, December 31, 2013, http://aleteia.org/2013/12/31/illiberal-catholicism/.

76. David Bentley Hart, "Mammon Ascendant: Why Global Capitalism Is Inimical to Christianity," First Things (June 2016), http://www.firstthings.com/article/2016/06/mammon-ascendant.

77. "World Bank Forecasts Global Poverty to Fall Below 10% for First Time," World Bank, October 4, 2015, http://www.worldbank.org/en/news/press-release/2015/10/04/world-bank-forecasts-global-poverty-to-fall-below-10-for-first-time-major-hurdles-remain-in-goal-to-end-poverty-by-2030.

78. See Anthony C. Sciglitano, Marcion and Prometheus (New York: Crossroad, 2014).

79. Pius XII, "In the Holy Gospels, the Divine Master does not condemn justly acquired riches," from "Allocution to Directors and Employees of the Bank of Italy," April 25, 1950, in Rupert J. Ederer, *Pope Pius XII on the Economic Order* (Lanham: Scarecrow Press, 2011), 224.

80. Frédéric Bastiat, *The Law* (1850), http://bastiat.org/en/the_law.html#SECTION_G037.

81. Todd Hertz, "Two-Thirds of U.S. Bishops Allowed Accused Priests to Go on Working: No Motive in Monday's Monk Shooting and Other Stories from Online Sources around the World," *Christianity Today*, June 1, 2002, http://www.christianitytoday.com/ct/2002/juneweb-only/6-10-32.0.html.

82. "Exposing Planned Parenthood's Cover-Up of Child Sex Trafficking," Live Action, https://liveaction.org/traffick/; Lauren Keiper, "Anti-Abortion Group Releases More Video of Planned Parenthood," Reuters, February 4, 2011, http://www.reuters.com/article/us-abortion-video-idUSTRE7130JI20110204.

83. Denis Coday, "Bishops' Conference Releases 2015 Abuse Audit Report," National Catholic Reporter, May 20, 2016, https://www.ncronline.org/news/accountability/bishops-conference-releases-2015-abuse-audit-report; John L. Allen, Jr., "Catholic Bishop of Kansas City Convicted of Failure to Report Child Abuse Resigns ," Crux, April 21, 2015, https://cruxnow.com/church/2015/04/21/catholic-bishop-of-kansas-city-convicted-of-failure-to-report-child-abuse-resigns/.

84. Harriet Ryan, Ashley Powers and Victoria Kim, "For Roger Mahony, Clergy Abuse Cases Were a Threat to Agenda," Los Angeles Times, December 1, 2013, http://graphics.latimes.com/mahony/.

85. "Stephanie Kirchgaessner, "Catholic Church Accused of Using 'Mafia-Like' Tactics to Fight Sex Abuse Bill," *The Guardian*, June 17, 2016, https://www.theguardian.com/us-news/2016/jun/17/pennsylvania-catholic-church-sexual-abuse-bill-mafia-tactics.

86. "Racist Planned Parenthood Founder Margaret Sanger Was Not So 'Pro-Choice,'" Live Action, September 14, 2011, http://liveaction.org/blog/racist-planned-parenthood-founder-margaret-sanger-was-not-so-pro-choice/.

87. Jason Scott Jones, "David Daleiden in Prison," The Stream, January 28, 2016, https://stream.org/david-daleiden-prison/;

88. For a detailed history of the American eugenics movement and the Catholic opposition to it, see Robert G. Marshall and Charles A. Donovan, *Blessed Are the Barren* (San Francisco: Ignatius, 1991). See also Lutz Kaelber, "Eugenics: Compulsory Sterilization in 50 American

States," University of Vermont, 2012, https://www.uvm.edu/~lkaelber/eugenics/.

89. "Margaret Sanger Quotes, History, and Biography," Live Action, http://liveaction.org/research/margaret-sanger-quotes-history-and-biography.

90. Jonathan P. Henderson, "Planned Parenthood: Eugenics & Organ Harvesting under China's 'One Child Policy,'" PolitiChicks, July 22, 2015, http://politichicks.com/2015/07/planned-parenthood-eugenics-organ-harvesting-under-chinas-one-child-policy/.

91. Mark Tushnet, "Abandoning Defensive Crouch Liberal Constitutionalism," Balkin Blogspot, May 6, 2016, http://balkin.blogspot.it/2016/05/abandoning-defensive-crouch-liberal.html?m=1http://balkin.blogspot.it/2016/05/abandoning-defensive-crouch-liberal.html?m=1.

92. "Gender Identity/Gender Expression: Legal Enforcement Guidance," New York City Commission of Human Rights.

93. Jason Scott Jones and John Zmirak, *The Race to Save Our Century* (New York: Crossroad, 2014).

Index